CW00766421

IS THERE A CHURCH OF ENGLAND?

REFLECTIONS ON PERMANENCE AND PROGRESSION

Also by C.H. Sisson from Carcanet

POETRY
Selected Poems
Collected Poems
God Bless Karl Marx!
Antidotes

PROSE
Christopher Homm (novel)
The Avoidance of Literature
English Poetry 1900-1950
On the Look-out (autobiography)
In Two Minds: guesses at other writers
English Perspectives: essays on liberty and government

TRANSLATIONS
Lucretius, *Poem on Nature*
Virgil, *The Aeneid*
The Song of Roland

EDITIONS
The English Sermon 1650-1750
Christina Rossetti, *Selected Poems*
Jonathan Swift, *Selected Poems*
Jeremy Taylor, *Selected Writings*

C.H. SISSON

CARCANET

First published in 1993 by
Carcanet Press Limited
208-212 Corn Exchange Buildings
Manchester M4 3BQ

A CIP catalogue record for this book
is available from the British Library
ISBN 1 85754 010 7

The publisher acknowledges financial assistance
from the Arts Council of Great Britain.

Set in 10½ pt Bembo by Bryan Williamson, Frome
Printed and bound in England by SRP Ltd, Exeter

Contents

Introduction

The Church of England is falling. Should it be saved? I am one of those who think that it should be, and that is my only excuse for publishing a volume of miscellaneous articles which is something of a jumble and does no more than represent the difficulties of one who came, belatedly, to love the Church, only to find that it was being mined by people hostile to many of the characteristics which had most attracted him to it. This is not a unique position, and many of the difficulties are probably shared by a larger or smaller number of people in every parish in the land. I am far from having any general solutions to offer. Indeed, the volume offers no solutions, only evidence of difficulties which must be overcome if this crucial institution is to be rescued.

If there is a peculiarity about the views which are here expressed it is in the extent to which they represent public rather than private concerns. I have no spiritual history, or none that I am myself able to recognize as such. The concern I recognize is for the future of England, which I cannot see otherwise than as having the Church at the centre of it. This is clearly not a general view, in a society which is seen by Christians and non-Christians alike, with varying degrees of anxiety or of satisfaction, as slipping, decade by decade, or even day by day, further from any such conception.

What is addressed in this volume is not this grand situation, for there is no cure for history and no certainty as to its future developments, but only specific worries which have come to me because of the chances of my own life, now in its eighth decade, and of my own interests as reader and writer. The nature of the latter interests is now as public as the somewhat limited circulation of my books allows. I have been much drawn to the seventeenth century, and that colours what I have to say; the attraction has not been due to any sort of antiquarian interest but to a sense of contemporary relevance. I have lived in the modern world, in a succession of milieux in which this bias had no place and could not have appeared, and my sightings of the Church have been from the ordinary workaday and domestic situations.

My concern is therefore with practicalities – those of ordinary parish life, those of the national community in which we are all set, those of language. As to the last-named, I cannot escape from the perspectives which the composition and translation of poetry have given me: I have an absolute distrust of the facilities which pass for communication in the media and, increasingly in the last few decades, in the Church. The mere wilfulness of so much of the spoken and written matter which now surrounds us takes it outside the bounds of any properly human, let alone Christian, expression: its prevalence has darkened the world it is supposed to enlighten, and made the truth about human nature, which the Faith was made to fit, less widely accessible.

A concern for practicalities, however sophisticated, must be an inadequate basis for a defence of the Church, which this book is intended to be, but even in the best of causes one must not pretend to do more than one can. I cannot claim an academic acquaintance with theology, nor more religion than, like it or not, is built into the ordinary make-up of the human race. If my position in that regard is no worse than human, I have learned, from traditional Christian teaching as well as from observation, not to share the exaggerated respect for our fallen nature which is common in a world of alleged consumer choices and alleged human rights. But what of belief? What of the ultimate nature of truth?

These questions are simply too hard for me to answer. As to truth, no one has yet invented a conclusive definition, so that any true scepticism has to rummage at the foundations. As to belief, this very uncertainty clears the way for it more than is commonly thought in the present age, and I feel none of the difficulties some eminent churchmen appear to find about accepting those articles of the Creed which appear to conflict with the latest news from the laboratories. That is not to say that there can be no difficulties about the Creed, but when I began to profess and call myself Christian it was because I had come to think that it could be swallowed whole, and that, taken neat, it corresponded perfectly with the world as I saw it, and in particular with the nature and needs of the human race. Not that I am claiming any extraordinary degree of conviction; indeed, my position, so far as I can be said to have one, is rather that it is the Creed or nothing, and that I hold these two possibilities in my mind. I see nothing to tempt me to the half-way houses which are now so popular both in the Church and outside, where people who find the Creed insufferable have no difficulty in believing in various panaceas for misplaced hopes.

These deep matters are not explored in the miscellaneous pieces which make up this collection, but I felt I could not present it to the public without attempting to give at least a summary and inadequate account, if not of exactly where I stand, at least of where I do not stand. Those who have read my partial autobiography, *On the Look-out*, will know that my first introduction to the practices of the Church Militant was at the hands of United Methodists in a working-class suburb of Bristol, and that my mother's family were of that now extinct race which I have called agricultural Anglicans. These origins have left their traces on my approach to the Church of England; from both sources I have a sense of the social importance of Christianity which my later explorations have much modified, but not erased. So it is that I have been able, as David Martin put it, in an essay (in 1984) on my then published works, 'to uphold the Church of England in its political and historical role, without glossing over her social condition.'

Because of my uncertainties, and the fragmentary nature of what I have to say, I have arranged the material in this volume chronologically rather than on the basis of subjects. It is divided by decades, beginning with the Fifties. I did not bother my head about the Church in the Thirties, except so far as it was forced on my attention by Eliot's apparent aberrations from modernity in *For Lancelot Andrewes, Ash Wednesday, Thoughts after Lambeth, After Strange Gods* and *The Idea of a Christian Society*, and the good fortune I had in having the seventeenth century as a special subject in my degree course in Philosophy and English Literature at Bristol University. In the Forties my attention to such matters was slight, a matter of chance encounters which, later, seemed relevant to the development of my interest in the Church. It was the Fifties which saw the consolidation of that development, and it is with that decade that this collection starts.

The first years of the Forties saw the war begin in earnest, and the war took me to India. It was thus that I came to know Cecil De Vall, and so made my first acquaintance with a High Church clergyman, indeed my first more than casual acquaintance with an Anglican priest of any kind. He was the garrison chaplain of Barrackpore, an old military station which was then the headquarters of Eastern, later XIVth Army, though I did not penetrate those august circles but merely sweated in the impressive barracks where many must have sweated since the Mutiny. I went sometimes, with a properly trained fellow-soldier, to Mattins or Evensong at his church – I was not qualified to go to Communion – and I still remember the ringing, metallic tones in which De Vall would utter the opening sentence: 'Enter not into judgment with thy servant, O Lord, for in thy sight shall no man living be justified.'

This first contact was soon followed by invitations to the padre's bungalow. There De Vall was no longer the imposing character he had been in church. He was sharp, sardonic, even a trifle silly, with his flow of what might be called High-Church social shop, and what seemed like impatience and arrogance with his servants. But he was amusing – certainly a change from the barrack-room – and to me instructive. It was from him that I first heard the name of Gregory Dix, whose works I was to read some twelve years later. He also introduced me to the *Hindu Manners, Ceremonies and Customs* of the Abbé Dubois, who had been in South India from 1792 to 1823. Impressed and vaguely appalled by the evidences of Hinduism which irrupted on one on the banks of the Hooghli, I was avid of the scraps of the Abbé's learning which came my way.

Dubois was an extraordinary man. A portrait of 1820 shows him in his missionary years with a light fringe of beard – presumably the local style at the time – and dressed completely in the local manner. 'A man singularly free from prejudice,' Max Müller says, 'and... a scholar with sufficient knowledge, if not of Sanskrit, yet of Tamil, both literary and spoken, to be able to enter into the views of the natives, to understand their manners and customs, and to make allowance for many of their superstitious opinions and practices, as mere corruptions of an originally far more rational and intelligent form of religion and philosophy ... There are few men now left' (it was then 1899) 'who, like the Abbé Dubois, have actually been present at the burning of widows, or who can give us, as he does, direct reports of eye-witnesses who saw a king burning with two of his queens joining hands on the burning pile over the corpse of their husband.' In Bengal there were 706 officially reported cases of suttee in 1817.

I have given, in Part 2 of *On the Look-out*, such impressions as I could gather, a few years later, of the impact of this Hindu world of which I was profoundly ignorant but which surrounded me like a miasma during my first days in India. The effect was obscure but profound, and I allude to it here only because a faint residue must have remained, somewhere at the back of my head, and perhaps made an unnoticeable contribution to my slow and intermittent approach to the Church. It certainly contributed to the relief I felt when, after Barrackpore, I found myself in the monotheistic world of the Punjab and the North-West Frontier Province. The atmosphere seemed to clear. There it was at least admitted that there was such a thing as the truth, and the endless elusiveness of Hinduism was an aberration.

My effective approach to the Church began only at the end of the 1940s, when I was settled at home, in the village of Dunton Green near Sevenoaks. It was about this time that our second daughter appeared, and was baptised. One way and another I had come, over the years, to think the Creed was not absurd and, *propter hoc* or otherwise, I began to be a regular attendant at Mattins.

It was only in the early 1950s that I actually joined the Church. Baptism had been omitted, in my case, though not in the case of the two older children and one younger child in the family to which I belonged, so I had to begin with that. It is a sort of indignity for a man of nearly forty, as I then was, and I daresay it was none the worse for that. It was soon followed by confirmation, and henceforth I was a regular and unnoticeable Anglican. Within two years, the vicar of Dunton Green asked me to be his churchwarden, and I succumbed, not through parochial ambition but, I suppose, because I was feeling vulnerable. My predecessor as vicar's warden had also been a lay reader, and the vicar pressed me to assume that office as well. I still have the letter, dated March 1955, in which I was informed, by the canon who managed these things for the diocese of Rochester, that I had passed both the qualifying papers 'very satisfactorily', and that he looked forward to my admission in the following June. Perhaps fortunately, this ceremony took place without me. There was a change of vicar in the parish and the new one, with whom I was soon on excellent terms, made it clear that he did not want a lay reader or, possibly, that he did not want me in that role. So I became a simple churchwarden, which was trouble enough for both of us.

At the beginning of the decade I became a regular reader of the monthly *Theology*. It was then edited by Alec Vidler, a *New English Weekly* connection, and I daresay I first looked into it on that account, that journal having been virtually the only outlet for my writing from 1937 till it came to an end in 1949. I continued my reading of the monthly as long as Vidler was editor, and indeed beyond that, for over fifteen years in all. But throughout the 1950s I did a lot of unsystematic reading which might be described as theology-linked – Alcuin Club publications, as well as odd books such as the 1604 Canons, Salmon's *The Infallibility of the Church*, and a variety of volumes both more obscure and better-known. The works of Gregory Dix were, perhaps not surprisingly, an important element in this mixed diet, but so were odd collections of liturgical texts picked up in second-hand book-shops: in this way I became acquainted not only with the older Anglican liturgies but, through such books as Maskell's *Monumenta Ritualia*, with the medieval uses which preceded them and, with the help of Hall's *Fragmenta Liturgica* and *Reliquiae Liturgicae*, with the so to speak more amateur attempts at reform which were made during the seventeenth and eighteenth centuries. I do not pretend to any real knowledge of these subjects, but they are part of the background of the not infrequent incursions into the subject of liturgical reform which occur among the pieces in this volume. Those pieces are not merely the literary aberrations of a vaguely Christianised poet.

The little appendix of poems at the end of this volume illustrates the obscure haunting which has made it inevitable that religious topics should surface in my verse from time to time over a long stretch of years. If none of this passes as devotional poetry, my preoccupations have been such as to produce work which cannot be understood without a Christian context, and indeed Donald Davie has allowed it to figure somewhat prominently in his *New Oxford Book of Christian Verse*. One of the poems included there – and in the appendix – begins with the line 'Christ is the language which we speak to God,' and it might be said that, in the western world, it is impossible to speak of religion without reference to the Logos. I would go further, and suggest that any discourse about the profounder human concerns which attempts to avoid all reference to the Christian tradition is hopelessly impoverished.

In the twentieth century, there are certainly many who would regard such claims as excessive, or plainly wrong, but those who care for poetry at all can hardly do other than admit that the language of religion has inescapable affinities with that of poetry. This takes one into territory which is difficult and disputed, both theologically and linguistically, and involves the claims made by dogmatically irreligious, as well as the religious, that poetry conveys some kind of exactness and some kind of truthfulness. It is not a matter of denying the truth of science, but only of asserting that the language of science is incomplete, and that there are other elements in ordinary human communication. This is not the place to develop such an analysis, but such problems are clearly relevant to the arguments which have emerged – belatedly, I would say – about the intelligibility of the liturgy, during a decade which has seen the relegation of a Prayer Book of admittedly superb literary quality, in favour of a relatively shallow production.

Poetry has deep roots, and one may safely assert that its surface perfections would not exist without the energies it derives from such sources. The name of poetry is much abused, and much that is called by it lacks the rhythmic and verbal qualities which are inseparable from the genuine article. Language without these qualities fails to convey more than a shadow of our human concerns – enough for the ordinary crudities of our practical occupations but always something below the possibilities of human communication. It is to those who are unaware of these possibilities that the composition of liturgies and the translation of sacred texts have, in recent decades, been largely entrusted. What is at stake in these controversies is not some literary frivolity about the 'old' and the 'new', but the profoundly important distinction between the more and the less meaningful.

If religion is concerned with the truth – and surely any religion which is not is no more than a tiresome obfuscation? – this distinction is of importance in ecclesiastical matters as in all human affairs. Languages rise and fall, and we are the poorer – in that we understand less – if we cease to value the great ecclesiastical as well as the great political works of the past. We need a strong infusion of literacy in our bishops and clergy as well as in those who reflect on our more general communal concerns. A concern for the use of words lies behind everything in this volume, as well as in my political essays (*English Perspectives*, 1991), no less than in the literary essays of *In Two Minds* (1990), where it would be more readily admitted to be appropriate. One does not have to be a poet to see the interconnection between the matter of the three volumes. In the case of the somewhat idiosyncratic piece from the 1960s, 'Native Ruminations', the balance between ecclesiastical and political matter hangs so evenly that it has been included both in *English Perspectives* and in the present volume, to avoid a cross-reference which could be a nuisance to a reader who did not have access to both.

If the contribution of the present volume to the practical issues facing the Church of England is small, that does not mean that the book has nothing to offer. Arrogance is not the exclusive preserve of such marginal critics as myself; if it were, the Church would not be in its present mess.

THE FIFTIES

A Political Note

Whether or not the opinion, 'that there is no such thing as Christian politics',[1] presents perplexities to the theologian, it undoubtedly presents some to the political theorist. And by this I mean to the political theorist as such, as one attempting to operate in an independent province, and not to the man who happens to entertain at the same time an interest in political theory and the hopes and beliefs of a Christian. The anxieties of a man in the latter capacity will contain nothing of which the theologian will not take account. But the theologian is not obliged, nor indeed as such is he able, to pursue the implications of doctrine into a secular field. And so the political theorist may be able to add a note of marginal interest on an inessential extension of the theologian's field. That is all that is attempted here.

Without making a foray into Mr Auden's article at large, which may be treated for our purposes as a sort of theological hinterland, it may be advisable to quote a little more extensively. Mr Auden's view, which he presents as a reading of the text 'Render unto Caesar', is 'that there is no such thing as Christian politics, or a Christian art, or a Christian science, any more than there is a Christian diet'. The conception of a Christian art and of a Christian science each presents its own difficulties, and we shall not be concerned with them. The comparison with *diet* is instructive. For one might have thought it very possible that there should be such a thing as a Christian diet, in the sense of a series of acts of eating; and one may recall that the term has been in use in the more general sense of a way of living or thinking. Mr Auden goes on: 'There is only politics, or art, or science, which are natural activities concerned with the natural and historical man. The standards of efficacy, beauty, and truth, by which they are measured, are valid irrespective of faith, but the Christian layman

[1] *Theology*, Vol. LIII, No. 366 (December 1950).

is conscious of exercising his natural gifts in the presence of God.' We will leave aside, as appropriate to the theologian, some doubts as to whether the latter half of the last sentence describes a consciousness specifically Christian, and exercise a dangerous surgery on the text to the extent of extracting, from Mr Auden's next paragraph, the words 'what a layman should do is answerable in terms of his individual gifts and his particular historical situation'.

There, as I read the article, we have an important clue to Mr Auden's view of politics, which may be abstruse but is certainly not peculiar. It represents an historical subjectivism. Within this doctrine, the injunction to love God and one's neighbour as one's self has no meaning. But it is not obedience to this injunction, in Mr Auden's view, which is, in his odd expression, 'serious'. What is serious is the intention of the will to love God and one's neighbour. Rightness hovers on the edge of action, but as it were succeeds in never alighting on it. So action remains completely 'lay', an affair of particular gifts in an individual situation. The eternal and the absolute are in no way implicated. No wonder that, in listing certain preoccupations of the natural man – politics, art, science – Mr Auden paired with each of them a different standard by which it was to be measured. Thus science is to be measured by truth, art by beauty, and politics by efficacy. In this way it is hoped that none of them will be entangled in the net of the absolute. Without entering upon over-subtle speculations as to the nature of beauty, we may think truth as the measure of science a dangerous criterion to introduce into this separatist world. It might accidentally get out of its compartment and measure something other than science. It might, in particular, suggest that 'efficacy' is an inadequate criterion for politics.

Efficacy does, however, pair as neatly with politics as beauty with art. For as it is a tautology to say that a work of art is beautiful, so it is a tautology to say politics involves a capacity to produce intended effects in a society. But whereas beauty is an end, either in itself or as part of a more complicated system of ends, efficacy is a technical expression and has to do merely with means. Politics, therefore, can only be understood in relation to something outside them. It is true that, the more precise our political studies become, the more apt we are to lose this something from view. For this reason some of the most profound minds engaged in political studies have been popularly regarded as cynics indifferent to ends. Machiavelli is a case in point. But a mind as profound as Machiavelli's is perfectly aware of the limitations of its subject-matter, and does not forget the nature of its ends merely because it does not happen at the moment to treat of them. There is, however, a tradition of imperfect political philosophy which attempts to ignore ends so far as may be and to convert all to means. The various forms of historical relativism are in this tradition. None of them succeeds in practice in excluding ends, for the bent of the human mind is that way. But all succeed more or less – to use Mr Auden's phrase – in not taking ends seriously, in denaturing them by setting arbitrary limits to inquiries concerning them.

This is the classical fallacy of liberal democracy, which is nowhere more compendiously set out than in Locke's 'Letter concerning Toleration'. The 'temporal good and outward prosperity of the society', says Locke, 'is the sole reason of man's entering into society, and the only thing they seek and aim at'. One is reminded of the aside, a little later in the 'Letter', that 'some enter into company for trade and profit, others for want of business have their clubs for claret'. Locke could maintain his position only by producing the civil reasons for not tolerating atheists and sceptics. 'Promises, covenants, and oaths, which are the bonds of human society, can have no hold upon an atheist. They taking away of God, though but even in thought, dissolves all.' These are but the misgivings of an innovator who, fearing he has gone too far, has not the courage to turn back. Locke's successors have dispensed with his misgivings, and their philosophy is no longer radically distinguishable from that of those whom they oppose. The answer to political questions 'in terms of... individual gifts and... particular historical situation' is one man's guess which is as good as another's.

To Locke's indifferentism we must oppose Hooker's comprehensive system of laws which ties the most trivial action to the highest good. Then we shall not suppose that 'God had ordained kings for no other purpose but only to fat up men like hogs'. No doubt it is rash for a political society to claim to serve the spiritual interests of its members. It is fatal for it to aim at serving only their material interests. In this latter purpose it may succeed.

A Literary Note

The English Church cannot escape from the accidents attending her reform. The shape of her liturgy is determined by the theological cross-currents of the sixteenth century and her Thirty-nine Articles are a museum of controversy and compromise. Moreover, the prose to which we have been accustomed in her services is, as to its origin, in the main, and as to its form and style, entirely, that of pre-Elizabethan England. The seductions of these familiar cadences are very great. Indeed, anyone with an ear for prose may well have to ask himself, from time to time, whether he not too much an Anglican to be a Christian.

Although one of the objects of the reformers was to enable the English people to worship in a language understanded of them, it is now only for a literate minority that the language of the Prayer Book has much of its original immediacy, and Anglicans must reflect seriously on the loss of impact which that entails. The object of this note, however, is much more limited. It is to draw attention to a literary problem, which is also by implication a theological one, in the style of certain prayers and, in the first place, to the uneasiness a layman who has literary susceptibilities may feel at the introduction into mattins and evenson of prayers which are stylistically discordant.

It is a widespread custom to introduce prayers not in the Prayer Book after the third collect, either in addition to or (regrettably) in substitution for the set prayers. In either case, the stylistic contrast with the language of the office proper and (where they are said) with that of the concluding prayers is marked. The revisers of 1662, who added the concluding prayers, were sufficiently near to Cranmer's time and style to be able to produce work not discordant with his. The movement which, with Sprat and Dryden and Swift, rationalized English prose, was only on the point of beginning. Once that movement has gathered force we are *en plein dix-huitième siècle*, and though Johnson, in particular, had older traditions in his bones, it was henceforward impossible to write, in all sincerity, a language which rang true with that of the Prayer Books of 1549, 1552 and 1662.

There have not been lacking, in the self-conscious literary decadence of the nineteenth century and after, makers of sham antiques who were well satisfied with their work. An interesting apology for this sort of activity is to be found in the introduction to Attwell M.Y. Baylay's *Century of Collects* (Alcuin Club Prayer Book Revision Pamphlets, No. III). Baylay does not make any appeal to antiquarian principles. His argument is from the necessity of expanding the Latin of his originals in order to give their meaning clearly and in rhythmical prose. The rhythm he has in mind is Cranmer's. It would hardly be too much to say that for him there *is* no other rhythm that could be used for this purpose. He describes Cranmer as 'determined to make the English of his collects rhythmical', and as perceiving that to do so he had 'to use more words than are needed' to give the bare meaning. Describing his own method of work, Baylay says that he has not been 'afraid of employing a much larger number of words' than were to be found in the Latin original. A fair sample of this work, with the Latin which Baylay gives side by side with it, is the following Leonine collect for St Stephen:

> Omnipotens sempiterne Deus, qui primitias martyrum in sancti Levitae Stephani sanguine dedicasti: tribue, quaesumus, ut pro nobis intercessor existat, qui pro suis etiam persecutoribus supplicavit.

> Almighty and everlasting God, who this day didst hallow the first-fruits of thy holy martyrs by the blood of the blessed Deacon Stephen: grant, we beseech thee, that we may be assisted by his prayers in heaven, who on earth was willing to pray even for his persecutors.

That is what might be termed a plausible piece of prose. It is reasonably neat, and follows the structure of its more terse original. But it does not go home to us as Cranmer's language does. It has no traffic with the living speech of the day in which it was written. The mere use of the old second person singular, as the only form proper in addressing the Deity, is an embarrassment to us now. There are other embarrassments here. Observe the second part of the collect: 'grant, we beseech thee, that we may be assisted by *his* prayers in heaven, *who* on earth . . .'. The syntactical contortion is dignified rather than direct. An ordinary member of the congregation might think it quite normal for a parson to talk like that in church, but he would be very surprised indeed if he heard it anywhere else. In other words, we are here asked to pardon a lack of colloquial force for the sake of preserving the ecclesiastical atmosphere. Observe, too, how the padding, the additional words put in in accordance with the translator's principles – 'that we may be assisted by his prayers in heaven' for the terse 'ut pro nobis intercessor existat' and 'on earth' for nothing at all – is designed for the same purpose.

It is sobering to remember that, even in the days when the English Church said its offices in Latin, it was the custom to bring home to the congregation their part in the service by bidding their bedes in the plainest vernacular. There were no stylistic inhibitions about the priests who turned to the people and said:

> "Ye shulle stonde up and bydde your bedys in the worshepe of our Lord Jhesu Christ.... Also ye shulle bydde for the gwode man and the good wife, that the charite hid brought to pay, and for tham that it first voonden and longest holden ye shulle bydde for tham that this Cherche honour....[1]

It is instructive to turn to one of the English Primers of pre-Reformation times. In the following petition the rhythm is not yet that of Cranmer, but it is interesting to note that the simplicity of the first three clauses gives way, in the second two, to a pairing of substantives which suggests the loose style of the great liturgist.

> God gyve grace to the quike, and to the deede reste, and forgyuenesse to the chirche, and to the kingdom pees and concorde, and to us synneris liif and endeles glorie.

It is, however, when we turn to the collects which appear both in the Prayer Book and in one of the medieval primers that the stylistic effect of the development of the language and the genius of Cranmer is most clearly seen. Take the collect for St Michael and All Angels. The Latin of Sarum reads as follows:

> Deus qui miro ordine angelorum ministeria hominumque dispensas: concede propitius, ut quibus tibi ministrantibus in coelo semper assistitur: ab his in terra vita nostra muniatur.

---

[1] A form of Bidding the Bedes, used on holy days in the diocese of Worcester, AD 1349 (*Forms of Bidding Prayer, with Introduction and Notes*, Oxford, 1840).

In the Primer given by Maskell, which is dated 'before 1410', this is given as:

> God, that in a merveilous ordre ordeynedist seruysis of aungels and of men, graunte thou mercifulli that oure liif be defendid in erthe bi hem that stonden nyg euermore seruynge to thee in heuene.

Cranmer's version (with the word or two added, in the same tradition, by the revisers of 1662) is notably more florid:

> O everlasting God, who hast ordained and constituted the services of Angels and men in a wonderful order: Mercifully grant, that as thy holy Angels always do thee service in heaven, so by thy appointment they may succour and defend us on earth.

The difference between the two English versions is by no means due merely to Cranmer's invention. The language has grown more supple. But Cranmer's own stylistic developments are of the telling force they are because they were in full sympathy with the developing genius of the language. They at the same time went with the current of the language and went beyond it, much as Shakespeare's went with and beyond the common speech of his day and the pentameters of Kyd and Marlowe. Like Shakespeare, Cranmer is, by his very achievement, a hindrance to his successors in the same field.

It is difficult for us to conceive of vernacular prayers in a language which owes nothing to Cranmer. Yet to use language which echoes those old rhythms is to slip away from the speech of the day into a miserable ecclesiastical dialect in which our living thoughts cannot be expressed. To introduce into our services more recent rhythms may be a little discordant, but it is a graver fault, even of taste, to admit the sham.

While prayers intended for the service of the church should be in a language which has access to our deepest feelings, and so should be a natural not an imitated speech, they should certainly not be idiosyncratic. It is necessary to tie them to the common tradition as well as to release into them our individual devotions. No one can say how such prayers can be written. If it were possible to devise an exercise which might prepare the way for them, it would be the uninhibited translation, into the living language, of some of the terser collects from the old sacramentaries. But it must be admitted that it needs a writer of genius to be uninhibited in the face of a powerful tradition.

Responsible Positions

To the Editor of *The Frontier*

Dear Sir,

On page 1 of your Vol. I the Christian Frontier Council is described as 'a fellowship of 30 or 40 laymen and women who hold responsible positions in secular life...' On page 34 is an article entitled 'The Spiritual Need of Men in Responsible Positions'.

What is the sense of this 'responsible'? It is, without a doubt, that of the most worldly usage. The responsible person, in these contexts, is meant to be one who is commonly recognized as some kind of Nob or Big Cheese. This is not, from a Christian point of view, a very important thing to be.

It seems to me that the word 'responsible', used as *Frontier* has used it, does not belong to the same universe of discourse as the words 'fellowship' and 'spiritual need', used in a Christian sense. If that is so, there may be confusion in the mind of the reader: of the writers I say nothing.

The various pooh-bahisms by which we earn our livings, even most of those we engage in in our leisure out of 'a sense of service' or on some such pretext, are surely the equivalent of the great possessions of the young man in the gospel, and 'men and women in responsible positions' must have all the difficulties which were likened to those of a camel going through the eye of a needle. At best, the pooh-bah is of no special importance for the Christian understanding of society. What the dish-washer, the clerk, or the mere idler understands from his situation is equally important. All that matters is the depth of the understanding.

Is not *Frontier* in effect suggesting that Nobs have some special part in exploring what are called (oddly enough) the practical implications of faith? And is that tenable?

Yours faithfully,

C.H. Sisson.

Church and State

1

In the classic controversy between Church and State the State has been mainly concerned to assert the independence of its own authority. In our day its apologists have several times shaken themselves to be rid of the last shackles and in doing so they have been, not the prophets of enlightenment they announce themselves to be, but the respectable fag-end of a considerable tradition. In one respect, however, they have shown what would almost amount to originality, if it were not absurd to speak of novelty in connection with a quarrelsome marriage in the course of which everything possible has happened. While usually disowning all theology, they have been insistent that, so far from merely seeking more power for the State, they are deeply concerned for the spiritual good of the Church. If they were wolves, one would say that they came in sheep's clothing. They express sympathy with the Church because it has to suffer a Prime Minister not necessarily bound by its rule having a hand in the appointment of bishops, and in general because it is entangled with the affairs of men. This is a trick, we must admit, that has been learned from some in the Church. The fate of the 1928 Prayer Book – which in retrospect does not necessarily seem to have been a bad one – causes many churchmen to speak a little rashly about the control of the State over the Church. It is hardly surprising that the apologists of the State should say: If you want your sanctity, you can have it. While Milton could not praise a fugitive or cloistered virtue there are many who prefer it that way.

It is evidence of the complexity of the problem of the relationship of Church and State that some of the basic arguments of those who would like to see disestablishment because they do not like the Church might have been taken direct from one who was not only a churchman but the author of a classic defence of the Establishment. Warburton's case was that Church and State should each be sovereign in its own field and independent, but united by 'free convention and mutual compact'.[1] Such was the nature of the union he contended, which produced 'a Church by Law established'. The established religion was protected by the State not for its truth but for its utility. Warburton assumed that truth and public utility coincided, and that the civil magistrate would therefore 'promote truth in religion'. In the high spirits of his apology, Warburton forgot that it was the statesman's view of utility which he had declared to be congruent with the churchman's view of truth. Behind this optimism was a basic principle which is now common currency of those who are indifferent to the Church or against her. 'The care of the State', Warburton says, 'extends only to the body and its concerns, and the care of the Church only to the soul.' The principle is entirely unchristian: the bishop could have learned as much from the words of administration. It asserts the existence of two co-existent realms, with governments quite separate so that the activities of the one need not worry the other. It is almost as if we were back with the Manichees; certainly we are, precisely, with those who wish the Church well so long as she merely carries on innocent Sunday entertainments and does not meddle with the affairs of the world.

Those who are anxious that the Church should not impinge on public life have a justification in some of our popular ideas about sovereignty and in certain aspects of our constitutional practice. The popular notion of sovereignty is that all power resides in the people. It is a principle which sounds well at the hustings and in the press. To any instructed person it is merely one of the several theories of politics, with a definite and traceable history like the others, which contain a part of the truth but no more. In its modern form it has come to us through Locke, Rousseau, and the French Revolution, and it has gained a little colour since from an entirely opposed theory, the Marxist. It hangs in the air now rather as a sentiment than as a theory, and it is perhaps as a sentiment that it is most respectable. So far as it suggests that the 'ideals and desires' of the majority are a criterion of truth it is nonsense, or means that the liberty given to minorities, in a democracy, to express their views is merely nefarious. A churchman, moreover, will inevitably reflect that

[1] William Warburton, *The Alliance between Church and State, or the Necessity and Equity of an Established Religion and a Test-Law Demonstrated*, 1736.

'the devices and desires of our own hearts' are not exactly the best guides. The support given to those who want to keep the Church out of public life by certain aspects of our constitutional practice is more solid. Our administration operates on a balance between the laws as they are and the popular pressures to change them. An existing law has to be so administered as to make life possible for the minister who has to answer for it in Parliament. If a law is such that it cannot be administered in a way that can be defended in the House, it has to be repealed or amended. The Queen's ministers, and the officials who work under them, have the paramount duty of holding the country together and ensuring the continuity of the administration. Their constant concern is to avoid trouble. If pressure for certain action is strong and continuous they are bound in the end to bend, lest the administration break. Their essential characteristic is pliability, not love of the truth. They use as much truth as they need to do their job. It is quite a lot, of a certain kind. A high degree of consistency and accuracy is necessary if one is not to be caught out in the game of recriminations. But the intrinsic value of what is said or done does not matter to the politician or official as such. This is not a peculiarity of our times, though it appears to be so when men compare, as they are apt to do, the practices of the present with the principles handed down from the past. It is the point Warburton has before him when he says that the State will protect religion for its unity.

For many the assertion that religion was useful to the State would merely raise a laugh. They have great difficulty in imagining that it could be useful for anything. That is partly due to inattention to what goes on in churches and what psychologically happens in prayer and worship. It is only a hasty and superficial observation which could yield the conclusion that something real happens when a man drinks a pint of beer at a pub and nothing real when he goes to church. And in the recorded history of man, if inns and ale-houses have had their agreeableness and usefulness, temples and churches have had their importance. We need not fear the intelligence of those who attach no importance to religion, though we may blame ourselves for the defects in our apologetics which have failed to make many people see even what is under their noses. One might, however, admit that there was 'something in' this business of religion, while maintaining that its usefulness to the State was nothing at all. The Erastians of the eighteenth century could think of it as binding the consciences of men, and there will always be those who have the impertinence to tolerate the Church because they think their property will be safer in a community of hands not given to picking and stealing, and those who hate religion but love respectability, of which they cannot believe the Church to be the enemy. One might argue with truth that the Church runs a tremendous social service far more cheaply than any government department would do it; one might argue that certain of the Church's doctrines are worth promulgating merely for the usefulness that a sceptical social worker might see in them. Even if these arguments succeeded individually they would, taken together, hardly convince anyone that the State should recognize the Church. The condescending answer would be that there are lots of other voluntary organizations which are equally worthy.

In putting the Church back among the other voluntary organizations, those who want disestablishment are able to pretend that they are concerned that it should live more in accordance with the objects for which it was founded; and those objects, they wrongly say, were of such a nature that the Church was concerned only with a Greek thing called the soul and not with the body as it is known in Westminster and Wigan. They are, moreover, grounding themselves on a notion of sovereignty which is more comprehensive in the support it has than in the truth it contains. Further, they are reasonably finding comfort in the constitutional practice of listening for the loudest and most persistent voice and then obeying it. In all, they have a good, tough, popular case, of the kind that often settles things in practice. If we were dealing with the political crisis of a decade it might be good enough. But what is proposed in disestablishment is the abolition of a relationship which in principle is as old as Constantine or, in these islands, as Anglo-Saxon England where bishops and nobles sat jointly in the Witan. There are those for whom the very antiquity of an institution is a reason for destroying it, but, happily, they have rarely been numerous enough to carry the day among the English.

2

It is unfortunate for the solution of this problem of the relationship of Church and State that we can hold out no hope to our opponents that the Church will disappear. If we could give that assurance, there would certainly be those who would be willing to extend a generous toleration during the interim period. The Church will, however, always continue to make the same claims as it has always made and to proclaim the same gospel. There can be no expectation that it will be more accommodating in future so that the nature of the problem might change. It will continue to assert that it is different in kind from other voluntary organizations and it will refuse to go away and give harmless entertainments of which nothing is heard in the outside world. It will not even consent to reserve its gospel for its members, as Freemasons do the oddities they indulge in. These things sound so unconciliatory as to be out of place in a temporizing, politicians' world. But they are facts which the most pliant of politicians will have always to reckon with. The martyrs are there for proof. The fact that the Church will go on and will have its martyrs is by no means adduced as an argument for it remaining established. Nor is it suggested that anyone would be martyred in defence of establishment nor that death on such an occasion would have any claim to be considered martyrdom. We know that disestablishment is a thing that would be welcomed by many devout churchmen. It is the thesis of this article that they are ill-advised. And it is the purpose of the second part of this article to indicate some reasons which should make agnostic supporters of the State as well as churchmen hesitate before committing themselves.

The relations of Church and State which make up Establishment are small things as seen against the background of the total activity of either, but they are of great significance. The State, which long fought for a certain control over the Church, though it now sets little store by it, has the right to summon Convocation, to hear appeals from Church courts, to nominate bishops, and to 'make laws as to Church Discipline, to unite with Convocation in dealing by legislation with matters of faith and substance, and to adjust the administration of Church endowments'.[2] It is curious that, in an age which above all others has been marked by an extension of State control, this one instance of a shedding of powers exercised for centuries should find such hearty recommendation. The privileges of the Establishment are few but prominent. There is the obligation of the sovereign to belong to the Church, the right of the Archbishop to crown the

---

[2] See Sir Lewis Dibdin, *Establishment in England*, 1932, pp.115-16.

sovereign, and the right of certain bishops to sit in the House of Lords. It is easier to understand the contemporary objections to these privileges than the desire to see the State shed its powers over the Church. The objection to the bishops in the Lords might take the form of the question: Why should one voluntary organization, rather than another, have members in the Upper House? The obligation of the sovereign to be a churchman might present itself to the popular mind as a violence to his conscience, for it is not to be supposed that anyone in the twentieth century could possibly benefit by such chains. To abolish the Coronation would certainly spoil the people's fun, but perhaps it would be proposed that Westminster Abbey would anyway be a nice place for a show of that sort and that any bits of the service which meant anything could be taken out by a vote in Parliament.

The significance of the fact that the Church will go on whatever the State says about it is this: that so long as the State goes on it will have to reckon with the Church, and the question is not, therefore, whether certain problems of either of the parties would be simplified by the disappearance of the other but, assuming that both go on, what are their relationships to be? They cannot escape having some. It must not be assumed that the only alternative to the totality of the present arrangements is complete disestablishment. 'The Establishment', says Sir Lewis Dibdin, 'has survived so many modification that, whatever we may think, it would be rash to assert that the irreducible minimum has now been reached.'[3] The basic question must be whether it is better for the relationship between Church and State to be defined so that both parties know where they stand, or to leave it to be settled *ad hoc* whenever the two make contact, as they must continue to do, on the pretence that the vast and ancient organization of the historic Church in England is no more than just another voluntary organization with private objects which amuse its members.

Those whose predilections are for this pretence would do well to reflect on the fact that the problem centres upon the Church of England because that is the most numerous and deep-rooted ecclesiastical organization in England. The problem does not arise in the case of the Nonconformist churches because, with one exception, they are ancillary and in the main derivative. The

---

[3] Op. cit., p.116.

Church of England in a sense fights their battles for them, and is the voice of Christianity in the State. If that voice were not heard, other churches might have the satisfaction of knowing that their mother had been placed by the State on an equality with themselves, but it is difficult to believe that they would not thereby be weakened. There are few Methodists, one imagines, who would be glad to see the sovereign profess no religion, or enter upon his office with a mere affirmation of good intentions. Few Christians of any kind would wish to see the proceedings of Parliament open without a prayer. The one Nonconformist body which might have cause for satisfaction is the Roman Church.

It is worth considering for a moment the politics of the Missal.[4] There are prayers provided with the design of undoing the work of the Reformation and no doubt, if that work were undone, the English State would qualify for a more central place in the Missal than it now occupies. The Introit for 4 May (The English and Welsh Martyrs) is no doubt a bemoaning of our reformed condition: 'O God, the heathen have broken into thy inheritance.' The Collect which follows is more specific and recalls those who were 'champions of the true faith *and* of the papacy' (my italics), and the third collect roundly asserts that 'from the beginning' of their church the English were 'the dowry of the blessed virgin Mary and subjects of Peter'. A Postcommunion prayer for the same day, said, like the third collect, to be 'For England', describes 'this nation of ours' as 'illustrious for its ancient loyalty to the apostle Peter' and concludes, in case there should be any ambiguity in the former reference, with petition that users of the Missal may be strengthened in obedience to the Apostolic See. More specifically political is the note, among the Bidding Prayers for Good Friday, under the heading 'For the Emperor', which explains that this prayer is 'omitted, the Holy Roman Empire being vacant'. Users of the Missal are apparently to count the restoration of the Empire among their political aspirations, even though they may now omit the remembrance of it from their prayers. This vestige of the better days of the Roman polity is of interest as a succinct demonstration of the patience of the Curia, and of its political tenacity. An Englishman accustomed

---

[4]The references are to *The Missal in Latin and English, Being the text of the Missale Romanum with English rubrics and a new translation*, 1949.

to the Book of Common Prayer will recognize in the rubric a political disposition exactly parallel with that taken up by his own church in relation to the English crown. The only odd thing, to the Englishman, will be precisely that the Missal, even as edited for use in this country, should take that disposition in relation to someone else's crown, which not only does not now exist but never at any time had the slightest connection with our own or meant anything to it.

The Roman Church is far from having abandoned its political objectives. In this country it plays the role of a minority biding its time. If it were as strong in England as our Church now is, the State would be forced to define more or less regularly its relationship to it. The State would, ultimately, have not merely to define relationships with its own subjects in their church but with a foreign power. That is, from the national point of view, the most significant difference between the Roman Church and our own. 'If we lived in Plato's commonwealth', said Bramhall,[5] 'where every man did his duty', there could be no danger in following the Pope. But the seventeenth century could remember Englishmen being relieved of their duty of common loyalty by a bishop in Rome. It was no accident that the Canons of 1604 began with the assertion of Royal Supremacy. It might be said that the authors of the Draft Canons of 1947 showed a lack of historical sense in not following a similar arrangement. It is popularly supposed that these political questions are dead, but they are not. Even the most outrageous of papal political claims have found apologists in our own time, and since the Reformation Rome has emphasized her apartness still further by the formal assertion of papal infallibility. In the seventeenth century it was still possible for a devout Frenchman, a member of the Roman Church, to write that the Jesuits had rendered themselves guilty not only of a heresy 'but of a manifest impiety, in levelling God with a creature, and asking us to render to the mere word of a man (the Pope) the same devotion as is due to the eternal word'.[6] In our day a Frenchman, and one of the most enlightened, can still defend the old thesis of the Elizabethan Jesuits that excommunication of a Prince by Rome relieves the subject of all duty of obedience, and that a Pope is indeed a temporal sovereign

[5] See John Bramhall, *The Consecration of Protestant Bishops Vindicated.*

[6] See Jean Racine, *Abrégé de l'histoire de Port-Royal.*

because if he were not he could not avoid being a subject.[7] In 1789 English Roman Catholics could lay a protestation before Parliament declaring that they acknowledged no infallibility in the Pope. They would not dare to show such independence now nor, since the Roman Church, once wrong, is infallibly wrong, will they ever dare again. They have their politics, however subduedly for the present, and they are not in their obedience bound to England.

They have their politics: need we really be ashamed to have ours? Embodied in the Book of Common Prayer is a simple loyalty to the Crown, which itself is further bound to us by the obligation on the sovereign to be a member of the Church. The making of the State Prayers optional, at Morning and Evening Prayer, in the Book of 1928, was a defection which only the intervention of Parliament (however motivated) prevented becoming part of the law of the Church as it has, regrettably, become part of its practice.

---

[7] See Jacques Maritain, *Primauté du Spirituel*, 1927.

Newman's Politics

'Newman thought that social and political affairs were not his "line", but this does not mean that what he has to say about these matters, nor indeed, what he fails to say, can be ignored.' Thus Terence Kenny in his *Political Thought of John Henry Newman*. This amounts to saying that it is because of Newman's general importance that the positions he took in political matters deserve to be studied. As to that general importance, Mr Kenny reports the surely immoderate opinion that 'Newman is widely considered among Catholics today to rank among the great doctors of the Church, even, some would say, to be of the stature of St Augustine and St Thomas Aquinas himself.' Mr Kenny has undertaken his task with a thoroughness appropriate to such an estimate. He has scraped the barrel of Newman's works for such political content as it has. This is a useful performance, even if it rather proves, in the result, that Newman's view that these things were not particularly in his line was a true one.

The political positions adopted by so subtle a mind cannot fail to be of interest. When Newman turned to explanation the subtlety had full play, yet the motives which exercised it were perhaps not extraordinary. One may regret that Mr Kenny's treatment of his subject is not more frankly historical or even biographical, for Newman's unsystematic utterances about politics were occasioned by his successive personal positions, and would, one suspects, have been rendered more fully intelligible by such treatment. Much in his early views represents attitudes common in the England in which he came to maturity; much in his later views represents the current of thought in those days. If there is a 'great gulf' between 'the Newman of 1829 who was alarmed at the prospect of the disestablishment of the English Church' and the later Newman who 'came to prefer the mediocre, neutral, tolerant State', the movement from one position to the other is, after all, natural enough in one who had abandoned the English Church for a species of non-conformity. It would be interesting to enquire whether there is not a relation between what Mr Kenny speaks of as Newman's 'life-long obtuseness to the vexing social problems of his age', or as his 'notorious lack of a social conscience', and his abandonment of the English Church in favour of an institution with its finger less securely on the pulse of this country. Yet Newman was in some ways well rooted in England, and much that strikes Mr Kenny as remarkable (e.g. his non-Thomistic approach to politics) is remarkable from a Roman, or more generally from a Latin point of view, but is not so if one views him as an Englishman.

THE SIXTIES

Church and Town

A layman of the Church of England, who has the misfortune to think about his position, may well be puzzled. To what discipline is he subject? He lives in a particular parish. Is he to be content with everything he finds there? There is a strong argument for saying that he should be. For this much is clear. Whatever differences there may be among his bishops, priests and deacons, they are united in their adherence to this outward order of the parochial system. Among people who disagree about so much even this measure of common ground is notable. Unless they are to be supposed merely to be concurring in ancient abuses which, from sloth, they are unwilling to put right – and that is not to be thought of – they must be saying to the layman: You will find the faith taught, and the sacraments administered, where you live. Go to your parish church.

So the layman goes. What does he find? He may be sure of finding a priest, ordained by a bishop in accordance with the ordinal, administering the sacraments and reading the Bible. He cannot be certain of much else. The Book of Common Prayer will be in use, but this does not mean that the order of service will necessarily be followed or the rubrics obeyed. The Prayer Book will be used, not according to the use of Salisbury or Hereford or York but according to the use of the parish or rather of the clergyman who happens to be in charge. Even the parishes which make most pretence of following the Prayer Book depart from it, and in the most important particulars. It is for example known for such parishes to admit to Communion persons who are not confirmed and are unready and undesirous to be confirmed. At sermon-time many oddities will be heard. The parishioner may be told at Christmas not to think of God with arms and legs. On the Sunday before Lent he may be exhorted not to fast. He may be told, in defiance of the Calendar in front of his Prayer Book, that in the Church of England there are no fasts. To be content with everything in the parish church is difficult, even for the most submissive, unless they have the gift of being blind to all contraries.

The layman who wishes to submit has to choose between his conscience and his parish priest. Happy the man who finds an identity between the two! But the man who does not? Even the stoutest Protestant must admit the possibility of a dilemma. It can hardly be that the layman must accept everything he is taught, however eccentric it may be. The martyrs roasted at Smithfield secured at least some freedom. Yet if the layman listens to his conscience he may have to dissent from the priest to whose care the Church, by its parochial arrangements, commits him.

The common answer to the man who finds himself in a dilemma of this kind is that he should abandon his parish church for another where the priest is more of his own way of thinking. This solution certainly makes for the pastoral and professional quiet of the clergy. They gather round them a laity, High, Low or Medium, according to their own preconceptions, and do not trouble themselves about the disarray in the next parish. The solution should also provide a sabbath calm for the layman, so long as he is not alive to the implications of leaving what the Church has appointed for him in his own parish in favour of what she has appointed for others in the next parish. If, however, he thinks of himself as a Christian baptised and confirmed in accordance with the rites of the Church, he may well wonder that the Catholic and Apostolic appointments are such that it is thought proper for him to pick and choose among them. It is intelligible that one should be recommended to hear one clergyman preach, rather than another, as being more likely to enlighten. But it is not intelligible that one should choose one celebration of Holy Communion rather than another, for they are the same Communion. The mass celebrated at the north side is neither more nor less than the Lord's Supper celebrated with bits out of the Roman Missal. (I speak as a layman.) Can I choose between them without dividing myself from those from whom I am not to be divided?

There is a *Protestant* answer to this question, and a *Catholic* answer. The *Protestant* answer is that the outward sign is nothing, and that you need not go to Communion at all if you find it more convenient to make an act of faith under the bedclothes; that for the sake of the minister you should, however, attend a church where they say mass at the north side; such a minister's words are not outward symbols like the bread and wine; and his expositions of scripture are scriptural, whereas those given where the celebrate differently are interpretations. This is a sort of proof, so long as you do not ask how one man can talk for hours without departing from mere exposition, while another cannot help slipping in glosses at every word. The *Catholic* answer to the layman who asks whether he should leave the mass of his own parish for the Lord's Supper with bits from the Missal is that this Lord's Supper, though no more valid than the mass at the north side, is more in accordance with the faith of the historic Church. At least that answer involves no blasphemous claims to a personal infallibility. But it leaves the root of the matter untouched. It is equivalent to the recommendation to hear one preacher rather than another, as being more edifying. It says nothing to the man who fears that to leave the priest and sacraments proposed for him in his own parish is a wilful election which he cannot make without detraction from the claims of the Church – as if he had said that the opinions of the minister hinder the effect of the sacrament. Neither the Catholic nor the Protestant answer admits the reality of this scruple.

The Anglican tradition allows a certain diversity. The Preface to the Prayer Book recognizes this, if not the Prayer Book itself. But our present diversity is no matter for complacency. The reforming fathers, like the Fathers before them, were concerned with how the Church should be, what its nature was. It did not occur to them that there could be a number of answers to this question. Their question was about the One Church; they were concerned with particular churches only in a geographical sense. They had not reached the late Protestant sloppiness of supposing there to be a variety of 'churches', all nice and respectable as one another. That is a nonsense which has no place in the Christian faith. There is no *Catholic* reason for allowing members of the Italian communion to practise in this country. The reasons for allowing that are the protestant and political ones on which the practice of the English dissenting sects is based. We certainly cannot avail ourselves of these reasons to justify differences within the Church of England itself. We can tolerate among ourselves only such differences as do not call the catholicity of the Church in question. To hesitate on the threshold of another's celebrations of Holy Communion does precisely that. And this is what happens, Sunday by Sunday, in this town [Sevenoaks, Kent].

There is no escape from this except in an extreme subjectivism which proposes to put a few threadbare ideas in place of the Communion itself as the bond between us. This is a Protestantism which has driven itself to the point of solipsism and ego-mania. '*And he that places any religious safey in theological Decisions, Scholastic points, in particular Doctrines and opinions, that must be held about the Scripture Words of Faith, Justification, Sanctification, Election and Reprobation, so far departs from the true worship of the Living God within him, and sets up an Idol of Notions to be worshipped, if not instead of, yet along with him.*' Those who value their opinions will go their own ways; but what are the others to do?

What Kind of English?

To the Editor of *The Church Times*

Sir,

The question, what sort of English should be used in public prayer?, is a more fundamental one than it is usually thought to be. It is *not* a matter of taste, if by that is meant a matter in which one opinion is as good as another. It is a matter of truth, of the authenticity with which we speak.

No doubt the matters with which the Prayer Book deals have always, in some degree, eluded human speech. They elude our language more completely than they did the English of the sixteenth century. There are profound and complicated reasons for that. One of them is to be found in a comparison of the state of the general language then and now, as to which I will say only that our language is thinner, vaguer, slicker. Another is in the fact that the sixteenth century was a theological age in a sense in which ours is not; people thought in theological terms, whereas now it is often difficult even with educated people, to jockey up to a position from which the most elementary theological discourse could begin. No wonder it is difficult to write prayers which ring true, and can be used in public.

It seems to me that the question, what kind of English should the prayers be written in?, is not one which would present itself to minds absorbed in their task. It is not a question which a serious writer could ask. He writes what he can, in order to make his meaning plain. He does not *choose* a style from a menu including the language of the Press, the language of the Athenaeum (if there is one, as one of your correspondents suggests) and various kinds of Wardour Street.

Your correspondent says: 'Historically our Prayer Book was written at a time where there was an accepted literary English.' It would be hard to speak more un-historically than that. The Prayer Book was written at a time when a language which *later* began to be thought of as 'accepted literary English' was in process of painful parturition. It is as absurd to think of Cranmer as imitating some 'accepted' language as to think of the Tudors ornamenting their churches with the ludicrous bric-à-brac which too often passes for appropriate furnishing in ours.

Very likely we are not capable of constructing an enduring liturgy in the language of the twentieth century. I should be more hopeful if, when I went to church, I more often heard a few terse words which conveyed some meaning as serious and precise as the key words of a contract the churchwarden might put his name to in the course of his business. When someone shows me laconic and forceful new collects, addressing the mind to God, I will begin to take the re-writing of the Prayer Book seriously. Meanwhile it strikes me as something of a frivolity.

Native Ruminations

INTRODUCTION

The conduct of government rests upon the same foundation and encounters the same difficulties as the conduct of private persons: that is, as to its object and justification, for as to its methods, or technical part, there is all the difference which separates the person from the group, the man acting on behalf of himself from the man acting on behalf of many. The technical part, in government as in private conduct, is now the only one which is publicly or at any rate generally recognized, as if by this evasion the more difficult part of the subject, which relates to ends, could be avoided. Upon 'the law of nature and the law of revelation', Blackstone said, 'depend all human laws'.[1] This quaint language, which would at once be derided if it were introduced now into public discussion, conceals a difficulty which is no less ours than it was our ancestors'.

It was reasonable for Blackstone, using this language, to use also language of a certain nobility in describing the functions of Members of Parliament:

> They are not thus honourably distinguished from the rest of their fellow-subjects, merely that they may privilege their persons, their estates, or their domestics; that they may list under party banners; may grant or withold supplies; may vote with or against a popular or unpopular administration; but upon considerations far more interesting and important. They are the guardians of the English constitution; the makers, repealers and interpreters of the English laws; delegated to watch, to check, and to avert every dangerous innovation, to propose, adopt, and to cherish any solid and well-weighed

---

[1] Sir William Blackstone, *Commentaries on the Laws of England* (1765-9), Introduction, Section I.

> improvement; bound by every tie of nature, of honour, and of religion, to transmit that constitution and those laws to their posterity, amended if possible, at least without derogation.

This is so unlike the language we should use, in relation to Members of Parliament, that it has an air of comedy. Honour and religion are – many would say, happily – subverted, and nature has become uncertain, so it is not clear what binds the Members. Are they there after all merely 'that they may privilege their persons'? They would for the most part shy away from that explanation. Many might say they were there to make innovations, as Blackstone thought they were there to avert them: and while for Blackstone 'dangerous' was the adjective which went naturally with 'innovation', for our Members other, more approving qualifications would come more readily to mind. They might well be so busy about change as not to catch sight of the fundamental problem, which remains, however. What are they there for, if not merely to 'privilege their persons'? If not tied by honour or religion, they are perhaps tied by nature, which science may study, and their innovations are in her service. It is a possibility.

A POSSIBLE ANGLICANISM

1

The real difficulty of the Creed is the first word – I – the number and person of the *Credo*. The *ergo* of Descartes, like many others before and since, now looks like a confidence-trick.

This is a difficulty which is least in youth, when the force of desire makes a certain animism easy. Surely a spirit must dwell in that body which is the object of nascent desires? But later the reflection comes that that spirit is like one's own, which is less impressive. A more wholesome reflection, perhaps, is that one's own body is like another's. That is to say, one can explain one's own spirit in terms of another's body, and so of one's own; re-assure oneself that, however uncertain it is to be oneself, one must at least be like other bodies, which seem plausible enough. This is a pagan reflection, but it may also be a Christian one, though it is self-regarding, perhaps, in a way that the young man's animism in relation to another body may not be – but that is only perhaps, too.

Whichever way one approaches the subject, one arrives at the identification of the self and the body, whether or not the two are co-terminous. There is nothing but the body, its actions and manifestations, that has any claim to be thought of as a self. Is spirit something different? If it is, I am quite without understanding of it. Unless of course it is a hall-mark, set on the body by God, or a sort of standard pattern, the image of the Creator. But that must be an object of faith, because it cannot be perceived – believed in if at all in sheer despair at what can be perceived, and out of need for a re-assurance of one's identity, not so much with oneself as with other creatures. It therefore looks like a metaphysical projection of the common need to be like another body, and to be re-assured that the other body contains consciousness, or whatever it is that one perceives in oneself. I have always slid over these difficulties to the resurrection of the body, so little believed in, incredible certainly, but more understandable than any other apology for the life everlasting – the only understandable one, I would say. It is that or nothing.

That, as distinct from nothing, is, it seems to me, what religion is. There is nothing but God to choose. Apart from that, which we properly call Him, not on account of sex but because of an identity with ourselves, there are only the miscellaneous performances of the human body, of any sort of body – not merely that of a cat but of a stone, for if consciousness has to be inferred from external appearance stones have their performance as well as those who are more usually thought of as our neighbours. If He does not exist the miscellaneous performances of the human body are not *sui generis*, the sums you do are no more than the sums done by a calculating machine, your punch is like that of the boulder that falls on you. Indeed I am afraid we believe in Him in order to be *sui generis*, in order not to perish. And if our faith is right he chooses us – we are a mirror and there really is someone looking in.

The Christian faith is that God was made man. And what is man? Why, he is the image of God – there is no other meaning I can attach to the expression. He is the broken image which was re-made at the Incarnation, for our re-assurance. There is a circle here which may be a deceit. If we believe it is because we want to choose and be chosen. If our belief is true it is because we must so choose. Otherwise the desire to choose and be chosen is the illusory appearance of something else, a mere accompaniment of being driven on by forces which indifferently drive everything. One cannot say that that alternative is improbable.

There is a trick in the abstraction of language which could deceive us either way. Because there is nothing of us but our bodies and their manifestations, the language which reminds us least of them seems most promising of a truth beyond them. But in fact what we say is said in words which have their start in the operations of the body. Words are not ours but the words of a myriad, having point only because of their history, ultimately of their prehistory. The man who speaks, if there is Man, is the same who (I think it was Frobenius who put me on to this) at some stage of pre-history – and it may be in some of contemporary consciousness – could have sexual intercourse without being aware of it, as I might scratch my head without knowing it. We speak as historical persons – well, to say persons is to beg the question, but we do not speak as ourselves. If we are selves, it is by virtue of other selves that we are so. And our speaking is that of a race, of a tribe, of a time. There is no speech which is not of a here and now and it is nothing except in terms of other times and elsewhere. That is why the historical church is so apt to our needs and meaning. It is a congregation of meaning and there is no meaning without congregation.

There is no meaning except in terms of a time and a place. If one could understand it would be at one altar, in a stone building, in such a place, at perhaps eight o'clock on a Sunday morning. If there were no sacraments there would be nothing. If there were not England there would be no church, for me who happen to have been born here. I am an Anglican.

2

If the *ecclesia anglicana* is the vehicle of meaning for me, it is the centre of England, however little it seems to be regarded. That is to say, it is so so far as England enters my consciousness – to which word I prefer *conscience*, and consider the French are more fortunate (and more exact) than we in having only one word for the two (English) conceptions. The *ecclesia anglicana* is the centre of the political England no less than of the others, and the political conceptions which omit it are not merely incomplete; they are without middle. It is no less true, however, that any consideration of the Church which ignores the vulgar exterior of doing and intriguing

– the ordinary behaviour of men – is an abstraction of an individual mind, the invention of a non-imagination – a partial, protestant mind like Kant's, trying to elevate our thinking above the world of sense. The truth is that churches have their politics, in the most vulgar sense, no more deserving of pity than other politics. There is no reason to adopt a soppy, Christianish way of talking about these things, as if everything to do with the church demanded the manners of the Ladies' Working Party. This soppiness is of course a new thing, the product not of sweeter and more gracious ways of thinking but of the progressive realization that the church is socially unimportant and can (nearly) be ignored. It was not very nice that people should burn one another for their faith, or that Archbishops should be executed for their political devotion to their sovereign, but these things were done because, at the time when they were done, there was not the present facility in extracting from theological conceptions all trace of practical meaning.

The progress of democracy – for which Locke's *Letter on Toleration* is an early apologia – has been a process of laicisation. It has succeeded in driving religion into the recesses of a thing called the individual conscience, which has to be less than the *consciousness* people have of their physical environment, including themselves, so that it bothers nobody. Then, it is said, we can ignore people's beliefs, indeed the proprieties of our politics demand that we should do so. We will debate in parliament about the things we can really agree about – what we all want, food, keeping the enemy away, never mind who we are or what form we give to the food we eat. The end of this is a material world which there is no-one to observe. There is the food secured for us by our governors, the fuel that warms our bodies, the machines which carry us around or replace our labours. All this system is to be promoted and no questions asked, for *conscience* has nothing to do with it. It is the Neanderthal man, with his mind closing upon him as he reaches the end of his path. Of course the conception is muddled. If politics are planned as a system of doing things to people (which, so far as it ignores consciousness is the same things as doing things to things) it assumes a supreme political group who do the doing, who are not merely some *thing* but some *bodies*, not merely some bodies but bodies with consciousness. There could be a new serfdom which would make this possible, but it is an oppression which would so much impoverish the human race, the conception of what man is, that even for the governors it would in the end be of little interest.

Under this negative debate of our public affairs, once excused under the name of liberty and now, more often, under the name of economics or production, the conscious, including the ecclesiastical, groups still stir. Not only stir, but exhibit all those political symptoms which are admitted to exist only in relation to groups concerned with the matters the consciousness of the commonwealth admits. Just as, in westernized Africa, black habits are likely to break out and disrupt the internationally admitted plans for a century ahead, the suppressed political forces of ecclesiastical politics are likely to irrupt one day, amidst profound misunderstanding, on the surface of our political life which denies them. The forces are, in the last analysis, only those of the *ecclesia anglicana*, with its tail of protestant sects fading imperceptibly into the great mass of what might be called the *prejudice of disbelief*, and the Popish non-conformity which has its political centre elsewhere. Meanwhile, so far as a residual theory of establishment is still admitted, the *ecclesia anglicana* is inhibited by (its own and others') belief that it occupies a seat of political influence, while the Roman conspirators, unhampered, plan the destruction of the whole edifice, political and social. Coleridge, so far as I know, was the last man of first-rate intellect who took this possibility seriously.

3

Does it matter an awful lot? one might ask. I will not here enter upon the doctrine of papal infallibility, which is an absolute bar to liberty of conscience, as it used to be called, or to the free admission of all that comes to our consciousness, as one might more lucidly put it now: except to say that it is also an invention, in its final form, of the democratic eighteen seventies, the earliest moment at which it became politically possible for the Curia to get the explicit endorsement of its long-nurtured, but hitherto always partially thwarted, ambitions. The essential thing is whether we want, in this country, a Roman *imperium in imperio*; as to which I agree with Coleridge that we do not. Rome has since the Middle Ages understood the necessity of government, and she has progressively insisted on the superiority of her own. But her government is like other people's, as was well enough understood in the old Catholic monarchies and given rational form in the Reformation conception of the Sovereign as Governor of the church in his own dominions – a conception of greater antiquity, it could be claimed, than the notion of papal infallibility; it is, indeed, much the conception of Constantine. It has often puzzled people, in recent times, that in the sixteenth century men should have attached so much importance to the subject following the religion of his prince. What we may think of as mere tergiversations, however, conceal a profound sense of the identity of the church and the commonwealth, as aspects of the same body, so that a failure to follow the prince in his religion partakes of the nature of schism. And as for the theology of it, given that the Church is one, but is torn, is our Catholicity more injured by being out of communion with the Bishop of Rome than by being out of communion with our prince and those among whom we live? Note the *non-conformist* quality of the papists among us.

Of course the identity of church and commonwealth was never more shadowy than it is now – or never since, say, the days of Constantine. But one cannot be complete without the other, and the notion of the solitary catholic is ridiculous. We are a broken-down lot, whichever way you look at it. If you look at it from the point of view of the ordinary non-Christian subject – he is not now even legally called that, he is a citizen, if you please – is there any point in monarchy at all? There is because the truth is not a matter of his or of anyone else's opinion. He cannot help being human, poor devil, if that is what we are. Therefore he exists as we (the obscure Christians) do, in virtue of the existence of others. And if Man exists only by God, the fact is not altered by Mr Jones thinking otherwise. And if he does not think – a better and happier condition than being all the time in exacerbated error – he may still feel that a King or Queen can stand for us as policies and the ministers who promote them can not. Already in the Cabinet, with its score of ministers, whose policies are the subject of analytical discourse, the human mind – which is the same as the human body – has begun to disintegrate; but it is one in the crown, which is as mysterious and unknowable as we are ourselves. It is by virtue of that that we are one. The need for this identification is not likely to become less, in the future, whether the future lies in an abstracted world of international organizations or in a physical devastation which sends us back to our primitive concerns. It is probably only for the local group that this can have any meaning. Others should not be discouraged from shedding the burden of loyalty. It may well be that the Crown will end, as it began, as the Crown of England.

AN ESSAY ON IDENTITY

1

It is, indeed, very hard to understand what makes up 'I'. And the mere existence of the pronoun should not at once persuade us of the existence of the thing.

There is, of course, a sense in which 'I' is self-evident. But it is a pretty silly sense, a sort of tautology. 'I' is the fact of the assertion being made. It does not get one out of the prison of solipsism, but when we say 'I' exists, what we are really hoping is that there are other 'I's. If we do not mean that we do not mean anything, indeed there would hardly be such a thing as meaning.

We are therefore talking about the existence of 'Man', and this is a very difficult conception indeed. Moreover, it is a conception rich in history; it is history. It is also biology. To discuss 'Man', in fact, one can only proceed by taking some traditional universe of discourse, and defining him in terms of it. There is nothing else.

The answer to 'what am I?' can only be that I am one of those two-legged creatures of which we see so much. Biology and history tell us something about them – their relations with other species of animal, their relations with one another. 'I' becomes at once a term for a variant, though it could also mean one of two identical twins, identically brought up, if that were possible. In any case what makes 'man' is not the fact of 'I', the individual, but the fact of the species. Unless one can say 'I am a man', i.e. one of a kind, 'I' does not say anything. Yet what is meant by 'I', the individual, is something more overweening than that. The something is historical and conceptual. It has been invented by man, I suppose as a comfort. It is a reason why you should not kill me – which is something living creatures seem to be constitutionally against, though few take it as hard as man.

Taking it hard, however, is merely a function of consciousness. And consciousness – as is not perhaps widely understood – is purely traditional. Adam did not know what he was doing. That was his innocence. There was a point at which consciousness emerged, presumably out of the frustration of wishes. It has grown and been handed down. What it amounts to is determined by the traditions of particular societies. A 'culture' is partly a style of consciousness. It can however be more easily studied as a style of behaviour. Behaviour and consciousness are two related aspects of 'Man'. They are not identical; there is plenty of behaviour without consciousness. But the style of one affects the style of the other.

The individual 'is', or may certainly be identified as, a sub-style of consciousness and behaviour. The variant is not important, except in terms of a tradition which says that it is. Tradition, once developed beyond a certain point, has to say something about 'Man'. The subject is so difficult that it usually starts by saying something about gods. These are projections, which is not to say that God might not be there all the time, watching all this. But mythology is about man, the first sketch of a difficult subject.

The individual is nowhere in this. And what did God become, in Christian history? He became Man, one for all. The meaning of the first Adam was Man, and so with the second. His incarnation was like the descent of a Platonic form into physical shape. It was a re-affirmation of the kind. Every bit of the kind was important. In the end the bits thought they were important as 'individuals'. The claim is ill-founded.

2

The incarnation is a tall story. But of course if you believe in God you can believe it. If you do not believe it, you can still believe that the kind is important, though without giving a reason for it. Is the difference between the importance attributed to kind by the Incarnationist and that attributed to it by the rest of the world of any significance in relation to the 'individual'?

The matter is not free from difficulty. Is every 'individual' included in the Christian salvation? It has generally been supposed not. The saints are a subkind. Those who believe in Christ shall not perish, but have ever-lasting life. The rest shall perish in some sort. Cowper thought himself one of these: ACTUM EST DE TE, PERIISTI. The saints are, as it were, a wealthy class, those to whom, having already, more shall be given. The Christian looks for a more precise identification by hoping to approximate to this class, he is a kind of snob. His 'I' is not merely the two-legged animal; it is an 'I' with paraphernalia, more or less realized. The rest of the world no doubt has its own snobbisms, their 'I's are variants of sub-kinds, more sharply defined on that account. Is there any possibility of an 'I' which is not, as it were, re-defined by a snobbism?

It is in fact impossible to conceive it. Is an Idiot a man? Yes. A monster? Yes. A man in a long coma preceding death? Yes. I give the answers of fashion. At other times it might have been said that the idiot was possessed, and so out of kind. And so on. But in fashionable terms where does the man begin? At the mouth of the womb? How premature must a foetus be to be disqualified? Are the ovum and sperm constituent parts of a man? You must choose your snobbism rather arbitrarily. And when you have chosen it, you say to those outside it: Periisti. Identity implies the election of a sub-kind, and henceforth a course of conduct which may be described as the management of the sub-kind. The object of this management is to collect the sub-kind into some ark or paradise. For the Christian it is theologically prescribed. For the self-justifying abortionist – as distinct from the abortionist who is willing to murder for money, who belongs, of course, to a species with wider terms of reference – it is the group of healthy people, as contemporaneously conceived. The two-legged may be handled without scruple in relation to those outside the group. This health is something which can be ascertained in relation to other people. Medicine and surgery at large are the treatment of other people. They are the technics of humanist management. Its objects are the preservation of a kind. It ought not to be too scrupulous about incidental 'individuals'. The Christian should not be too careful with the damned; the kindness so often exhibited is a symptom of weakened faith.

Is there a Christian management of the sub-kind? Since God became Man, would it not be reasonable to seek an objective salvation for the holy, to attempt a kind of eugenics for God's people? 'Not one of these little ones should perish', to be sure, but what about these and these? The ones not yet born? The ones whose parent orgasm is being mounted at this moment? Those who will tear one another's eyes out, in a hundred year's time, for the last food in Asia? Is every bit of mankind important? What does number mean in relation to holiness? Would it not be a kindness for old men to kill themselves?

3

What makes up the 'I'? If the separate parts of our kind are 'individuals' there would have to be identifiable minds in the separate bodies. But are there? 'Creation's matter flows through us like a river.' It flows, but the question is whether there is an 'us' that it flows through. And so with consciousness. It flows, but its contents are historical rather than individual. It is a matter of 'culture' what we are conscious of. The 'thought' is a common thought; only so could it be understood. A stream loaded with old bottles, the vegetation of several countries, rags of clothing perhaps, flows around the world. It makes no sense to talk of the individual mind. The individual body, perhaps. That is made of matter that flows in this changing form, comes from and goes to other things. But for its limited history of growth and decay it is defined by its skin, it is one in the clear sense of being separable from other things. The individual, if anything, is this, without regard to consciousness. It begins with the egg and the sperm; it ends, not with certified death but with the disintegration which follows. In the end it is not there, as an identifiable thing. There is no 'personality' apart from it. If that were ever collected again, it could only be at the resurrection of the body.

'CALL NO MAN HAPPY UNTIL HE IS DEAD'

1

Conduct is supposed to be of the individual. And so, it is supposed to be directed from the inside, for that is how the individual is conceived of as being directed. That is what used to be called being a 'rational creature'. There are no such creatures nowadays, but the conception of being directed from the inside persists. Indeed it was never so popular. The preferred theory is now that not only the direction, but the rules of conduct themselves, come from inside.

There is something in this. Man, like other machines, moves according to the laws of his construction. There may be question as to how absolute those laws are, but nobody doubts that there are limits within which he must operate, whether or not those limits are held to be fully known. The limits are the range of human conduct, and it is generally held that the individual has to choose points within that range, and that this is his freedom.

It may be so. But, whether or not freedom is an illusion, there is at any rate an apparent question of how I should act. And so of where to look for the rules. Or what motives to admit, which is the same thing. Those in search of the individual usually prefer the motives of non-conformity, or said to be so. If the differentiation goes far enough, whom may they not find? Them 'selves', no doubt, as the unattainable end; meanwhile in observable particulars their conduct resembles that of other people. At best they contribute to the fissiparousness of groups; more generally merely share in the popular fickleness, which heaves to and fro between accepted opinions.

It is better, perhaps, to accept the external direction of one's conduct. There is then no nonsense about one's 'self', no attention to the pathology of the moment. The mind can be used to reflect the outside world, as is the case with the best animals. There is a duty of discrimination, which cannot be avoided, but one makes as little as may be of internal doubts and hesitations – the flaws in the mirror, the ripples on the surface of the reflecting water, or the unidentified objects lying below the surface.

One should be glad to find social conceptions one can conform to. They represent possibilities of one's nature, and the most one can hope to do is to embody certain of those possibilities.

2

The person who takes this orientation finds a kind of renewal. The 'individual' sinks from sight and is extinguished; in exchange, one has all the benefits of history, not as an emporium to choose from, but as they bear down upon one at a particular point of time, like a column of air. The famous 'conflict between the individual and society' – that Byronic conception – is resolved, because one term is lost. One enters, as a negligible quantity, on a vast playing field and has all the possibilities of the game being played there. One chooses roles and tries to perfect them – not one role, but as many as one can discern. Instead of the 'problem of conduct' there is the matter of discernment. The attention is shifted from the subject to the object. Indeed one does not bother about the subject; perhaps it is not there.

'Call no man happy until he is dead' is a paradigm of this conception of things. The happiness is not an affective condition, it is a state of prosperity, judged as such by others rather than by the subject. Or if the subject judges of himself, he judges as he would of another man, because it is of a man that he is judging, not of a 'self'. Health, wives, children, cattle or other riches according to the custom of the time, the marks of honour accorded by other men – these are the constituents of this happiness. In all this there is room for a large discrimination. One need not keep many cattle to be sure of one's milk, in a society in which it comes to door in bottles. One may not get an honour one cares for by owning a bigger car than one's neighbours. Diogenes is an early example of sophistication in this kind. He sought an objective condition, as much as any patriarch in the Old Testament, but he was on the brink of the terrible discovery of him'self' which would ruin everything.

3

The role one chooses – the husband, the father, the soldier, the man of affairs – one plays them more or less well according to the richness of one's inherited conceptions. There is no way of acquiring such conceptions except by inheritance, but of course whereas any fool can inherit money the ability to inherit conceptions depends a little – though less than is usually thought – on the capacity of the heir. This capacity of the heir is, however, a small thing compared with the capacity of the society he lives in to remember and to transmit, in short to embody. You cannot be Plato in Bechuanaland or George Herbert in Connecticut. You cannot be in the Italy of the twentieth century a man of the first century A.D. So in fact you are largely directed from the outside, however little you like to think so, and it is not so much a recommendation I am giving you as a short view of the nature of things.

To seek to discriminate among your inherited possessions, to understand more profoundly the roles it is your chance to be called upon to play, is more than enough to occupy anybody. Of course there are wilful persons who imagine that they stand outside society and change it, but it is merely that they have struck a not very rich vein of tradition. Their ideas of changing come from where other people's ideas come from; they cannot be got from anywhere else. And if those who talk most of changing society also talk most of individual liberty, it is merely that they are confused. To make a change is to make other people bend. If one can do that at all it is only by putting them in the way of a current. And what is the meaning of acquiescence, to the reed the stream catches?

4

Acquiescence is perhaps a joke. At any rate it is clear that, for the most part of our lives, there is no more in it than is involved in going quietly. What opinions do you hold about being born, growing, declining, and dying? You will do these things even if you are against them. And how? You will do them as they are done in these parts, at this time. How much less acquiescence is involved in being compelled by someone who says he understands your role better than you do yourself? Is there really much difference between persuasion and compulsion? The mythologies of the moment say that there is, and they have to be obeyed. In the very act of obedience to them the man who understands his role will see that there is no freedom of choice, that a compulsion underlies all our persuasions. But if it does, should we deny it?

The word 'democracy' is now so full of air that it is about to burst. Its bursting will not be the end of everything but the recognition, in passing, of a truth. There is reason to believe that it may mitigate the boredom of our society. If hunger does not drive us, do we not need more than ever those who will put us in a corner and make us fight? The ease of technology will, in any case, in the end produce a race of diminishing consciousness, for whom the only persuasion is by force. The triumph of technology would be to leave people with so little consciousness that they did not notice the change.

ON THE EROS OF POETRY

1

Ernst Robert Curtius says, in *Europäische Literatur und lateinisches Mittelalter* (1948), that most of the themes employed by modern lyrical poets, 'out of their own experience', are to be found in late classical antiquity, where they appear as the themes of rhetorical exercises. It is uncertain how much is swept away by this observation. Certainly most of what has been thought about poetry in the last two hundred years, at any rate in the form in which it has been thought. The poet was after all not expressing *himself*. The very existence of the conception of *self* may be in doubt, from other causes, and what Curtius says comes to demolish the notion of expression.

Certain literary curiosities fall into their place. It would generally be said that Shakespeare, in his sonnets, was expressing himself in some more personal sense than in his plays. But this is an absurdity, from several points of view. In the first place, it is ludicrous to suppose that the author of the plays was the helpless victim of his own biography, when it came to inventing material for the sonnets. And secondly, if the notion of self-expression is fundamental to the notion of poetry, how does it come that Shakespeare is expressing himself more radically in the sonnets, because of their supposed biographical reference, than in *Lear* or the other great plays of his maturity?

2

It would usually be thought that Spenser and the other Petrarchans wrote lyrics of a more 'artificial' character than, say, Donne, because they are more evidently the coherent members of a group – those who succumbed to the 'Petrarchan tradition'. They might well not be expressing 'their feelings', because their sources are known to be literary. Because Donne is outside this tradition, he is often thought to be not only 'more original' but writing more directly from his own experience. It is the very notion of experience which Curtius is, by implication, questioning. The difference between Donne and the Petrarchans is perhaps not the closeness of the relationship between the subjects of their verse and what actually happened to them, but the degree and nature of the psychological insight which these authors respectively brought to their themes which, like 'experience' itself, are merely traditional.

It is too readily supposed that there is a 'personal experience' which can be conveyed in words. In fact, the consciousness we have is a product of history, and we think we feel as we do as much as feel that way. We can only feel as we do, because only so will our forms of words and thoughts allow us to feel. There may be some uniformity between the feelings of men who have their legs cut off, whether in the forests of hundreds of thousands of years ago or in London now, but certainly even in so patent a matter there will be differences. But when it comes to the feelings of a woman abandoned by her lover, the whole force of a civilization is in play. There is no original feeling of such a situation, and no overlay of tradition. The whole is an invention of thousands of years, places, times, religions, cultures. The individual variant which could be 'expressed' – if we admit the conception – must be negligible by comparison.

5

The fact that our thoughts are not our own does not mean that there is no distinction to be made between the thoughts of one and another. There are degrees of relevance of thoughts to situations; there is a variety in the capacity of different people for assimilating and applying what they have assimilated. The first symptom of a wide intelligence is its receptivity. The colour-blind who cannot distinguish red and green are the type of imperfect awarenesses – imperfect that is within the possibilities of a particular culture. The depth, coherence and relevance of what one person has to say will immeasurably exceed those qualities in what another says, and the poet has his place in this scheme of things. In a sense he will be less concerned than other people to be original, because he will be seeking among forms of thought long current for the formulation which will apply most exactly to the new situation.

4

The prominence of the erotic in the thought of the twentieth century is not the mark of any increase in the activity of the erotic organs, or even of the reverse. It is a result of the desuetude of other thought-forms which are recognized as being of general interest.

The problem – which was perhaps one of the problems of Catullus – is how much weight the contemporary Eros can bear. It will clearly not bear very much unless it is re-inforced by streams coming from more profound sources. There are only two – the stream of classical mythology and that of the Christian faith. Both are erotic, though they have proceeded side by side through the centuries, burbling at one another like quarrelsome water-gods.

The poet who can still draw on these sources will not merely illustrate the contemporary Eros. He may revivify the popular apprehension of the Christian and pagan worlds, so that, for example, in fifty years' time, people might sing hymns of which the imagery did not seem grotesque. But it would need more than a few bedraggled poems to have such an effect.

A NOTE ON MORALITY

To say purpose would be to beg the question, but the effect of moral rules is to produce coherence – and from one point of view, perhaps an important one, it does not matter what the rules are so long as the coherence is there. Of course coherence is also a word that begs some questions. There are modes certainly, but the essential thing is that everybody should think the same, or same enough. When that happens you have a culture in which, typically, all the vases are the same shape. The importance of the sameness, from the individual's point of view, is that it provides expectations. It is immoral to disappoint this expectation, roughly speaking. The sameness also produces conventions about the meaning of actions, which again is reassuring. For it is above all meaning that actions are in need of, if we are to be human. This means attaching actions to traditional patterns of thought, preferably the general view, at any rate a view which enough of us hold to make it respectable. In an evolved society it seems that everything has been thought about, and everything has a meaning. In a disrupted one the meanings are inadequate.

Are there any morals apart from those of particular societies? 'Thou shalt not steal', 'Thou shalt not commit adultery', are already notions with a particular sort of society in mind. This 'thou shalt not' is not absolute; it relates to an existing idea of what is the done thing. It is dependent on the form of property and the form of marriage established. If there were Christian morals would they go beyond the needs of particular societies, and what would their relationship be with the laws of a particular society, formerly seen as the law of God? The first Christians solved this question, in relation to Jewry. Having burst into the Gentile world, they then found another question. Was there a Christian social form (sc. morality) to be imposed? The answer was yes, but it has never been an entirely satisfactory one. It is least satisfactory in the less stable societies. In the Middle Ages, and long after, Christian morality had taken the place of the Law, and the finer breath of Christianity blew over it, as it had over the Law. In an unstable world, Christian morals have to justify themselves, a task for which they are not altogether equipped because, like all morals, they prefer to be taken for granted.

Take the famous morality of marriage. It could not be said that the gospels do more than bless the morality of a society in which, by that time, monogamy had become general. Certain dicta may even be held to equate adultery with the ordinary thoughts of man. If there is a pattern of behaviour as well as the dicta, it is not of monogamy but of abstinence. The only family exemplified is strictly inimitable.

Is it then the duty of Christians to establish a certain relationship with the morality of the day, whatever that may be? This is not antinomianism but it may be held to come too near to it. The alternative is to wage a war of Christian morality against whatever else is current, as if an agrarian or even a sheep-rearing society could replace a society of contraceptives and euthanasia.

ON POETIC ARCHITECTURE

1

There is no reason to suppose that the state of mind of the poet, when he writes a poem, is reproduced in the mind of the reader. It has sometimes been said that the poem represents an 'organisation of impulses' which is transmitted – it is generally supposed with beneficial effects – to the reader, who in this way manages to live for a moment with the sages. If you believe that you can believe anything about the relationships existing between members of the human race.

In the first place, one should try to be clear – or as clear as one can – about 'the state of mind of the poet, when he writes a poem'. What sort of correspondence has it with the poem produced? The poem is, of course, some of what is passing through his mind. It is certainly not all, even though he is likely to be more nearly absorbed by this activity than by many others that he engages in. And 'passing through his mind' is not an easy conception either. The only proof, really, is that the words get written. What accompanies the act of writing may be various. The poet may be exalted or he may be merely numb. He is just as likely to feel the emotion he is (as they say) 'conveying', *after* he has written as at the time of writing. He may be frozen as it comes to consciousness. In any case he is using words which are not his own (words are not a man's own), though his organization of them owes something to his own physiology and, of course, history. He speaks with the voice of a civilization and if anyone understands him it will be people who 'understand' what he 'understands', whatever that may mean. But what does it mean?

2

Does it make sense to talk of 'understanding' a person as distinct from 'understanding' a thing? There probably is no distinction, except so far as affinity between the subject and object (the same sort of animal, the same civilization) give a peculiar quality to one's relationship with things like oneself. That people share states of mind is obviously true in the sense that consciousness is historical and within a particular civilization there will be commonly accepted explanations of various classes of events. But the only proof of your understanding of a motor-car is your ability to handle it in various ways and to do what it wants to do (if it is to go at all). The more complex the machines the wider the range of mutual adjustments, but one is usually more stupid than another, as a car is more stupid than a man, and will normally come sooner to the point of exercising its will, i.e. refusing to adjust itself any further.

3

'The poem' is words on a piece of paper, or spoken, just as 'the building' is erected before you and you must make of it what you can. Nobody supposes that you feel what the builder or architect 'felt', as he sweated through his work, even in cases where there is one man to whom a 'feeling' or an original creative act could with any plausibility be attributed. Of course buildings are in styles as well as being in materials, and many people have a hand in them. And so have poems although one man will, these days, put his name on the title page. Take no more than a due amount of notice of it; it is to get the money, or the reputation, or in hopes of the same.

LE ROI SOLEIL

1

Does consciousness of one's own body differ from consciousness of other things? 'One's own body': an expression already heavy with metaphysic. At first it seems obvious that it must. 'One's own body': the one that is always there; the least interesting of bodies. If consciousness is the centre, or perhaps the maggot, then that body is the nut and the surrounding world the shell. Most of what goes on in our own bodies we are unconscious of;

it is the microcosmos. The macrocosmos is hardly more mysterious, or unknown; its size alone is impressive.

What we see, what we touch, we do with our own eyes, our hands, parts of our bodies. But it is also our eyes which see what we see of ourselves, our fingers which touch our skin or our tongue which touches our teeth. What of our consciousness of what goes on inside our bodies? The bellyache, the sudden lesion? These pains are not external to our bodies, but they are as external to our consciousness as events we perceive in Mars. Is not consciousness a convention, more or less, a matter of history? Could not an animal have a belly-ache without being aware of it? It would not be an ache, no doubt, but there would be the visceral disturbances, the vomiting would follow, and then quiescence. How much we perceive of the convulsions of the macrocosmos is a matter of the tradition we have inherited. But so it is, surely, with the belly-ache. If two states of consciousness could be compared (as they cannot, with any accuracy, because only one is known) the neolithic pain would differ from our own, for there is no pain, certainly no located pain, without meaning.

2

But if the relationship of the consciousness to the microcosmos and the macrocosmos is the same, what becomes of the notion of personality? It is more extensive. Instead of trying to conceive of a consciousness which corresponds to a physical person, as if such a person could float out of space and time, one takes the consciousness *de facto*, with all there is in it, which is something of the world as well as of a single body. A person becomes, not what he thinks he is, but what he is, or at any rate what is. The 'what is', like the person in other conceptions, can be seen from inside or outside; the more or less of correspondence there is between these two views is a commonplace of morality.

Who was Louis XIV? He was what he was seen to be, or if he was not, it was because there was more to be seen and not because a 'reality' was hiding in Versailles behind an appearance. Subjectively, he was what of his world he was aware of, and in building Versailles he was to some extent building himself. A whole skein of connections met in his hand, and it matters more whether a king dies than whether a beggar does. What profound sense has it that not a sparrow falls without the knowledge of your father which is in heaven? It is supernatural.

BY WAY OF EXPLANATION

About a month before George Herbert's death (according to Walton), a conversation took place between him and a Mr Duncon, who had been sent by Nicholas Ferrar:

> 'I desire you to pray with me.'
> 'What prayers?'
> 'O, sir! the prayers of my mother, the Church of England: no other prayers are equal to them!'

The point needs no illustration, but when he prayed, daily, 'Lighten our darkness, we beseech thee, O Lord' it was 'Illumina, quaesumus Domine Deus, tenebras nostras.' The prayer is in the breviaries of Sarum and York, in the sacrametaries of Gregory and Gelasius. The *mother* of George Herbert was the Church, looking on him with her English countenance. It was 1633, the year in which the King first greeted Laud, then Bishop of London, as 'my Lord's Grace of Canterbury', adding, 'you are very welcome.' It was only eleven years before the Archbishop, on Tower Hill, said: 'Cupio dissolvi et esse cum Christo' and passed through 'a mere shadow of death, a little darkness upon nature,' as he said in his prayer.

2

A less austere character, Robert Herrick, who welcomed the king into the west when he published his *Hesperides* in 1648, looked towards death through the ordinary sensualities, and hardly distinguished the sacred from the profane:

> Holy waters hither bring
> For the sacred sprinkling:
> Baptize me and thee, and so
> Let us to the Altar go.
> And (ere we our rites commence)
> Wash our hands in innocence.
> Then I'le be the *Rex Sacrorum*,
> Thou the Queen of *Peace* and *Quorum*.

Herrick had been deprived of his living before his book came out; and he is not heard of again till he goes back to Dean Prior in 1662, aged seventy-one. In this year was issued the edition of the Prayer-Book we now have, the use of the Elizabethan book, as it more or less was, having been illegal from the Ordinance of Parliament, Die Veneris, 3 Januarii, 1644, for the taking away of the Book of Common Prayer, and for the establishing and putting in execution of the Directory, until the Restoration.

3

Roger Clark, rector of Ashmore in Dorsetshire,

> When the Rebellion broke out... adhered Immovably to his Majesty's cause, and betook himself to the army under my Lord Hopton; for which he was Plunder'd of all that he had, the Soldiers Tearing a broad the very beds, and Scattering the Feathers out of the Ticking:... they took the Two Young Sons, being Twins, the Elder named Roger, and the Other, Richard, and laid them stark-naked in a Dripping-Pan before the Fire, with a design to Roast them; but a certain woman, whose name was Pope, came and snatched them away in her Apron. (Walker, *Sufferings of the Clergy*, 1714)

It happens that the minute-books of the Parliamentary Standing Committee, which sat in Dorset during the Rebellion and interregnum, have been preserved: perhaps the only ones of their kind; there was good reason for destroying such books: 'Whereas we are informed that Leonard Snooke of Stower pvost, one Combe of Fifehead and Thomas Dowden of Kingston have been in armes against the Pariament, it is therefore ordered that you seize, inventory and secure their estates...' It is a matter of taste, or perhaps something more, whether you sympathize with these men or with John Hampden, that model of the bourgeois who makes a virtue out of not paying his taxes. Somebody gained by the losses of such men as Leonard Snooke, one Combes and Thomas Dowden: 'shall hold and enjoie the farmes called Grange and Waddam, beeinge part of the sequestred estate of Robt. Lawrence, Esqr, for delinquencie...' And instead of ecclesiastical discipline – 'It is hereby ordered that noe minister whatsoever shall psume to preach in the pish church of Blandford in this Country without leave first obtained from Mr. Trottell, minister of Spettsbury.'

4

At the Restoration, Jeremy Taylor was consecrated Bishop – to an Irish see – and some other reparations were made to tired men.

Thomas Ken, whose sister Anne was married to Isaac Walton, was ordained in 1661 or 2. He became Bishop of Bath and Wells in 1684. In 1688, with six other bishops including Sancroft, Archbishop of Canterbury, he submitted To the King's Most Excellent Majesty (James II) the petition which humbly sheweth

> That the great averseness they find in themselves to the distributing and publishing in all their churches your Majesty's late declaration for liberty of conscience proceedeth neither from any want of duty and obedience to your Majesty, our holy mother the Church of England being, both in her principles and constant practice, unquestionably loyal.... nor yet from any want of due tenderness to dissenters, in relation to whom they are willing to come to such a temper as shall be thought fit, when the matter shall be considered and settled in parliament and convocation; but yet among many other considerations, from this especially because that declaration is founded upon such a dispensing power as hath often been declared illegal in parliament, and particularly in the years 1662 and 1672, and in the beginning of your Majesty's reign....

The seven bishops were taken to the Tower 'for contriving, making and publishing a seditious libel'. But Ken would not take the oath to William; nor would Sancroft and seven other bishops. Ken went to Wells and from his chair asserted his canonical right. The rest of his life he spent at Longleat, where he wrote two thousand pages of verse, as a form of laudanum, he said, which shows how dangerous it is for a man to have time on his hands.

5

One does not often think of Swift as a cleric, because his imagination was unbridled, and because he was Irish and the merits of a later (rebellious) nationalism are supposed to have washed away the stains of his loyalty. But Swift said: 'Might not those who enter upon any office in her Majesty's family, be obliged to take an oath parallel to that against simony, which is administered to the clergy?' And in *A Letter concerning the Sacramental Test*:

> As to the argument used for repealing the Test, that it will unite all the Protestants against the Common Enemy; I wonder by what figure these gentlemen speak, who are pleased to advance it.... 'Tis an odd way of uniteing parties, to deprive a Majority of Part of their antient Right, by conferring it on a

> Faction, who never had any Right at all, and therefore cannot be said to suffer any loss or injury, if it be refused them. Neither is it very clear, how far some people may stretch the term of Common Enemy. How many are there of those that call themselves Protestants, who look upon our Worship to be idolatrous as well as that of Papists, and with great Charity put Prelacy and Popery together as terms convertible?

6

Queen Anne died in 1714 and the country has been more or less given over to Whiggery ever since. In 1717 Convocation was suppressed so that it should not condemn the invisible bishop of Bangor, Dr Hoadly, to whom William Law wrote (in the *Defence of Church Principles*)

> But, my Lord, as human nature, if left to itself, would neither answer the ends of a spiritual or civil society; so a constant visible government in both is equally necessary; and I believe, it appears to all unprejudiced eyes that, in this argument at least, your Lordship has declared both equally unlawful.

7

George Hicks, the non-juror who in 1694 was consecrated titular Bishop of Thetford, used the First (and more Catholic) Prayer Book of Edward VI, and in 1717 the Nonjurors published their own office, which was closely allied to it. Those who followed the latter book were called the *Usagers*, from the mixing water with the wine, saying the prayer for the dead and other usages prescribed in it.

> What can be more heinously wicked [wrote Law, himself a Nonjuror], than heartily to wish the success of a person on account of his right, and at the same time, in the most solemn manner, in the presence of God, and as you hope for mercy, to swear that he has no right at all.

From Johnson it is enough to quote the *Dictionary*:

> TORY. One who adheres to the ancient constitution of the state, and the apostolic hierarchy of the church of England.
> WHIG. The name of a faction.

Not wholly irrelevant are certain curious verses of Charles Wesley about Methodist preachers:

> Rather than suffer them to dare
> Usurp the priestly character,
> Save them from arrogant offence,
> And snatch them uncorrupted hence.

Omitted in the second edition. John did not like them.

8

The Tories of the nineteenth century are Samuel Taylor Coleridge and the Duke of Wellington, and the latter was already intent upon ruinous calculations: 'What I looked on as the great advantage of the measure (for Roman emancipation) was that it would unite all men of property and character together in one interest against the agitators.' Coleridge upon fanciful conditions:

> a declaration, to which every possible character of solemnity should be given, that at no time and under no circumstances has it ever been, nor can it ever be, compatible with the safety of the British Constitution to recognise in the Roman Catholic priesthood, as now constituted, a component Estate of the realm, or persons capable, individually or collectively, of becoming the trustees and usufructuary proprietors of that elective and circulative property, originally reserved for the permanent maintenance of the National Church.

But, on any terms, the emancipation of the Papists was the end of even the possibility of that system which Coleridge himself defined:

> the Constitution, in its widest sense as the constitution of the realm, arose out of, and in fact consisted in, the co-existence of the constitutional State.... with the King as its head, and of the Church, that is, the National Church, with the King likewise as its head; and lastly of the King, as the head and Majesty of the whole nation.

The political device of the latter part of the seventeenth century was not the Restoration but the Revolution which is sometimes called glorious, and indeed you might call it that by comparison with the one which took place in France in 1789. From the time Charles raised his standard at Nottingham, Toryism as defined by Johnson has almost always been a doctrine of opposition, and so it will remain.

Is there a Church of England?

The Church of England can be puzzling enough if one is English, and an Anglican. A Frenchman who wants to understand this situation has a long course to run. M. Guy Bedouelle starts in the right place, with the Celtic Church, and one could wish that more Anglicans were instructed to the extent, at any rate, of the admirable summary history he gives in the early pages of his book, *L'Eglise d'Angleterre et la Societé Politique Contemporaine*. He is not, however, writing a history of the English Church, nor an account of its (elusive) theology; he is concerned, as is appropriate in a book emanating from the rue Soufflot, with its legal position, its influence in our political life, and its operation in our society, whether as a constitutional force or as a pressure group, (all as at present, or as near present as the exigencies of composition and publication allow).

It is inevitable that, for Anglicans, there is little novelty in most of M. Bedouelle's discoveries. After his general historical sketch he probes, with admirable tact, the nature of the vague and tenuous unanimity which goes under the name of Anglicanism, indicating beyond the domestic scene the ghostly and social communion now extending so far overseas. He then looks at those particulars which constitute the Establishment and which are so much less, when one comes to look at them, than the uninterested man in the street commonly imagines. He looks at the legislative function, so slow, so diffuse, and so little binding, to judge by what goes on around one. He explains, with a moderation more than British, the place of the parson in his parish and the bishop in his diocese, points to the mumbling reports which purport to study our dilemmas, notes the interventions of what is still grandly called the bench of bishops, well appreciating that they amount, for the most part, to a few humanitarian platitudes emitted by individuals, rather than the voice of the Church.

Becoming more explicitly sociological, M. Bedouelle then

looks at the place of the clergy in society, the dim respectability that surrounds them, and their modest (some would say totally inadequate) financial status. He concludes with an understandably inadequate chapter on political thought of which, after all, there is so little now, either within the Church or outside it. Here his key points, conventionally but, in a study of this kind, not inappropriately are, after the great Hooker, T.S. Eliot and William Temple. After this gentle survey of an institution so faulty, so divided, so inept, and so weak, one can admire the charity which can still note that the spirit of Anglicanism has raised, in the Church itself, 'a number of defenders so ardent that one cannot but be struck by the vehemence of their love for her'. No one can doubt that the Church of England is the object of loyalties, none the less strong because they are, in a sense, those of a remnant.

Is there a Church of England now? In some sense the answer must be, Yes. We cannot doubt that, in this country and within this communion, the sacraments are being duly administered and the pure Word of God preached. There is strong inclination, laudable enough in some contexts, to look beyond this to the daughter churches scattered throughout the world who send their bishops, from time to time, to confer and fraternise at Lambeth, as if the failings of Church here were somehow compensated by the geographical distribution of her friends. How easily, however, the rapture of these wide horizons becomes a substitute for looking at the mess under our own noses. It is the imperial vice, become even more soggy in the post-imperial years. Just as, in secular politics, people pride themselves on a vague 'moral responsibility' where they used to have duties, so it is pleasanter to smile benignly at those who live a long way away than to try to find a response in the uncomprehending, well-fed faces who fill the factories and offices and the cars queuing along the holiday roads.

Within the field surveyed by M. Bedouelle, and without intruding upon that of the theologian or of the father in God and the curate of souls as such, there is a range of difficulties which are important for the Church of England and are for the most part ignored. The Establishment, in the most limited sense, is something that people do worry about from time to time, generally now with an anxiety to give away any privileges it may involve, as if the habit of giving things away, when that is the easiest course, had not become a vice in the nation. Of that Anglicans need only say that if the Establishment gives privileges, and we are indeed the Catholic and apostolic church in England, we are the right people to have them and it is our duty to make the most of them. There is another argument, of a more theological kind, for giving away the Establishment, which it would not be appropriate to pursue here. But there is no doubt that, in the field cultivated by M. Bedouelle (that of the Church as a legal and social entity), the discussion of the Establishment has had much too prominent a part.

We should bother about the Church and deal with the problem of the Establishment when we have to. But bothering about the church means, *inter alia*, bothering about it as a social entity. It is a society like another, differing from others less than is commonly supposed in its need for order, discipline, property, accounts, education, architects, management – yes, management – though differing in what it incarnates, which means that it is more, not less criminal for the Church to treat these things sloppily than it would be for another institution. And from its position in the Middle Ages, when it was the model administration, the centre of education, the manager of vast properties, the guardian of the poor and the nurse of the sick, the Church of England has sunk to a ramshackle, out-of-date body, ill-adapted to the world it is in, incapable of recruiting, training or paying its ministers properly; receding year by year from its influence on the education of the young; respectable in the sense of being largely coloured by the back waters of the suburbs, with bishops who have no serious control over their dioceses and parochial clergy who obey them only when they agree with them; a whole apparatus of nominal control, from archbishops to rural deans, which would be laughable in any other organization and ought to be derided in the Church.

The most sickening form of defence used by the apologists of this decay is to suggest that the general dissolution is merely evidence of freedom of conscience, or even of unworldliness. But Laud mounting the scaffold or Cranmer going out to be burnt were not more worldly than the bishops who consume long hours on indifferent committees, or at ladies' coffee mornings. They were merely much more deeply implicated in the society of their times, so that they could not choose but take decisions which led them into trouble and locked them in unending struggle with the most brilliant and most powerful men of their time. A coffee morning is not, of its nature, a more spiritual thing than a council of state; the demands it makes on the abilities and resources of the participants are commonly less. And a clergy which moves too much among its kind friends, and too little among its enemies, is bound to grow soft. Our clergy has grown soft, as a class, and despite notable exceptions. Not softer, of course, than millions of the laity but that *tu quoque* gets you nowhere.

It could be argued that the Church of England ceased to exist, as a juridico-theological entity, after what was revealingly called the Catholic emancipation. Ken and his fellow bishops had been right after all in thinking that an indulgence to Roman Catholics was a blow at the constitution. It was not merely that James II was using a dispensing power to which, it was contended, he had no legal right. If the Church of Rome was to set up altars beside Anglican altars that was to say that the Church of England was not, after all, what it claimed to be. Those battles are long past, and the Catholic emancipation was really the declaration of the modern state which would regard it as favouritism to be partial to the established religion. Does it matter that we now live in a state in which it is important that Sikhs should publicly exercise their customs but is thought wrong that a child should be taught the creed or the catechism at the public expense? At any rate the ethos which produces and accepts these things is one which is utterly foreign to the origins and history of the Church of England. It reduces that institution to a body of opinion, no more, and one less to be considered than many minorities, because it is supposed to be privileged and is therefore marked for a diminution and not for an increase of rights.

What, in this situation, should Anglicans do? There is no one thing to be done. To mock up a hurried programme of regeneration would be the most damaging thing of all. But, in innumerable ways, we should begin to treat the church as a social entity more seriously. As M. Bedouelle says, talking of Lambeth, *'on pourrait imaginer une administration'*. It is absurd, indeed presumptuous, to suppose that an archbishop or a bishop in twentieth-century England can function without an office as efficient as an oil company would expect to have. There must be, surely, some overt signs of obedience in the clergy before much can be done about the dissipations of the laity. It is odd that an organization founded on 'saying to that man go, and he goeth' should now be manned largely by people who can hardly be given instructions by anybody. There must be much more money, and Anglicans are not unworldly because they give a shilling where they ought to give a pound.

THE SEVENTIES

The Schism between Church and State

'To deal plainly with his memory, he was a flaming incendiary.' That is how Jeremy Collier spoke of John Knox. Collier was not exactly docile himself, except in principle, but no doubt for sheer turbulence he came a long way behind the hero of the Scottish Reformation.

His docility in principle carried belief in the virtues of non-resistance to lawful authority to the point of treating William III as no king. Collier was a Nonjuror. He managed in the relatively benign times in which he lived – benign as compared with the sixteenth century – to survive to the age of seventy-six, but he saw the inside of Newgate. Not being troubled with a lawful sovereign after 1688, unless you so reckon the extremely ineffectual king over the water, he was, you may say, happily placed for a turbulent spirit of scholarly tastes and literary gifts.

Besides being the author of *A Short View of the Profaneness of the English Stage* – a book with more merit than it is now usually credited with – and numerous polemical works, he wrote *An Ecclesiastical History of Great Britain* which was reprinted in the 1840s in nine large volumes. It is in this work that he gives his characterization of John Knox.

There is probably little to choose, in point of doctrine, between the attitude to the civil magistrate recommended in the Scots confession and the attitude which found its way into the Book of Common Prayer. There could hardly be. Knox was not an original thinker, and his sources were certainly not narrowly local. He was open to the same European streams as Cranmer, and indeed had been more exposed to them than Cranmer was. Where he differed from Cranmer was rather in situation and temperament. Cranmer was much aware, subjectively, of the realities of power; his situation reinforced this awareness until the last bitter days. Knox was naturally combative, the very type of boring indomitability. When he saw an enemy he flew to denunciations.

There is an element of the scold about him, in the best tradition of Scots 'flytings' from Sir David Lindsay to Hugh MacDiarmid. But it was his situation above all which determined his stance in the matter of Church and state. In England the Reformation was being played out, in its various stages, in the forum of the court. The country was moreover comparatively settled.

In Scotland, Knox found the old world and the old doctrines still entrenched at court. What wonder if the Reformation seethed below and loosened the stones of the structures in which, in medieval times, Church and state had been interlocked? The new ideas grew up in disjunction from the Crown, and Knox became, for Scottish history, or mythology, a strident and outspoken proto-democrat as well as proto-reformer, suggesting a Glasgow trade unionist rather than an Edinburgh minister or lawyer.

There is a world of difference between the problem of Church and state in an age when religious notions are in common currency and in an age like our own in which they are on the way to being an oddity. The argument, formerly, was about the Christian Commonwealth, and what it should be like to live in it. Now there is nothing of that. It would be very offensive to reasonable people if it were suggested that we should live in a Christian country. Even Christians, for the most part, hold that democracy is to be preferred. Democracy is, indeed, the public religion of the age. No one is allowed to say a word against it without heavy penalties being exacted. With such a religion, it may be said, the problems of relations with the state are removed for all time. The Church is the state, so to speak. The medieval tensions are resolved.

Only it is not the Christian Church that is thereby put in security. What we have is a sort of Roman state religion, with public gods who are not the Maker of Heaven and Earth and certainly not the one who suffered under Pontius Pilate, was crucified, dead and buried, and on the third day rose again from the dead. Indeed that one would be regarded as a dangerous intruder in our Pantheon, as indeed he is.

In so far as there is now a doctrine of Church and state which is believed in by Christians it has, in our situation, to be something like this: (1) It is for people to believe according to their consciences; (2) democracy is the form of state which leaves most freedom to the conscience; (3) therefore democracy is the form of state which Christians should support.

That is a respectable argument, if the second premise is sound. No one could say that there is not good contemporary evidence in favour of it. But it is far from self-evident. It was a popular majority which asked for the crucifixion. There is no mischief that a majority might not get up to. So however benign our political world for those who hold the religion of democracy, by Christians it has to be looked at warily, just as any other form of government has.

For the state the perspective is different. A democracy, by definition, does not see one view as better than another, except so far as the crowd goes along with it. In reply to a statement as uncompromising as the Creed it says politely: If you think so – which it also says when people proclaim themselves Hindus, Marxists, Humanists or indeed anything else except, possibly, anti-democrats.

Whatever the advantages of such undifferentiated politeness on the part of the state – and it has advantages – there should be no illusions in the minds of Christians or of those who proclaim any other belief (other than that of the religion of democracy) that they are getting anything which amounts to sympathy from that quarter. The consequences for Christianity are severe – much more severe, for example, than they are for Hinduism, which practises a sceptical inclusiveness much more akin to the democratic spirit, or for Marxism, which at least shares the materialism of democracy. But the Christian religion, which proclaims the uniqueness of a particular local event, and insists both on its universal significance and its present consequences for every man and woman alive and – worst of all – that it is necessary to mankind as no other religion and no human thoughts are, finds itself dogmatically opposed to the state's broadmindedness.

The state dogmatically holds that Christianity is not unique, that the Church is not a special sort of society, certainly not a divine society, for divinity means nothing to it and it would be unfair to accord to the Church a kind of recognition which it did not accord to other bodies of opinion. If the Church says: It is the truth, the state can only answer: Well, that's your opinion.

All this is far from the world of the Reformation, when the argument was between governors whose thought moved, however clumsily, in a religious system as surely as that of British politicians of the twentieth century moves in a democratic one. That is to say it moved hazily, and often not in accordance with the suppositions of the system, but recognized that it had always to come back to that point, and to look – if one looked quickly – as if it were obeying a certain set of rules.

When John Knox denounced a ruler or the ways of a government, it was on the assumption that they would have to show – would indeed want to show – that they were acting in accordance with the divine will. There might be some difference of interpretation, but that was all.

Now, to thunder from the pulpit – if one can talk of thunder in relation to so negligible a noise – about matters of public concern the preacher has to appeal, not to the common basis of the Creed but to the political catchwords of democracy – freedom, self-determination, self-expression – a list to which non-discrimination, the most arrogant and nihilistic of them all, has in late years added itself.

Truth to tell all these catchwords, even or especially this last-comer, can in many practical contexts stand for impulses of which the Christian can only approve and to which he is bound to give his assent. They may represent a proper stance against the cupidity and cruelty of the world. But this degree of congruence with the consequences of Christian belief is in some sort an accident. It represents a trick of language, even of behaviour, of a post-Christian society. No reason to suppose that the words will not progressively be emptied of the dregs of a Christian social tradition.

Meanwhile, it should give grounds enough for reflection that the Christian preacher cannot any longer appeal to the state except in a language of itself dogmatically opposed to Christianity, and indeed may speak only so long as it adopts the language of the state. In such a situation as ours, there may be a problem of the relations of Church and state, in the sense that the Church may have a problem. She indeed has the problem she always had. But the state has no such problem any longer, for it regards itself as alone among the pressure groups, and the one that calls itself the Church gives it less to worry about than a lot of others.

'The ministeris exerce not the civill jurisdictioun.' I should think not! 'Bot', the quotation from the *Book of Discipline* goes on, 'teich the magistrat how it should be exercit according to the Word.' That's what you think! the politicians reply.

The novelty is not their reluctance to listen, but their determination to show that they are not exercising their magistracy 'according to the Word' – which they would regard as a highly partial way to proceed – but in accordance with the prescriptions of quite a different religion, that of democracy.

No Christian can be content with this, however little he expects to see things much otherwise in his lifetime or believes that any alternative political form, which could be achieved in his lifetime, would be more 'according to the Word'. These reflections on Church and state are not an essay against democracy, though they may be a little against the uninhibited and abstract theory of it. They are an exhortation to think rather of the actual complexities of our constitution, now so neglected in favour of a disembodied theory. And in particular to go back to the roots of the argument, in the sixteenth century and beyond, and to consider how their grandchildren may reach a position in which the dialogue between Church and state could be resumed in language which recognizes the existence of both parties.

Politics and the Pulpit

In relation to the seventeenth century in England, whether one's main interest is in its literature or its politics, some understanding of its worship and theology is indispensable; just as, for the theologian, some immersion in the politics and the literature is necessary in order to understand the bearing and motivations of the theological arguments then so heftily bandied about. So the appearance of *Worship and Theology in England: from Andrewes to Baxter and Fox, 1603-1690*, by Horton Davies, the Henry W. Putnam Professor of Religion at Princeton University, is much to be welcomed. The volume is the last to appear, but the second in sequence, of five volumes covering between them the years 1534-1965. The imprint of the Oxford University Press, which appeared under that of Princeton in the earlier volumes, is missing here, and the binding is not uniform with that of those which appeared on this side of the Atlantic. *Andrewes to Baxter* can, of course, be read as a separate study by those whose main interest is in the seventeenth century.

How wide is Horton Davies's conception of 'Worship and Theology'? One has to turn to the first volume, *Cranmer to Hooker*, for his own elucidation. 'Worship', he says, 'is understood in no narrow or rubrical sense, but as the corporate offering of thought, emotion and decision-making as a response of the Christian churches to the saga of Christ and His followers throughout history.' The language is not very clear, at least to me it is not. Apart from the rather inappropriate use of the word *saga* – as if Christ were some sort of Norse or Icelandic hero buccaneering around the world – how is one to understand this 'offering of thought, emotion and' (ghastly fugitive from the business schools) 'decision-making'? Is it something less than 'our souls and bodies' which, as the Book of Common Prayer compendiously puts it, are to be 'a reasonable, holy and lively sacrifice'? Professor Davies goes on, a little more intelligibly:

> This series, then, is a study of the art of Christian adoration as expressed through the ritual and ceremonial of the major Christian denominations of England in the past 400 years. It is an adoration expressed in prayers and preaching, in sermons as in sacraments, in religious architecture and sacred music, in devotion and duty.

A history of duties and devotions must be even more uncertain than most history. That of music and architecture has to be understood against the background of the general performance of the age in those two fields. The theology itself has to be understood in relation not only to the longer history of the Church but in relation to the non-theological thought of the time. There is economic change to be taken into account, and the ugly face of politics. It must be uncommonly difficult to set the limits of such a book as this.

Another difficulty is the orientation of the author within his chosen field. Professor Davies claims that, in all but the final chapter, his 'exclusive interest has been to understand by way of empathy the most varied rites and ceremonies'. It is a fetching way of asserting one's impartiality, or rather one's ability to put oneself in the skins successively of Parsons and of William Prynne. In some measure no doubt one can do this, but 'exclusive interest' is rather strong language. In pursuit of this even-handedness Professor Davies concentrated, throughout the five volumes, 'on three traditions: the oldest, the Roman Catholic; the new Anglican; and the newest, the Puritan, the two latter originating in the sixteenth century'. Yet the question throughout the seventeenth century was, precisely, what the 'oldest tradition' really amounted to. Andrewes would not have seen the matter as Professor Davies summarizes it, though the summary would have suited the Jesuits and their friends from Douai. If it would have suited some of the Puritans – and for them Davies can speak without calling too much on empathy, for he is a Congregationalist, born in Wales – it would have been because the independents believed in 'reformation without tarrying for any', as Robert Browne put it, and did not have to concern themselves overmuch with the historical Church. Swift, whom Professor Davies ignores in his third volume, perhaps as too rough, had his own succinct version of the 'three traditions', which he called Peter, Martyn and Jack, 'and all at a Birth, neither could the Mid-Wife tell certainly which was the Eldest'.

Swift and his tart language are not out of place here, for if he came to have an appreciation of worldliness, sharpened successively at the hand of Temple and Harley, he was at bottom a disciple of Sancroft, with his roots in Caroline High Churchmanship. Something of his robustness in the great world has been missing from Anglicanism ever since. It is usual to attribute this deficiency to a superior delicacy of conscience and respect for the individual in more recent times, but it is possible to see it rather as the oblivion of certain aspects of reality. At any rate there is no understanding the world of the seventeenth century if one cannot make one's own some of the language in which what then seemed the crucial events in church and state were then discussed. One has to go back even to the *cuius regio, eius religio*, of the sixteenth. The sense of that phrase was not wholly in a worldly sycophancy to powerful princes. No doubt such dispositions as that, among churchmen, go back at least to Constantine. But there is in this now barely intelligible formula also a sense that it is scandalous and one might say unnatural for Christians not to be of the same communion as their neighbours. They are of one communion but, being human, they have infallibly muddled it.

To the shift away from this attitude the Puritans, and the Independents in particular, made a handsome contribution, not unconnected with their stubbornness in sitting or lying at Communion, which elicited what Professor Davies calls Herbert's 'intriguing denunciation': 'Contentiousness in a feast of charity is more scandal than any posture.' The politics and the theology were all of a piece, in those unenlightened times, and it was inevitable that the Royalist should, typically, follow Andrewes who stood for 'the Catholic heritage of the first five centuries in doctrine, polity and liturgy, as well as reason', while the Puritans were prophetic of the modern world. Professor Davies, with extreme justness of language on this occasion, speaks of 'the sitting *gesture*' at Communion, a gesture being, in Johnson's first definition, an 'action or posture expressive of sentiment'. He adds that it was 'rightly interpreted by Anglicans as an exceedingly revolutionary and democratic gesture'. It was their own sentiments that these Christians were anxious to display as they sat down or put their hats on the altar, and that places them at least as firmly as Herbert in the world of politics. The political bias of the Roman Catholics was never in doubt, from Parsons and the others who plotted against Elizabeth to Guy Faux, and the shadow of Jesuit intrigue remained with them throughout the century. They and the extreme Puritans were suspected, not altogether unjustly, of having some common interests against the peace of the kingdom, however antipodal their theologies might be.

It is in this horrible complex of politics and worship that the student of the theology of the seventeenth century inevitably finds himself. One is like a fly in treacle, the milieu is so enveloping. Yet it is because it is so difficult to escape that the study is so valuable. The difficulty comes from the engagement of the whole range of the faculties. In the closet or at the altar there is always the certainty that there are outside seething enemies, among whom most of life has to be lived. It is not only tinkers who have to make a *Pilgrim's Progress*; an archbishop may end on Tower Hill and a country parson may be ejected either for using or for not using the Book of Common Prayer – and although Professor Davies reminds us more often of the latter, he does show us Evelyn going up to receive the Sacrament on Christmas Day with a musket pointed against him. More important than these brawls, there is the fact that neither government nor preaching or praying are to be seen as segregated employments, but each as involving the whole man whether he likes it or not. It had not then been finally – and one might say, unrealistically – decided that everyone can freely follow his tastes and his conscience as long as he buys his insurance stamps.

The twentieth century in England and America still leaves the historian of worship and theology with a choice of approaches to his subject. That made by Professor Davies is perhaps the obvious one for the historian of 400 years whose final volume bears the subtitle 'The Ecumenical Century', and whose emphasis in what he calls the 'pre-ecumenical centuries' is on 'the unconsciously complementary character of divergent modes of worship'. He tries to give equal weight, so far as the subject he is treating allows, to the Roman Catholic, Anglican and Puritan strands. To be able to do so he must make good a claim to a catholicity superior to any of them. Failing that, his claim can only be to a fairness which is certainly not specifically Christian, if Christian at all, and which owes more to the politics of the 'ecumenical century' than to the facts of the seventeenth. There is no particular merit in setting out as 'The Roman Catholic View of the Sacrament' what was written by two Jesuit exiles in the Low Countries, to create an illusory sense of balance with 'The

Anglican View of the Sacrament' and 'The Puritan View of the Lord's Supper' in the succeeding sections. The same might be said of the sections 'The Roman Catholic Calendar', 'The Anglican Calender' and 'The Puritan Calendar'. There is of course a perfectly good Roman Catholic history of the worship and theology of seventeenth century England; there are several possible Puritan histories of the same subject, from the underside during the earlier and later parts of the century and the overside during the Commonwealth. There is an Anglican history, which shows the historic church of these islands, separated from Rome, unable to contain dissenters either papist or Protestant; overwhelmed and almost extinguished by the latter; and finally, returning to a rather hollow dominance.

One can sympathize with Professor Davies, wishing to steer away from these controversial interpretations and so avoid renewing quarrels which are better at rest. Yet one may doubt whether the method he has chosen is altogether the best. His 'three traditions' are three sets of administrative and political arrangements rather than exclusive vehicles of a comprehensive set of doctrines or manners of devotion. If he had laid less emphasis on them he might have done more to exorcize the politics, and one might have been left with more sense of the underlying unity. As it is we are left with Peter, Martyn and Jack at their clowning as usual, and with Jack claiming to understand his brothers by empathy.

If these are difficulties which the author has not entirely overcome, he has succeeded in packing into his books a mass of information about forms of worship. This will go without saying for those who have seen the earlier volumes. In the arrangement of this one, he has perhaps ridden off on a hobby-horse in devoting two chapters to church architecture and, as he says, attempting 'to derive the theology from the architecture which was its outward and visible expression'. In doing so he gives a proper prominence to Wren and has some interesting things to say about seventeenth-century Gothic and its possible relationship with the theology of Laud. He also has some fascinating material about the meeting-houses which are among the more delightful embodiments of Puritan and Quaker theology – even if not quite delightful enough to outweigh what one may call the negative architectural activity of Puritans in breaking up the furniture, smashing the glass, and generally making churches more suitable for their own 'utter simplicity and sincerity'. 'It was not', as

Davies says – twice, as a matter of fact – 'that the Puritans disliked art, it was simply that they loved religion more.'

There is a rather miscellaneous chapter entitled 'Spirituality' – never a very satisfactory word in English – which includes material about Ignatius Loyola, the poetry of Crashaw, the devotional works of Cosin and Andrewes, and a variety of manuals from *Holy Living* and *Holy Dying* to *The Saints' Everlasting Rest.* There is a chapter on sermons, which has to cover an even vaster ground. Both these chapters, while giving pointers to a fair range of valuable material, strain the general plan of the book a bit. For the readable literature of the period in these fields is overwhelmingly Anglican, and too much attention to merit must upset the sort of account of the 'three traditions' which Professor Davies has set out to give. The Puritans rated sermons more highly than Anglicans did, but the Anglican sermons were better. 'It may well be, of course', Professor Davies says, making the best of a bad job, 'that Puritan sermons seem much duller than they were only because we are reading them rather than listening to them.' Just as, one may add, newspapers may seem more exciting than the durable literature being produced at the same time. Deference to the 'traditions' apart, Davies feels obliged to give the boring and influential Tillotson a prominence scarcely less than that given to Andrewes or Taylor.

The second part of the book, entitled 'Cultic Controversies', contains chapters on 'Style in Worship', 'Calendary Conflict' – not a very happy expression, but the chapter has some interesting material on sabbatarianism and state services as well as the observance of the Christian Year – 'Sacred Music', with the subtitle 'Splendid or Scriptural?' which is rather an odd antithesis, and 'The Chief Sacrament'. It is hardly for a layman and general reader to raise an eyebrow at what a professor of religion says on this subject. Still one wonders whether it can well be introduced by the question 'how is the chief Sacrament to be evaluated?' – or represented as merely 'another debate . . . among the cultic controversies of the century'. The third, longest and most satisfactory part of the book is under the heading 'The History and Forms of Worship'. In this the author gives an account of the parts played by the Book of Common Prayer, the parliamentary *Directory* which was supposed to replace it, and the various forms of Presbyterian, Independent, Roman Catholic, Baptist and Quaker worship.

The volume as a whole, like its predecessors, is a valuable

compendium of material about theology and worship in the period it covers. As such, it will be useful to students of history and literature as well as, one supposes, to theologians. With the growing ignorance of these subjects among the public at large, there is a need for books which will give students an *entrée* into them, for without that the poetry of Donne, Herbert, Vaughan, Crashaw and Traherne – to mention no others – becomes, in varying degrees, insubstantial. The past is slipping from us, with the Synod of the Church of England following Cromwell's Parliament in hounding the Book of Common Prayer into the shades – one more manifestation of the erosion by technology of the old language and the old landscape. Whoever continues *Worship and Theology in England* a century from now will have to include chapters on Islam and Hinduism as well as on Professor Davies's 'three traditions'. The seventeenth century will be as remote as the Middle Ages. Already the England to which Scotland was united by the Act of Union has disappeared. However, there are always a few people who doubt whether invention and novelty for the future are best served by forgetting the past, and for them the strands which tie us to the Anglican and Puritan England of the seventeenth century are still worth a tug.

Some English Divines

The pieces here collected under this title have been extracted from *The English Sermon*, an anthology in three volumes published by Carcanet in 1976. The first is my 'General Preface' to the whole work. The three volumes each covered a century apiece, and the remaining extracts are from Volume II (1650-1750) which fell to me, while Volume I (1550-1650) and Volume III (1750-1850) were edited respectively by Martin Seymour-Smith and Robert Nye. The extracts from Volume II given here are the 'Introduction' and my accounts of the thirteen divines represented in that part of the anthology.

GENERAL PREFACE

One does not have to be a Christian to be interested in sermons, nor a non-Christian to be bored by most of them. For the three hundred years covered by the three volumes of this anthology, preaching was one of the main vehicles for current reflections about the way of the world. It was so because, at any rate until the latter part of the period, the Christian religion was generally regarded – as it still regards itself – not as a matter of private whim or opinion but as something which has to be understood, to the limit of each one's capacity, by anyone trying to understand the nature of man and the universe into which men are born. Many now think differently, but only those who are sure that their ancestors were bigger fools than they are themselves will think that they can discard the explorations which went on for centuries – and still go on, if less prominently – in the language of Christian theology. Moreover, anyone who wants to understand the literature in which Donne, Swift and Johnson are prominent figures must make some attempt to understand the notions of religion in which they and indeed all but a few very recent contributors to our literature were, to a greater or lesser degree, educated and which are intertwined in the texture of their thought. These considerations apart, the volumes of sermons now left so largely unread – or read only in short extracts for particularly colourful passages – contain what is, in its own right, an important branch of our literature. Much of the finest English prose is there, an indispensable study for anyone who is interested in the development and decay of the medium.

The pretensions of these three volumes are modest. There can be no question, in this space, of more than an introduction to the subject. With a few exceptions in the first volume, only complete sermons have been included, so that the construction and development of the genre can be fully appreciated. Not more than three sermons of any one author have been selected, and some forty-eight preachers are represented, including all the most famous and a number of those whose names are less familiar. Most of the material here reprinted is not now readily accessible, so that the volumes will enable many readers to acquaint themselves with the work of men who have hitherto existed for them only as figures in a history-book or as allusions in the writings of Coleridge or Eliot. The sermons have been chosen for their intrinsic interest and for their qualities as representing important streams of thought and literature. There has been no attempt at a consistent theological orientation. Among the editorial names appearing on the title pages, there are three who pretend to no religious faith, and two Anglicans. That the sermons themselves are predominantly – overwhelmingly – from Anglican sources owes something to the prejudices of one of the editors, but more to the fact that this literature is primarily the voice of the main stream of English Christianity, muddied by all our English affairs.

INTRODUCTION TO VOLUME 2

One of the profound difference between England and France is that in France the Revolution followed a century of widespread amusement at the mysteries of the Christian faith, while the English revolution took place after a century of reformation and counter-reformation, and while the language of Christianity was still the language of political and social aspiration, as of more intimate reflections. In France as in England, of course, many of the ideas in play in the revolutionary movements had a theological origin or colour – there is in the west no complete escape from the Church – but the process of laicization had gone much further, and bitten much deeper, in the Paris of 1789 than in the London of 1649. 1649 was still a long way from Locke, whose ideas, and those of the empirical rationalism that went with him, were popularized in France by Voltaire.

At the starting-point of this volume, in the mid-seventeenth century, the public disarray of this country was inextricably at once political and religious. The movement from Episcopacy to Presbyterianism, from Presbyterianism to Independency and so to chaos, marks the political progress, or declension, of those times. There are many shifts, in the century that follows, to 1750, and by that time we are in another world. Theological arguments have become frivolities, as far as politics is concerned. The Whig bishops and the Whig landowners overlay the country like a plateful of cold porridge. In 1650 things were not like that. The king had been put to death by a revolutionary tribunal. The bishops had been pushed out; the use of the Book of Common Prayer, privately as well as publicly, had been made a criminal offence punishable by fine or imprisonment; thousands of the parochial clergy had been deprived of their functions and their means of livelihood; there had been a great smashing of church ornaments, under parliamentary direction. The Church was, politically, a defeated and illegal opposition. No doubt it learned something from that, and it is worth reflection that a great century of Anglican divinity included this period in the wilderness.

When the revolutionary movement had played itself out, and Charles II came back in 1660 without serious dissent, the English Church was restored with him, and the remnant was swollen by many who were less sure of their bearings. There was some vindictiveness and much mutual incomprehension, but the Church was again there, visibly, in every diocese and in every parish, ministering the sacraments in accordance with a Prayer Book which was certainly not less Catholic than its proscribed predecessor. The bishops had a part to play on the public stage. It was a transitory phase. The moment of their greatest political – and only popular – triumph came in 1688 when seven of their number took a public stand against James II's Declaration of Indulgence (see note on Ken, p.96 below). It was the last time the hierarchy played a significant public role in England. The settlement of 1689 meant, in the long run, the resurgence, in more sedate guise, of the forces behind the revolution of 1649 and their integration with the new forces of scientific rationalism. The outcome was the Whig oligarchy which, so to speak, had its licence from the financial enterprise of the City of London and has hardly relaxed its grip since. Certainly the prosperity of the High Church party in the last years of Anne's reign was a flash-in-the-pan. Ever since, Toryism in the sense defined by Dr Johnson – a Tory, says the *Dictionary*, is 'One who adheres to the ancient constitution of the state, and the apostolic hierarchy of the church of England' – has been no more than an obscure opposition doctrine, held more or less ironically by a few scattered people who persist in thinking that it has a bearing on the orientation of the country, however unhandy politicians may find it. That Toryism, which was that of Swift and of Johnson himself, has nothing whatever to do with the present-day political party which sometimes appropriates the name.

The strand of political involvement can never be lost sight of for long by any reader of the sermons of this period. It shows up most clearly in this volume in Atterbury's sermon *On the Martyrdom of King Charles I* and in the sermons of South, but it is present also in Swift and Barrow, to name no others. Atterbury's subject was common to the divines of the age; the Prayer Book provided a form of service to be used on 30 January, the day Charles was beheaded. The word 'martyrdom' was used because of the King's final stand for episcopacy. It must always have been distasteful to many, and the service fell into disuse – not without protest from such men as Swift – as the Whig oligarchy tightened its grip. These remote political quarrels have to be accepted as part of the scene of the times.

The related, but more general, political theme which recurs with a frequency which is likely to surprise the casual reader of the literature of the age is that of passive obedience. This meant the duty of obeying civil authorities – the king and the king's government – whether one liked what they were doing or not. South's treatment of this subject will be found in his sermon on Romans 13:5, 'Wherefore he must needs be subject, not only for wrath, but also for conscience sake'. But the subject was not one only for party men. No one was ever less that than Berkeley, and he gave a series of discourses on the subject, in the most conciliatory vein, in the chapel of Trinity College, Dublin. It is a way of thinking remote from any that is now current, but there is a theological issue to be understood. The classic application of the doctrine, in this period, was to the difficult question of allegiance to James II after he had fled the country and William and Mary had come in. It was possible to maintain, and many, like Stillingfleet, did maintain – after more or less hesitation – that obedience was due to the *de facto* government, whatever it might be. But many of the most sensitive churchmen of the time felt, with Sancroft, the Archbishop of Canterbury, and Ken, that they could not rescind the oath of allegiance they had given to James II and so could not take the oath to William and Mary.

These events are important for an understanding of sermon literature of the age, not merely because they echo through it, but because those who felt they could not take the oath were an important group and the fact that they were turned out affected the character of the subsequent literature. For the Non-Jurors, who were catholic-minded and had strong affinities with the earlier Caroline divines, had no access to pulpits and delivered no more sermons. A valuable stream of Anglican thought went underground, re-emerging in various ways with Wesley and Newman. There was Jeremy Collier, whose *Short View of the Immorality and Profaneness of the English Stage* is less absurd than it is often made out to be and who was the author of a number of other works, including a most readable *Ecclesiastical History of Great Britain*. The greatest name is undoubtedly that of William Law, of whom every student of eighteenth-century literature should read at least *A Serious Call to a Devout and Holy Life* and the *Three Letters to the Bishop of Bangor* – charming and elegant masterpieces, the latter an ironic onslaught on the Erastianism of Hoadly. The chill on the English pulpit, as the century advances, would have been less if these men had had their say.

With the political involvement of the Church from 1650 to 1750 there developed another characteristic, a relative neglect of dogma, what seems a lack of curiosity as of passion in relation to the fundamental tenets of the Christian religion. This neglect is far from being general, or absolute, but there is enough of it to make a contrast with the preceding period, when the quarrels of the Reformation still reverberated. This is not to say that the essentials of doctine were not kept alive by the more Catholic part of the clergy – a Bingham or a Wilson, even Swift. But there is, undoubtedly, an orientation towards questions of conduct, which is marked from the very beginning of the period. Before the mid-point of the century Henry Hammond had published his *Practical Catechism*, a lucid, deeply considered work aimed at the 'heightening of Christian practice'. The book is uncompromising in its claims for the apostolic church of England, but one senses in the prominent attention given to conduct a desire to lay weight on those matters in which reconciliation between Christian opinions seemed least hopeless. There is something of this even in Jeremy Taylor, with whom this volume opens. *Holy Living* and *Holy Dying* are, after all, manuals of conduct, and in the latter part of his life what Taylor most valued among his works was the casuistry of *Doctor Dubitantium*. The sermon given in this volume, which belongs to his best period as a writer, shows a most delicate psychological insight. While one may miss, in this period, the doctrinal expositions of an Andrewes, one cannot make light of the longing for peace which must have been partly responsible for turning men's minds in the direction of practice. There was, however, also a more sinister motive for this development, which can be felt in France as well as in England. This is the movement towards deism, not to say atheism, which accompanied the fading of the imagination of the seventeenth century and the growth of the sort of rationalism which founded itself on empirical and mechanical philosophies. This movement did produce some direct theological reaction, in which Bingham played an important part. But there is still more of an attempt to meet the new prejudices on their own ground, one common sense against another, which leads only to the complacency and worldliness of the time-servers such as Tillotson. Butler, with talents and a personal forbearance which put him in quite a different class, is really a last serious bid to answer the eighteenth century on its own terms.

*

The form and style of the sermon alters during the period, in the same way as the form and style of literature at large. The great poem of 1650 is Marvell's 'Horatian Ode', which looks backwards to the Metaphysicals and forwards to the clarities of the Augustan age. The reform of the heroic couplet had already begun with Denham and Waller, but the way was so far only obscurely open to the ages of Dryden and Pope. By 1750 this aesthetic was in decline, though 'The Deserted Village', which would not have been possible without it, was still to come. The movement in prose style is well exemplified in this volume.

Jeremy Taylor, born seventeen years before any other divine here represented, belongs wholly to the world before the formation of the Royal Society, which however happened before his death. His abstractions are not the abstractions of science, and the new conception of rationality, as of eloquence, which marks the latter part of the seventeenth century and becomes dominant in the eighteenth, hardly shows itself. It is more marked in Barrow, who was a mathematician, and in Stillingfleet, yet they still drag their feet a little in the old rhythms. The watershed is marked by Tillotson, a man of much less ability than any of them. Tillotson was born in the same year as Barrow, and before South, but he was a man with his ear, as well as his eye, on the present, and perhaps had less strong attachments than they. He saw what was needed for the worldly success of the Church – if that is not a contradiction in terms – and it is he, more than anyone, who grasped what sort of thing decent people in that age would listen to, without feeling that they were in any danger of being disturbed in their complacencies. He set the tone of the eighteenth-century pulpit. This is not to say that there were not, in the first half of the eighteenth century, powerful minds among the clergy, who had absorbed all the new elegances – to a degree, indeed, far beyond Tillotson's capacities – and were capable of using them to convey orthodox and disturbing messages. Swift's tongue was rough as well as elegant, and, under all his armour of irony against the world of the Whigs, he was a Caroline High Churchman. Berkeley, one of the most brilliant minds in the Europe of his age, was not the man to throw away the imagination of the seventeenth century. Finally there is Butler, a man of the eighteenth century certainly, and speaking the language of his opponents, but holding fast to his orthodoxy in a world of deism.

No one can take the study of seventeenth-century literature very far without some acquaintance with the works of the Anglican divines who were among its greatest prose writers. So much of the intellect and imagination of the age went into these channels. Even if one considers that Hobbes, Locke and Hume swept the board, and that the science which followed them has made all theology a useless dream – which is a common enough assumption, even conclusion, in our own day – it is still necessary to know what it was they swept away. Moreover, the reader of Vaughan and Traherne will not be very near their poetry unless he has some knowledge of the world of Jeremy Taylor. The deficiency of Christian teaching in the latter part of the twentieth century has made the approach more difficult, for many readers, and this deficiency has to be made up for somehow, whether or not one thinks Christianity superannuated. This book at least contains a number of clues to what was involved in the transition from the seventeenth to the eighteenth century, and might well be found of value by any student or general reader within whose field of interest that large subject falls for one reason or another. It is not and does not pretend to be a comprehensive guide to the subject.

The sermons have been chosen both for their intrinsic interest and to give an indication of the drift of the times. To the newcomer to this branch of literature – which, because of the widespread suspicion, in our time, of theological writers, as if they were the only repositories of superstition, has been comparatively neglected – these sermons will at least indicate what variety there is, and what sort of entertainment is to be found. There is at any rate a massive amount of good prose, written by men passionately concerned for the truth of what they were saying and perfectly primed in the intellectual difficulties of their contemporaries which are, of course, no more than more or less our own.

In the seventeenth and eighteenth centuries the clergy, as a matter of course, attracted to its numbers a high proportion of the ability which, in the twentieth century, would be more likely to find its way into ordinary academic work, the civil service, or any one of a variety of professional and business pursuits; and that can be said without aspersion on the able men in orders now. Moreover, a variety of literary talent, which would now be more likely to find vent in imaginative or analytical writing of an entirely lay character, then found an outlet in the pulpit and in other forms of theological writing. So the mind of those times is not to be known without some acquaintance with the sermons, nor can any comparison of our own with the older literature be made without it.

JEREMY TAYLOR

Taylor was born in Cambridge in or about 1613. His father was a barber; Heber and others have tried to make out that he must have been at least a *surgeon*-barber, but those who are anxious to prove the respectability of the bishop could rest content with his own life and works. He was admitted to Gonville and Caius College, Cambridge, in 1626, having been to school in the same town. He was elected a fellow of Caius, and ordained, in 1633. He spent little time in the college, however. He went to London to preach at St Paul's in place of a Cambridge friend, and made impression enough for news of his performance to reach the ears of Laud, who was attentive to such matters. He was invited to preach before the Archbishop at Lambeth. Laud's only adverse remark afterwards was that he was too young, a fault Taylor is said to have promised to cure, if he lived. In 1635 he was nominated to a fellowship at All Souls, Oxford, by Laud, who expressed the hope that the fact that he had been educated at Cambridge would 'be no prejudice to him'. Taylor thus started his ecclesiastical career under the most favourable auspices.

He stayed at All Souls no more than three years, and then became rector of Uppingham in Rutlandshire, and married. Shortly afterwards he became chaplain to Charles I, and it is probably that which took him back to Oxford in 1642. He became a chaplain in the Royalist army. Naturally his house in Uppingham was 'plundered, his estate seized, and is family driven out of doors'. He seems to have been taken prisoner in the struggle around Cardigan Castle, and the same year – 1645 – was released and went to live as chaplain to the Earl of Carbery, at Golden Grove in Carmarthenshire. Carbery seems hardly to have been a hero; after some initial gestures for the royal cause he apparently preferred to stay at home drinking, and not to imperil his estate. It was this circumstance which gave Taylor the safe seclusion in which much of his best work was produced. At Golden Grove he wrote not only many of his best sermons but *The Liberty of Prophesying* and *Holy Living* and *Holy Dying*.

In 1655 Taylor was imprisoned for a time in Chepstow Castle. After that he did not go back to Golden Grove. Royalists were by then forbidden to keep chaplains, or tutors for their children. After some comings and goings among Royalists in London and elsewhere, Taylor went to northern Ireland in 1658, under the protection of Lord Conway. He was back in London in 1660 and able to declare his support for Monk. With the Restoration he was appointed Bishop of Down and Connor and Vice-Chancellor of Trinity College, Dublin. It was perhaps a mark of distrust due to literary ability that he was not offered an English bishopric; 'a man of dangerous temper,' as Sheldon said later, 'apt to break out into extravagances.' His Irish see brought him troubles; it was full of Scottish Presbyterians who could not be pacified. Taylor's work at Trinity College was, however, a success. He found 'a heap of men and boys' and set the place on its feet as a university. He died in 1667.

Despite adversities – which were hardly to be avoided by anyone who took a firm stand in the internal struggles of the seventeenth century – Taylor had a fortunate life, if anything too much under the protection of great men. His writings are among the most seductive in the great literature produced by the Anglican clergy of the period. *Holy Living* and *Holy Dying* are full of wisdom, charm and eloquence; no one should let a prejudice against works of piety stop him from exploring them. *The Worthy Communicant* is a book for the practising Christian, but can be read with pleasure and other advantages by anyone who wants to understand the temper of Anglicanism.

ISAAC BARROW

Isaac Barrow was born in London in 1630. His father was Linendraper to Charles I. He had an uncle who became Bishop of St Asaph. He was said to have been a pugnacious boy, and not attentive to school-work. He was thought to have done little good to himself at Charterhouse, but improved when afterwards he went to school at Felstead. His father 'often solemnly wished, that if it pleased God to take away any of his Children, it might be his son *Isaac*.' This opinion changed, and Thomas Barrow, who outlived his son by some years, regretted the loss to his old age. He also found it 'no small mitigation' to his sorrow, that while his son lived 'he was not unprofitable to the world', and he himself published his son's collected works. It cannot have taken Isaac long to settle down to his studies, for he did well at Felstead and was thought fit for Cambridge at the age of fifteen.

He was not well off at this time, his father being impoverished through his adherence to the King. Barrow apparently received some support from Henry Hammond, one of the chaplains of Charles I, who was in due course deprived and imprisoned. He took his B.A. in 1648 and became a Fellow of Trinity in 1649. He was a discreet and reasonable man, and managed to live with the Puritan authorities in spite of his Royalist connections and his own independence of mind. The Master of the college is said to have placed his hand on Barrow's head with the words: 'Thou art a good Lad, 'tis pity thou art a Cavalier.' His talents and industry were valued. For some years he took to the study of medicine, and thought of becoming a physician, but concluded that not to make divinity the end of his studies would be contrary to the oath he had taken when he became a Fellow.

In 1654 he sold his books and went abroad on the proceeds, though some other aids must have been found before he returned for his travels lasted till 1659 and he went as far as Constantinople. Off the coast of Italy he once manned a gun against pirates. He made notes on Mohammedanism, on Turkish proverbs and Turkish officials. He was a learned man when he went abroad, and he came back with numerous additions to his armoury.

At the Restoration he became Professor of Greek at Cambridge, then Professor of Geometry at Gresham College. In 1663 he became the first Lucasian Professor of Mathematics at Cambridge, and not the least sign of his unusual fitness for the post is that he recognized the superiority of Isaac Newton and gave way to him in 1669. His collected works were edited by Tillotson. They include, besides sermons and mathematical works, a treatise on the Pope's supremacy. Barrow died of a fever in 1677.

ROBERT SOUTH

South was born in Hackney in 1634. He was the son of a London merchant. He went to Westminster School and was there when Charles I was beheaded outside the Banqueting Hall a few hundred yards away. There is a story that he mentioned the King's name in the school's Latin prayers on that very day. It is certain that the scholars will have heard the great shout or groan of the crowd. In 1651 South went on to Christ Church, Oxford. He is said to have shown some Presbyterian leanings there but he certainly received episcopal ordination in 1658, when it could not be done openly. He travelled on the Continent.

His public career began with the Restoration, and he sided uncompromisingly, and some might say at times intemperately, with the victorious party. He became Public Orator at Oxford, chaplain to Clarendon and a prebendary of Westminster; on Clarendon's fall he became chaplain to the Duke of York. In 1670 he was made a canon of Christ Church and in 1676 went to

Poland as chaplain to the ambassador. In 1678 he became rector of Islip and he was chaplain to Charles II. In 1689 he hesitated, then took the oath to William and Mary, but he is said to have declined a bishopric vacated by a Non-Juror. In the years immediately following he became involved – again in no very temperate spirit – in controversy with Sherlock and others about the nature of the Trinity – a subject which Swift later summed up, with trenchant orthodoxy, by saying that God commanded us 'to believe a Fact that we do not understand'. In Anne's reign, South, naturally enough, took part in the Sacheverell affair, but he ended with dignity, refusing in 1713 to become Bishop of Rochester on the grounds that 'such a chair would be too uneasy for an old infirm man to sit in'. He died in 1716.

South was a man of learning, and if he could get head over heels in controversy he could also stop to observe. In his mission to Poland he noted the beneficial effect of public baths, 'from the use of which, in all probability, it happens that the Polish children seldom break out in their head or face, and that not one of a thousand is distorted, crooked, or ill-shaped, as in other countries.' He had some fairly lucrative preferments, but he was generous and gave away a large part of the proceeds and his benefactions included provision for the education of the children of parishioners as well as church repairs out of his own pocket. He was often plain-spoken to the point of brutality, in the pulpit or elsewhere. He had a ready wit, and apparently found it hard to refrain from using it. He had all the talents required to make a churchman respected at the court of Charles II – an ambiguous testimonial, no doubt.

EDWARD STILLINGFLEET

Stillingfleet was born in Cranborne, Dorset, in 1635 and educated at St John's College, Cambridge, where he was elected to a fellowship immediately on his graduation at the age of eighteen. No doubt he was a brilliant student; it may be concluded also that his views were not offensive to Presbyterians. He received ordination, however, at the hands of Brownrig, the deprived Bishop of Exeter. Brownrig was a man with whom Stillingfleet must have felt at home. A Cambridge man himself, he was a Calvinist who did not like Laudian ways but said he liked the

Church of England 'better and better as he grew older'; and it is recorded that 'persons of all denominations' were present at his funeral. In 1659 – when he was only twenty-four – Stillingfleet produced a book called *The Irenicum*, in which he advocated a union between episcopalians and Presbyterians.

In 1655 Pepys 'heard the famous young Stillingfleet', whom he had known at Cambridge; he reports that 'he did make the most plain, honest, good, grave sermon, in the most unconcerned and easy yet substantial manner'. It is the impression one gets from Stillingfleet's works. He was a man of great ability, and had great learning but, even more notably, active practical sense. He preached in an outspoken manner at Court, but maintained good relations there as well with the dissenters. In 1678 he became Dean of St Paul's. He was not prominent during James II's reign, but 1689 saw him Bishop of Winchester, a member of the Commission which considered the revision of the Prayer Book and the possibility of comprehension. Nothing came of the Commission's proposals. In his later years Stillingfleet engaged in controversy with Locke. He died in 1699.

Stillingfleet was a man to whom practical objectives were important, yet – as many men of affairs are – he was of an abstracting turn of mind. He was a close reasoner, and apparently believed that by reasoning he could persuade. At the end of his book on *Idolatry Practised in the Church of Rome* (1671) there are a few pages in which 'The Faith of Protestants' is 'Reduced to Principles'. It is a characteristic production. Such work points forward to an eighteenth-century rationalism of which Stillingfleet would not have approved, for he was himself very much a man of the seventeenth century and a convinced, if at times Latitudinarian, churchman.

THOMAS KEN

Ken was born at Berkhamstead in Hertfordshire in 1637, the youngest son of an attorney. He was educated at Winchester and New College, Oxford, where he graduated in 1661. In 1663 he became rector of Little Easton, in Essex, and two years later went back to Winchester, where he undertook to look after a small neglected parish on the outskirts of the city. From 1672 he taught at the college, and it was about this time that he composed his *Manual of Prayers for the Use of the Winchester Scholars*. In 1675 he travelled as far as Rome. In 1679 he was appointed chaplain to Princess Mary at the Hague, and seems to have got on less well with William. He afterwards became chaplain to Charles II, who took in good part his refusal to allow Nell Gwynn to lodge in his house in Winchester. Ken apparently thought he should not countenance the King's irregularities and the King thought this was a perfectly proper line for a clergyman to take. The following year Ken was made bishop of Bath and Wells. He attended at the death-bed of Charles II, giving him an absolution to which the King perhaps paid little attention, and he was outwitted by a Roman priest at the last moment.

The most important public events in Ken's life were in connection with the changes of 1688-9. He was one of the seven bishops who protested against James II's order that his Declaration of Indulgence should be read in all churches. The matter of the declaration was no more than everyone now takes for granted; there was to be full liberty of worship and an end to discrimination on grounds of religion. The bishops' protest led to their arrest. They were provided with good lawyers. An initial argument on a purely technical point about their standing as peers led to their being incarcerated in the Tower of London. To those who didn't understand the issues this must have looked like the first of those acts of popish oppression which they were expecting from James, while the more knowledgeable of his opponents must have been delighted at the misunderstanding. When the main case came on the bishops themselves had only a passive role to play. The case was entirely managed by their lawyers. First came a long argument as to whether the bishops were properly before the court; then as to whether the petition and the signatures were in the handwriting of the accused. All this niggling looks odd in relation to the position of the bishops as political heroes. The lawyers were forced in the end to the substance of the argument, which had been made in the protest itself, and was the constitutional issue as to whether the King could dispense with laws passed in due form by Parliament. The charge was one of issuing a seditious libel, and the jury returned a verdict of 'Not guilty'. By the time he heard the verdict James II was already in camp with his troops at Hounslow, and soon he was out of the country and William and Mary were on their way over from Holland.

For Ken this was only the beginning of the end. When William was in the saddle he required an oath of allegiance. Ken with four other bishops and about four hundred of the clergy felt that they could not take it. It was a matter of conscience. They had sworn allegiance to James. There were two sides to the question, and Ken recognized this. It could be argued that there was a duty of obedience to the *de facto* government. When Ken made his decision he wrote to the Non-Juror Dodwell: 'Only in one thing I cannot go as far as you seem to do, in condemning those who are of another persuasion, because I think there are more degrees of excusability in what they have done than perhaps you will admit.' Ken and the other Non-Jurors were deprived and ejected. For many of the clergy and their families this meant extreme hardship. Ken retired to the protection of Lord Weymouth's mansion at Longleat, with no more than seven hundred pounds from the sale of his effects in Wells. He continued to take an interest in the affairs of his fellow Non-Jurors, but opposed the consecration of further Non-Juring bishops when others sought to continue the succession – and the schism – in that way.

Ken was a man of great generosity and charm, ascetic and assiduous in his devotions and morally fastidious. He can hardly be said to have been intellectually outstanding among the churchmen of his day. His prose works are not important, most of his verse is weak and self-indulgent, quite different in kind from the splendid Morning, Evening and Midnight Hymns for which he is remembered and which he used regularly in his own devotions. He took care of his diocese, while he had it, and was always actively charitable. He worked day and night for the relief of the hundreds of prisoners in Bridgwater, Taunton and Wells after the battle of Sedgemoor. After he was deprived he had, of course, no public function. There were twenty years of religious retreat at Longleat. He died in 1711.

JOHN TILLOTSON

Tillotson was born in 1630 at Sowerby in Yorkshire. He was the son of a clothier of good family, a man of Calvinist and Puritan views. Tillotson went to the grammar school at Colne and then, in 1647, to Clare College, Cambridge. The part of Clare where he and his friends lived is said to have been called 'Roundheads' Corner' and no doubt he held views acceptable to the time for he became a fellow of the college in 1651. He was acquainted with Cudworth, Henry More and the other Cambridge Platonists, but he was of a more practical turn of mind than they. On leaving the university, he became tutor in the family of Edmund Prideaux, who was Cromwell's Attorney-General, and almost exactly at the moment of the Restoration sought episcopal ordination. He became a preacher at Lincoln's Inn and married in 1663; his bride's reluctance is said to have been over-ruled by her father with the words: 'You shall have him, Betty, for he is the best polemical divine in England.' Through his father-in-law's influence he became a regular preacher at St Lawrence Jewry, where he made a great reputation, so that all the best people and all the most ambitious young clergymen went to hear him. In 1672 he became Dean of Canterbury, in which capacity he managed to meet and be of service to Prince William of Orange, who had just married the Princess Mary and was carrying her off to Holland. In 1688 he helped the Seven Bishops draw up the document explaining why they could not read James's Declaration of Indulgence. When Sancroft refused to take the oath to William and Mary, and was deposed, Tillotson was appointed Archbishop of Canterbury. William III said he was the best friend he ever had.

Tillotson was one of those ordinary able men, common enough in the world of affairs, who owe their eminence to the utter suitability of their opinions to the political requirements of the times. He was probably not particularly devious and he was always hostile to popery, even during the reign of James II when it might have paid to talk differently; though James, of course, was anxious to keep on good terms with the less orthodox Protestants. With his Presbyterian past, his tepid common sense and his tendency to drift with the growing rationalism of the age, Tillotson was the perfect ecclesiastical figurehead after 1689.

As a churchman he counts for very little. His mind was without originality and his expositions of doctrine are notably shallow. He achieved the distinction of a favourable mention in Collins's *Discourse of Free-Thinking* – a work which Swift characterized as '*a brief compleat Body of* Atheology'. Swift summarized Collins's tribute as follows:

> But *Arch Bishop Tillotson* is the person whom all *English Free Thinkers* owe as their Head; and his Virtue is indisputable for this manifest Reason, that Dr. *Hicks*, a Priest, calls him an Atheist; says, he caused several to turn Atheists, and to ridicule the Priesthood and Religion. These must be allowed to be

> noble effects of *Free Thinking*. This great Prelate assures us, that all the Duties of the Christian Religion, with respect to God, are no other but what natural Light prompts Men to, except the two Sacraments, and praying to God in the name and Mediation of Christ: As a Priest and a Prelate he was obliged to say something of Christianity; but pray observe, Sir, how he brings himself off. He justly observes that even these things are of less Moment than natural Duties; and because Mothers nursing their Children is a natural Duty, it is of more moment than the two Sacraments, or than praying to God in the name and by the Mediation of Christ. The *Free Thinking* Archbishop would not allow a Miracle sufficient to give Credit to a Prophet who taught anything contrary to our natural Notions: By which it is plain, he rejected at once all the Mysteries of Christianity.

It is Collins, rather than Tillotson, who is being held up to ridicule. On the other hand, no one could miss the undercurrents of irony directed at the great Whig mediocrity who had stepped into a better man's shoes. For Sancroft, Swift had had as a young man something very like a cult.

WILLIAM SHERLOCK

Sherlock was born in Southwark and educated at Eton and Peterhouse, Cambridge. He was ordained, and some years later became rector of St George's, Botolph Lane, in the city. In 1674 he published a work attacking Puritan spirituality, and in 1684 a book on the duty of passive obedience. This view he maintained throughout James II's reign, combining it with strong attacks against popery. His passivity did not extend so far as complying with James's command to read the Declaration for Liberty of Conscience. At the Revolution of 1689 he was at first inclined to side with the Non-Jurors, as might have been expected from his declared views. In 1690, however, he took the oath. It is reported to have been said as he walked through the city: 'There goes Dr Sherlock, with his reason for taking the oath.' The reason was Mrs Sherlock. In 1691 there was a new book, *The Case of Resistance*, in which Sherlock took the view, reasonable enough in itself, that the Anglican Church has always recognized *de facto* government. In 1691 Sherlock was rewarded by being made

Dean of St Paul's in succession to Tillotson, who was succeeding the Non-Juror Sancroft as Archbishop of Canterbury. In the nineties Sherlock gave much time and energy to a 'vindication' of the doctrine of the Trinity wich took him so far that he was accused of saying that there were three Gods instead of one. He later modified his position. During his last years he was rector of Therfield, Hertfordshire and continued to write vigorously against dissenters. He died in 1707.

It is hard to avoid the impression that Sherlock was a rather silly man. He was almost certainly a rather weak one. South, whose tongue was admittedly none of the kindest, said: 'There is hardly any one subject he has wrote upon (that of Popery only excepted) but he has wrote for and against it too.' One has the impression that he couldn't stop writing and couldn't stop talking. He certainly did not impress his contemporaries as a man of any great solidity. His sermons show a marked facility of language and, as to content, a little meaning goes a long way.

JOSEPH BINGHAM

Bingham was born in 1668 in Wakefield, Yorkshire, of which his father was 'a respectable inhabitant', though what other occupation he had, is not known. The boy went to school in the town and then to University College, Oxford. He graduated in 1688 and shortly afterwards became a fellow and then a tutor of the college. Everything points to his learning having been extraordinary, even at this stage. According to his great-grandson, who wrote his life and produced an edition of his works in the 1840s, he had 'employed the greater portion of his time in studying the writings of the Fathers, making himself intimately acquainted with their opinions and doctrines, and fully able both to explain, and to defend, their interpretation of the difficult or disputed passages of Scripture.' A formidable young man, and of the most dangerous kind, for he could not readily be corrected by his seniors.

By 1695 he had outstayed his welcome in Oxford, and was presented to the rectory of Headborne-Worthy near Winchester, a living worth about a hundred pounds a year. This was the scene of his labours for the rest of his life. Those labours were extraordinary. 'The duties of his profession', says his great-grandson, 'he punctually discharged, not only with great ability, but with devout and fervent zeal, directed by pious and conscious rectitude.' Every other moment, one might think, must have been given up to his studies. Yet he married, after about six years at Headborne-Worthy, and as if inadvertently became, 'in the course of a few years', the father of 'ten children, two sons and eight daughters'. This must have stretched the hundred pounds, and made the rectory rather less peaceful than a fellow's rooms. There is evidence that Bingham was extremely hard up for books; he had no resource but the cathedral library at Winchester. It was not until 1712 that he had any addition to his living.

Meanwhile, in 1708, he had produced the first volume of his great work, *The Antiquities of the Christian Church*, a sytematic compendium of information about the organization, rites, discipline and calendar of the Church in the first four or five centuries, which after two hundred and fifty years has not been superseded. The last of the ten original volumes appeared in 1722, and a few months afterwards Bingham was dead, it is said of old age, although he was only fifty-five.

Bingham is an engaging character, a scholar of great intellectual endowments, kind and affectionate, mild and charitable. When, in 1720, his books had brought him at least a little money which he put aside to maintain his family in case he should die, he lost it all in the South Sea Bubble. He met this trouble with complete equanimity or – a cynic might say – left his wife to worry about it, and did not let it interrupt his studies for a single day. He disliked pompous monuments, in an age which was certainly too fond of them, and had a plain tomb. A pity, perhaps, for his old schoolmaster in Wakefield wrote a splendid Latin inscription, which ended by saying that Bingham, who deserved a patriarchate, had no preferment but to Headborne-Worthy and Havant.

FRANCIS ATTERBURY

Atterbury was the second son of the rector of Milton Keynes, where he was born in 1662. He was educated by his father at home, then under Dr Busby at Westminster. In 1680 he went to Christ Church, Oxford. He seems to have been brilliant and engaging, with the weaknesses with which those qualifications usually comport. His early works included a Latin translation of

Dryden's *Absalom and Achitophel* and an essay in defence of the Church of England against Romanist innuendo, and he later became involved in the controversy with Bentley which is the subject of Swift's *Battle of the Books*. A taste for controversy was among his weaknesses. He was ordained in 1687, and was soon well known as a preacher, a success to which his social charm must have contributed as well as his manner of delivery. In 1691 he became lecturer at St Brides and chaplain to William and Mary; on Mary's death in 1694 he was the only one of the royal chaplains who was retained. Apparently he was already a favourite with Anne and he became her chaplain in ordinary on her accession to the throne. Other preferments were not lacking; he became Archdeacon of Totnes in 1701, Dean of Carlisle in 1704, Dean of Christ Church in 1711/12 and in 1713 Bishop of Rochester. No wonder Swift, who knew him well and was on good terms with him, characterized him lightly in the *Journal to Stella* as 'one that understands his own interests', and in his correspondence showed some sensitivity about his own less sparkling course and 'the deanery they thought fit to throw me into'. But if Atterbury had the art of pleasing he also had a more serious talent for friendship, and not only Swift himself but Bolingbroke, Pope, Arbuthnot, Gay, Prior and South were among his friends. Moreover he allowed himself to be swept along steadily by the causes to which he was attached and served them with more enthusiasm than prudence.

It was his determination, as well as his ability and charm, which made him the spokesman of the Lower House of Convocation against bishops of the Upper House. Behind the long and sometimes obscure procedural wrangles was a division with its roots deep in the history of the seventeenth century. Atterbury was the spokesman of those who were more royalist than the King and more episcopalian than the bishops. The bench of bishops had been filled up, after 1689, with Whigs and Latitudinarians and the tension of this situation was felt in the quarrels of Convocation. Atterbury was sympathetic – to put it no more strongly – with the Jacobite cause, and there is a story that in 1715 he offered to lead the way to a Proclamation in his lawn sleeves. His dealings or his reputation, or both, led in the early twenties to his arrest, imprisonment in the Tower and finally, in 1723, to his being deprived of all his ecclesiastical offices and banished from the country for ever. He served the Pretender for a short time in Paris but this seems not to have been a satisfactory situation and his last years were spent in the south of France. There is extant a letter to Pope in which he briefly describes the last hours he spent with his daughter, who came out to see him and died twenty hours after their meeting in Toulouse.

THOMAS WILSON

Wilson was born at Burton, in Cheshire, and went to school in Chester, then to Trinity College, Dublin, where he studied medicine. He was ordained deacon in 1686, and served as curate to his uncle in a Lancashire parish. In 1689 he became a priest, and three years afterwards chaplain to the Earl of Derby. It was through this connection that he was offered the see of Sodor and Man, which had been vacant for four years and was rather down-at-heel. He accepted, and was installed in St German's Cathedral, Peel, in 1698. Both the cathedral and the bishop's residence were in a ruinous condition, and the income was not more than three hundred pounds a year. Wilson 'had a practical turn', as his first biographer said. He farmed energetically and with success, planted orchards and woodlands, and ran a mill, besides for some years being the only doctor on the island and providing a free service to the poor. His economic preoccupations, which were strictly subordinate to his work as a bishop and certainly not undertaken for personal gain, enabled him to extend his care for his diocese in several directions. No doubt he infected others with his energy. Not only were the cathedral and Bishop's Court repaired at great expense and almost entirely out of his own funds; other churches were built and the grammar schools and parish schools of the island were improved.

Perhaps unfortunately, it was Wilson's administration of Church discipline that made most noise in the world, and he has been held up as a model of apostolical simplicity in this matter. In fact, he was the inheritor of a practically medieval system and continued it in a manner which would have been possible only in that out-of-the-way corner of the world. Warnings, penances and excommunications were the ordinary stock-in-trade, for offences ranging from fornication to playing with a dog in church. Wilson left the old 'spiritual statutes' of the island largely untouched and introduced Ecclesiastical Constitutions of his own in 1704. Whether one views these activities with the mawkish admiration of Keble, or regards them with more reserve, there is no doubt that Wilson was absolutely fearless in his administration. It was his mitigation of the fines in the ecclesiastical courts which first raised the hackles of the civil authorities, who were anxious about losing revenue. In 1721 he ordered the Governor's wife to ask forgiveness for slanderous statements, as a sort of mitigated penance; this naturally did not improve his standing among the 'best people'. There was a first-class provincial row. He suspended his archdeacon, who not only sided with the lady but approved the *Independent Whig* which Wilson had censured. The old-world customs of the island extended beyond ecclesiastical censures, and Wilson and his vicars-general found themselves confined in a dungeon. His later years in the diocese were less eventful.

Wilson was a man of energy and simplicity, and his devotion to his function and his diocese was irreproachable. Three times he declined an English bishopric, saying on the last occasion: 'I will not leave my wife in my old age because she is poor.' Nor should he be thought of as itching to manage the conduct of others. 'Generally speaking,' he wrote in his private notebook, 'men have more need of a confessor than of a director.' His most striking characteristic was a far-reaching seriousness. It was no doubt this which so attracted Matthew Arnold. There are a number of references to Wilson in Arnold's notebooks, and he wrote about Wilson's *Maxims* at some length in the preface to *Culture and Anarchy*. Less deep and powerful than the *Meditations* of Marcus Aurelius, Arnold said, they were a work of the same kind, with 'something peculiarly sincere and first-hand about them'. He admired their balance but, perhaps above all, 'that downright honesty and plain good sense which our English race has applied so powerfully to the divine impossibilities of religion'. Dangerous qualities, and a dangerous recommendation, but they probably sum up well the character of this man about whom there was so little nonsense.

JONATHAN SWIFT

Swift was born in Dublin in 1667; He 'happened, indeed, by a perfect accident,' as he says, to be born in Ireland, but he came of an old Yorkshire family and did not regard himself an Irishman.

His father, one of several brothers who had gone to Ireland to make a living, died before the boy was born, and his mother soon went back to England. Swift owed his education to an uncle. He was sent to school in Kilkenny, then to Trinity College, Dublin, where he seems to have been more noted for his independence than for his academic attainments. He became secretary, at Moor Park in Surrey, to Sir William Temple, with whom there were family connections. Temple was a Whig ex-statesman and *littérateur*, who was perhaps pleased with Swift until he found the young man was abler than himself. Temple certainly contributed greatly, both wittingly and unwittingly, to Swift's education, and it was to him that Swift owed his introduction into the great world. Swift showed as much independence as gratitude. In 1694 he left Temple and was ordained, but not before he had been offered a civil appointment which gave him, as he says, 'an opportunity of living without being driven into the Church for a maintenance'. He was not over-pleased with his living at Kilroot, and soon returned to Moor Park, but went over to Ireland again in 1699 as chaplain to the Earl of Berkeley and soon after became vicar of Laracor.

He spent the following years between Ireland and England, becoming ever more involved in affairs of state as well as of the Church. The period of his most intimate involvement in affairs of state was during the last years of Queen Anne, when he was on familiar terms with the leaders of the Tory administration, Harley and St John, though less in their confidence than he supposed at the time. The appointment as Dean of St Patrick's was on Harley's recommendation; it was 'no great prize', as Leslie Stephen says. The death of Anne brought in the Whigs who were to dominate the century.

The rest of Swift's life was spent in virtual exile in Ireland. He knew the country from top to bottom, as few knew it. He had acquaintance in the best circles; he took long solitary journeys across the countryside and was familiar with the condition of the people at large. He became a hero in Dublin for his opposition to the rapacity of the Whig administration and the forces of money. He was punctilious and unobtrusive in his duties as a churchman, and exercised charity with a rough tongue. He died in 1745 and was buried in St Patrick's Cathedral where, as the epitaph he wrote for himself says, 'savage indignation could no longer tear his heart to pieces', *ubi saeva indignatio cor ulterius lacerare nequit.*

GEORGE BERKELEY

Berkeley was born in 1685 in County Kilkenny, where he went to school, and entered Trinity College, Dublin, at the age of fifteen. In 1707 he became a Fellow and Tutor. He held various posts in the college in the years that followed, including those of lecturer in Greek and lecturer in Hebrew. Meanwhile, as his *Commonplace Book* shows, he had from the age of twenty, or earlier, been preoccupied with certain intuitions about the nature of reality to which he gave a philosophical turn. Trinity College had changed since Swift was there twenty years before. The impact of Locke and Newton had been felt. The speculative mind of Berkeley quickly absorbed these new influences. He was, however, a man of a different kind. Although he developed the empiricism of Locke and is a link in the chain between Locke and Hume, he has affinities with the Traherne of the *Centuries of Meditations*. He was a visionary for whom the external world was important. In his speculations, he quickly went to the point of convincing himself that to exist means to perceive or to be perceived. This notion he developed in philosophical writing of elegance and luminous clarity, unlike any other in the language.

The *Essay towards a New Theory of Vision* was published in 1709; the *Treatise concerning the Principles of Human Knowledge* in 1710; and the *Three Dialogues between Hylas and Philonous* – the most seductive exposition of his philosophy – in 1713. After that there were several years during which Berkeley travelled extensively, particularly in Italy and Sicily, and spent some time intermittently in London. He was appointed Dean of Londonderry in 1724. For some years after that his main energies were devoted to a scheme for a missionary college in Bermuda – first in London, where he looked for contributions and support, and 1728-31 in America. It was a fundamental part of his scheme that 'the children of savage Americans, brought up in such a Seminary, and well instructed in religion and learning, might make the ablest and properest missionaries for spreading the gospel among their countrymen'. There is more than a touch of Berkeley's vivid delight in the external world in his recommendation of the islands: 'no part of the world enjoys a purer air, or a more temperate climate, the great ocean which environs them at once moderating the heat of the south winds, and the severity of the north-west.' The project failed, through lack of support from the home government. After a year or two back in London, Berkeley was appointed Biship of Cloyne, and spent the years 1734-52 there, in intelligent and charitable care of his diocese. To this period belongs *The Querist*, a fascinating series of economic questions, the outcome of Berkeley's concern for the condition of Ireland and in particular for the poor of his secluded diocese. To this period also belongs the development of his interest in the merits of tar-water as a cure for and preventive against all manner of diseases. He not only used it himself and recommended it in the most practical manner to the people of his diocese, but made it the subject of a chain of reflections and inquiries, *Siris*, a work of Platonic and neo-Platonic character. Berkeley retired in 1752 and spent the last year of his life in Oxford.

Swift said that Berkeley was 'an absolute Philosopher with respect to Money Titles or Power' – meaning that he cared nothing for them – and there is a debonair unworldliness about him which would itself be very engaging, even if he did not make so many other claims on our admiration. He lived simply and when he says, in the course of his reflections on the South Sea Bubble, 'Frugality of manners is the nourishment and strength of the body politic', he is saying what he means. 'The same atheistical narrow spirit', he goes on, 'centering all our cares upon private interest, and contracting all our hopes within the enjoyment of this private life, equally produce a neglect of what we owe to God and our country.' Berkeley is deeply aware of the Erastianism of his century, and with a single puff blows it away.

JOSEPH BUTLER

Butler was born at Wantage, in Berkshire, of Prebyterian parents. His father was a retired linen merchant. As a dissenter, Butler was debarred from the universities, and went to an academy at Tewkesbury. At the age of twenty-one he was conducting a philosophic correspondence with Samuel Clarke, a divine noted for his talents as a reasoner. He conformed to the Church of England, and in 1714 entered Oriel College, Oxford, where divinity was treated rather differently. Indeed he thought of leaving Oxford, where he had to 'mis-spend so much time' 'in attending frivolous lectures and unintelligible disputations', in favour of Cambridge, but was prevented by various procedural difficulties.

He took his B.A. in 1718 and was ordained the same year. The father of one of the friendlier Oriel Fellows was a bishop, and through his patronage Butler became preacher at the Rolls Chapel, an appointment he retained until 1726. Some of the sermons he preached there he himself described as 'very abstruse and difficult'; he evidently felt free to develop his ethical analysis before an intelligent audience. He published *Fifteen Sermons Preached at the Rolls Chapel* in 1726. About the same time he was given a wealthy living in Co. Durham. His influential friends did not neglect him. He spent seven years at Stanhope, and there wrote his most famous work, *The Analogy of Religion*. He was also said to have discharged conscientiously 'every obligation appertaining to a good parish priest', although the 'retirement was too solitary for his disposition, which had in it a natural cast of gloominess'. Once again his friends – this time Secker, an old school-friend from Tewkesbury, who later became Archbishop of Canterbury – came to his rescue. He became chaplain to the Lord Chancellor and later Clerk of the Closet to Queen Caroline, on whom he was in frequent attendance. He was given the 'mean' bishopric of Bristol in 1738, but it was only on being made Dean of St Paul's in 1740 that he resigned the living at Stanhope. He was an accomplished pluralist, and must have moved with discretion among the rather bloated hierarchy of the mid-eighteenth century. In 1750 he was translated to the see of Durham, which was extremely rich. He died in 1752.

Through all his excessive number of preferments Butler proceeded in a singular spirit. He was of an ascetic temper, and his benefactions were immense. There is no question of his having lived indulgently on his considerable fortune nor of having kept much of it for himself. Yet he seems to have thought the appointment to Bristol rather beneath him, and one might say that he never refused a preferment, but for a story that he was offered the see of Canterbury in 1747 and replied that it was 'too late for him to try to support a falling Church'. Butler had immense intellectual endowments, yet there is something commonplace about him, so far as commonplaceness can be said to go with so much distinction. The *Analogy* itself is so directed to the mind of the eighteenth century that it proves little now except that religion might have been invented by analogy with the world of nature. The objectives Butler proposed were modest and timely. It had, he said, come to be 'taken for granted, by many persons, that Christianity is not so much as a subject of inquiry; but that it is, now at length, discovered to be fictitious.' That was as clear in the eighteenth century as it is now, for those to whom such things are clear. Butler aimed to show simply 'that it is not, however, so clear a case, that there is nothing in it'. There is a 'cool self-interest' – Butler's own phrase – about much of his writing which is entirely that of the more well-fed part of his amiable century.

Yet Butler was in some respects far from that complacency. Apart from his endless charities he has left evidence – slight, as such things are often the better for being – of personal devotion and care for religion. Despite his Presbyterian beginning he belongs rather among the High Churchmen. One of his most interesting pieces of writing, to those who are concerned with him as a churchman rather than as a philosopher, is his *Charge to the Clergy of the Diocese of Durham*, in which he laments 'the general decay of religion' in this nation and pleads for the *forms of godliness* to be kept up, not for their own sake, but for what they may bring. It says something of the extraordinary state to which the Whig supremacy and the spread of deistic rationality had brought opinion by the mid-eighteenth century that this charge, together with a marble cross which Butler had erected in Bristol, were thought, a few years after his death, to be bases on which a charge of popery could be brought against him; and still more that such a charge could be seriously enough regarded for Secker, by then Archbishop of Canterbury, to intervene in defence of his memory.

A Four-letter Word

It is an odd fact that, in a century in which it has, on the whole, paid writers to trade under a left-wing label, so few of the major figures have done so. For some of the most eminent figures – one need go no further than Yeats, Eliot, Pound, Lawrence, Wyndham Lewis – it has been necessary to enter special apologies, to explain how people so recalcitrant to the main stream of intellectual prejudice can be accepted as intellectually respectable in spite of it all. Something is wrong somewhere, and since the general managers of the trade cannot be at fault, something must be wrong with these eminent writers. It is fortunately not difficult to show that *something* is wrong, in each case, for anyone who dips a toe into the great sea of politics gets his feet dirty. None the less it is odd that none of these brilliant performers could quite swallow what might be called the great obligatory truths of the left, which all decent people can take without choking: put compendiously, a belief in the harmony of democracy, largescale organization, and individual self-expression. Of course the managers of the trade have become adept at various logomachies; one of the most useful has been the assimilation of literary innovation into the general notion of revolution, which has become a repository for all that is desirable. There are even people, not themselves anxious to promote the usual axioms of the left, who have been so far convinced by this as to be on the look-out for technical manifestations in literature which will reassure them that the world is not changing too fast.

But the world is changing fast, and not even formal rhyme-schemes will save us from this. The question remains, whether the hell-for-leather race for the incompatible goals of democracy, largescale organization, and self-expression is the most intelligent form of political sport which can be engaged in at the present time. In raising this question here, there is no design of dragging *PN Review* into the combats which entertain politicians and their supporters, either in Parliament, the constituencies or the various perhaps more powerful fora which now exist outside. These have their proper places and actors. What has been lacking is the sort of pre-political discussion which the poetic intelligence can hardly avoid, when it becomes discursive, and which is of moment to everyone who has the interests of literature at heart, as distinct from the interests of the trade and its managers.

It is with this degree of disinterestedness, and no more, that this essay ventures upon an explanation so unfashionable that even my inured typewriter jibs at the enigmatic word. The word is – but before I utter it I must ask the reader to exercise an enormous forbearance and not to choke at it until he has digested several pages of my qualifications – the word is, *Tory*. It is as shop-soiled as any in the dictionary, and has long been the property of a political party which has no conception at all of its meaning, so that a voter who was a *Tory*, in the sense about to be elucidated, might as soon find himself voting Labour or Conservative – so-called Labour as soon as so-called Conservative; or he might, truth to tell, not think it worth his while to vote for either. Only I beg the reader, for a moment, to dissociate himself from these quarrels and to turn his mind to the quarrels of three centuries ago. They have their relevance to our affairs.

Dr Johnson, whose Erse was not very good, thought that the derivation of the word Tory was 'from an Irish word signifying a savage'. My own Erse is no better, but the compilers of the Oxford Dictionary, whom one must suppose to be careful about such matters, say the root of the word is *toraidhe, –aighe*, a pursuer, from *toir*, to pursue. As it was English settlers that these tories pursued, perhaps Johnson's rough translation was not so far out. It was by Cromwell's charmers that the word seems to have been given its first tinge of constitutional respectability, for they used it of any Irish Royalist in arms. In Charles II's reign it was used of those who thought that the hereditary principle, so recently re-established by the Restoration, should not immediately be imperilled by the exclusion of James from the throne on the grounds that he was a Roman Catholic. The innuendo was that such persons, for the most part Anglican High Churchmen, were no better than a lot of murderous Teagües. Not for the first time in history, a name invented as a term of abuse was adopted as a label by the party so insulted. James did not repay this loyalty, but by the Declaration of Indulgence of 1687-8 attempted to remove the disabilities of all dissenters, Protestant and Papist alike. This unparalleled act of liberalism was not well received.

Like most liberal acts of government it was open to other interpretations. James was suspected of indulging the Protestant dissenters only to make way for the Papists. Moreover, the Declaration purported to set aside Acts of Parliament, which did not promise a very liberal course once the Papists were in the saddle. The strongest opposition to James came from the very quarters which had insisted on his right to succeed Charles II. It was headed by the Archbishop of Canterbury, Sancroft, with the support of six other bishops including Ken of Bath and Wells, and Trelawny of Bristol. James was tactless enough to imprison these seven in the Tower, which did their cause a world of good. Too much good, it may be, for it was not the bishops' cause which triumphed. Soon James was out of the country and William and Mary were in his place. That was the Revolution miscalled Glorious.

The consequences of that affair are as complicated as the subsequent history of England. There were scrupulous persons who could not in conscience take the Oath of Allegiance to William and Mary because they could not break the oath they had sworn to James II and his heirs. These included eight bishops – Sancroft and Ken among them – and four hundred other clergy. Many would say they had more sanctity than sense. At least their action makes a pleasant change from the temporizing which usually wins the day in politics. They lost their day, and the non-juring group dwindled to nothing in the course of the eighteenth century. They had chosen a quixotic course, to an extent that disqualified them even from being Tories.

The bits that remained, for the Tories to pick up, were few and unsatisfactory. Yet nothing is more striking, in the eighteenth century which was given over increasingly to Whiggery – the forces of money taking over increasingly from the old landed rights while deism and rationalism ate away at the old foundations of theology and, it might be said, imagination – than the tenacity of the older constitutional thinking. Blackstone's *Commentaries on the Laws of England* so to speak demonstrated the value of what was being lost, while it was being lost. There is of course a sense in which any general exposition of the law gives the illusion of a stability which never existed, and of a coherence which owes more to the mind of the expositor than to the current facts of any one age. Blackstone did not exactly invent the constitution, but he drew attention to the great, half-forgotten residue of laws, written and unwritten, explicit and implied in the practice of Englishmen over the centuries of the country's formation. It is for this reason that the *Commentaries* retain their interest, to this day, for anyone who still thinks that it matters how the country is put together. There is much that throws light on our deepest political attitudes. That the work caused some shock among Blackstone's contemporaries may be gathered from his *Postscript* to the *Preface* of 1765; one may also gather in what quarters the shock was most felt.

Many of the positions in the work 'were vehemently attacked by zealots of all (even opposite) denominations, religious as well as civil; by some with a greater, by others with a less degree of acrimony.' Blackstone was the first Vinerian professor at Oxford. He was by way of being an intellectual innovator, attempting not only a new systemization of English law but a new method of education based on his more systematic elucidation of the subject. But in constitutional matters he was so far from being an innovator that his one passionate concern was to draw attention to what was *there*, as he conceived it, embedded in the laws and customs of the country; and in doing so he drew attention to much that the Whigs did not want to hear of, that they hoped to see eroded or merely wished away. Wishing away does in the end get rid of constitutional attitudes people can be taught not to like, and perhaps the great result of Blackstone's work was to set up a programme of what was to be abolished. The next stage was the Benthamite construction of a system of law based on the reformer's fantasy of what people wanted, or what a reasonable man ought to want, if he was reasonable in the way that Bentham was.

What Blackstone saw was that mixed constitution which became famous in the misinterpretations of foreign observers.

> If the supreme power were lodged in any one of the three branches separately, we must be exposed to the inconveniences of either absolute monarchy, aristocracy, or democracy; and so want two of the three principal ingredients of good polity, either virtue, wisdom, or power... But the constitutional government of this island is so admirably tempered and compounded, that nothing can endanger or hurt it, but destroying the equilibrium of power between one branch of the legislature and the rest. For if ever it should happen that the independence of any one of the three should be lost, or that it should become subservient to the views of either of the other two, there would soon be an end of our constitution.

It is hardly too much to say that to bring about this subservience, and so to subvert the constitution as understood by Blackstone, has been the standing objective, viewed with varying degrees of clarity, ever since, by those who are generally regarded as enlightened persons.

None of the subversions of the constitution has met with more general and more persistent approval than those which aimed at the position of the Church. So great is the success which has attended these subversions, that even among practising Anglicans there is scarcely even a shadowy apprehension of what has been given up. Since these subjects are now out of most people's way, it is perhaps necessary to say that the roots of the matter go back beyond the Reformation which for Romans – but not Anglicans – was the start of the Church of England. 'Christianity is part of the laws of England', says Blackstone, and backs this with the recital of a bit of an Act of Henry VI: 'Scripture est common ley, surquel touts manieres de leis sont fondues'. There would have been some confusion any time after the thirty-fourth year of Henry VI if that provision had been invoked in a literal sense. Still, the medieval, and the original Anglican assumption, was that members of the state were members of the Church, and it followed that there were certain disabilities for any who were not. In the medieval view, such outsiders were fit only for burning, and the law provided accordingly. The modern English view was less extreme, once Bloody Mary, in the last fling of papal power, had sickened people at large by her roastings at Smithfield and elsewhere. The laws against recusants under Elizabeth were laws against treason, for the Pope claimed to have absolved the Queen's subjects from their allegiance – a very practical point which was welcome to the King of Spain. As late as 1605 Guy Faux and his friends showed, also in the most practical way, that loyalty could not be counted on in Papists. This aroma of disaffection was not dissipated in a hurry. After the murder of Charles I by a tribunal without legal standing a certain aroma of disaffection hung about Protestant dissenters as well, though perhaps less pungent, for it was a *homely* smell, whereas the smell of Papists was not only suspect but *foreign*. It was in either case a doubt about loyalty, rather than a scruple on a point of doctrine, which lay at the root of the civil disabilities – of increasing mildness – suffered by dissenters up to the time of the Catholic Emancipation Act of the early nineteenth century. The two were never entirely disentangled; dissent whether Catholic or Protestant implied a degree of dissociation from the Christian polity which the realm was supposed, however implausibly, to be. All this seems nonsense now, for it is thought that everyone has a right to disaffection, and that religion is not a matter of truth but of opinion.

Looking now over the volumes of Blackstone, which I browsed over more than twenty-five years ago, I recognize that many of my notions of government must have been, if not formed, at any rate sharpened, on that work. It was the epoch of the 'Reflections on Marvell's Ode', if that is not too grand a way of referring to my preoccupations at the time. That meant that such writers as Filmer and Algernon Sidney, key figures of the political discussions of the seventeenth century, were in my mind. It is perhaps fair to make the point that such reading was the work of my odd moments, and that my days were spent, within earshot, so to speak, of the centre of government: so that, whatever the appearances to the contrary, the essays written at that time were not the product of someone ignorant of the mechanisms of government in the twentieth century, but on the contrary of someone who, in his brief leisures, was concerned to identify the elements which had somehow gone missing from the political discourse of the day, even though the realities of politics seemed to call for them.

There is no question now of resuscitating Samuel Johnson's definition of *Tory* and offering it to anyone as a political programme. It is not merely than no one prominently on the scene in politics would be likely to understand it; there is the more radical inconvenience that it is simply unusable. For Johnson a Tory was 'One who adheres to the ancient constitution of the state, and the apostolic hierarchy of the church of England'. The term was 'opposed to a *whig*', and *Whig* was 'The name of a faction'. If these notions, and the history which lies behind them, are not directly usable in a party programme, they at least provide the elements of a possible criticism of contemporary political manners.

A *Toryism* of this kind not ambitious of political success but only of contributing a little, in time, to the reorientation of minds which – whatever else may be said about them – certainly require some treatment of that kind. One would have to start by washing away all that rubbish of imaginary rights which are conceived of as a sort of metaphysical property of each individual, as if there could be right which did not impose a duty on somebody else. 'The Rights of Man' is a cant phrase, covering a series of quite concrete problems involved in some proposed redistribution of social duties. The 'rights of women', as we have the phrase now, does not have quite the same degree of abstract futility, for no one is in any doubt that whatever is claimed is at the expense of somebody.

Once the abstract 'individual', with his imaginary 'rights' is out of the way, one can, starting from the limited physical person, who moves around on the earth, identify the particular obligations which arise from the presence, round about, of other physical persons in like case. The web is of great complexity, in the twentieth century, and one of the few certain things about it is that it is *local*, not quite the same in one place as in another, in spite of the kaleidoscopic effect produced by rapid transport. Another certainty, well understood in the past but now also subject to kaleidoscopic effects which produce a faint dizziness, is that the web is *temporal*, has its place in time and cannot be the instantaneous creation of someone who happens to be thinking something at the moment. In fact our thoughts, our language, our institutions, our *rights* – if the word cannot be escaped – are historical. The present moment was preceded by the previous moment which was preceded by... and there never was a moment when any of these things changed in a flash. So we are caught in space and time, whether we like it or not. If you go forward without looking back you are still impelled by the past. It is a highly inadequate realism, whether in literature or in politics, which pretends to take account only of contemporary influences.

One cannot argue from these considerations to the maintenance of ancient institutions. Everything temporal will also crumble in time. But one can argue from them to the need for understanding old institutions, especially those still surviving in some form, which may therefore still serve us, indeed other things being equal are more likely to serve us lastingly than is last week's so-called invention, about which the most certain thing is that it is not so new as is at the moment made out.

So much – and it is not much, except an invitation to reflection – for Johnson's 'ancient constitution of the state'. For the 'apostolic hierarchy of the church of England', its public character as a vehicle of truth was impugned by the temporizing of politicians.

The two key dates are 1689 and 1850. At the former date, under the same Crown, the religion of Scotland became different from the religion of England. At the latter date, a collateral apostolic line was brought to this country, with territorial claims which drove a wedge into the fabric of the Church of England. On both these occasions the state was announcing that it dissociated itself from the truth and was concerned only with political expediency. This should be understood by all who expect a government to espouse a cause, uphold a right or right a wrong.

So the surviving Tory lives on, in an obscure ill-understood opposition, profoundly sceptical in all those fields in which popular belief is most widespread and passion rises highest; credulous himself, most would say, in an ill-defined faith going back for two thousand years or established from all eternity, as he would by definition say. At least the profound scepticism with regard to contemporary politics will not seem out of place, to anyone who sets a value on any truth at all.

Intimations of the Eternal

It is perhaps illusory to look back on a Golden Age when people did not think so much, but certainly there was a time when they did not think so much about Society – that great threadbare garment which covers all our nakedness – and, above all, when they did not imagine that their thinking about it could do society so much good. The belief in socially beneficent thought is one of the marks of modern times, which one may take to have begun with the talkative theoretical preliminaries to the French Revolution. The Church tends to collect beliefs, as well as to perform its historical task of expounding afresh the few that are essential to it, and it has certainly collected this one. If it is so beneficial to the world to emit thoughts about the organization of society, *a fortiori*, it might be argued (by Christians) it must be pre-eminently so to emit such thoughts with a dash of Christianity about them.

It must be said that this is far from being the view of the world at large. Even in England, which has not only all those elements of opinion which owe their origin to the former prevalence of Christian beliefs and practices, but some vestiges of that religion in the institutions of the state, Christianity is dogmatically excluded from practical politics. The old maxim that 'Christianity is part of the law of England', is a laugh. Any minister would be highly embarrassed if it could be shown that he had accorded the slightest preference to Christian prejudices, in the field of education or any other involving the expenditure of public funds. The only state religion, for practical purposes, is democracy which is, in this context, not an actual system of government, such as we may all defend provisionally as the lesser of evils, but an extraordinary heap of superstitions which, for practical men, have taken on all the sacredness of the truth. The governing principle is not what the majority think – in the past usually thought to be a fair indicator of what wise men did *not* think – but the characteristic nihilism which comes from the resolution of all problems by giving way to the mere numerical pressure of opinions momentarily held by those operating in a particular field at the instant of decision. The absolute rightness of this proceeding once accepted, as it is, it follows that nothing else can have absolute rightness at all. No wonder 'church leaders' who irrupt on to the public stage from time to time cut rather curious and, generally speaking, altogether insignificant, figures on it.

It has not always been so. Yet it is nothing new for the principles of practical government to be those of the world and not of the Church. Indeed that has always been the case. This was clear to see in the early centuries of Christianity, and whatever the consequences of the conversion of Constantine they are unlikely to have included a radical change in the management of the Roman Empire. Nor were the Catholic Majesties and the Most Christian Kings of medieval and modern Europe particularly scrupulous in their operations, and even the history of the Papacy has some curious episodes, if indeed it is not curious all the time. What is different in the European past, in our own history down to say, the reign of Anne – though some would put it later – is the state's recognition of the Church as a spiritual institution – an expression which it would tax the wits of our politicians unbearably to give any plausible meaning to. It is not that the Church is utterly ignored, even now, for it may on rare occasions figure in the mind of some politician as a body of voters, even if in practice it is hardly a body of coherent opinion, on any matter of political importance.

In the two centuries covered by the Dean of Peterhouse's history, political conceptions of the Church's role became increasingly attenuated. Institutions have to be fed with thought to keep them standing, and if the national church looks sickly now, in a welter of ecumenicism, it is partly for lack of nutriment for the conception. Coleridge's essay *On the Constitution of Church and State according to the Idea of Each* was perhaps the only contribution to the subject from one of the first-class minds of the period, and notions are not kept alive by what passes for a first-class mind in the practical or academic worlds – at best a Gladstone. E.R. Norman says, fairly enough, that 'Coleridge's own debt to German Idealist philosophers, to the influence of Herder, was not such as to coincide with the English political tradition'; yet it is to be noted that Coleridge did precisely what the work of those who were more superficially in accordance with 'the empiricism of the British Constitution' did not – he drew deeply on the resources of the sixteenth and seventeenth centuries, making them live again by combining them with the original thought of his own time. It is significant that, 'as a practical contribution to the debate on the relations of Church and State, Coleridge's thought was nowhere near as influential as some modern commentators have supposed.' The lack of influence was symptomatic of the growing gap between the Church and, on the one hand, the original thought of the age and, on the other, the world of practical affairs. There was no possibility, in the England of the nineteenth century, of another Hooker; the political centre had moved too far away from the Church for anyone to be able to touch Church and State at so many points as Hooker did, while being concerned primarily with a theological exposition. Perhaps no one since Swift had taken enough notice, in this connection, of the destruction of England which followed the Act of Union with Scotland, the consequences of which Scotland is more likely to emerge from than we are.

E.R. Norman's *Church and Society in England 1770-1970* is not, however, about the constitutional position of the Church, but about a more modern subject, her 'social teachings and attitudes'. The more fashionable subject is not unrelated to the matters which were more apt to engage people in the earlier centuries, because the reorientation is in part due to the veering of the centre of government – at any rate in the popular imagination – from supreme authorities in the state to the many who hold opinions about what should be done. The doctrine of passive obedience sounds oddly now, though it still has its theological significance; what interests people now is the application of Christian doctrine to particular practical programmes, which are either governmental or lined up for the exercise of future governments, by more or less knowledgeable groups of those who were once referred to as subjects. This is a confusing matter, the programmes themselves are usually that, and the attempt to throw in a little theological advice rarely leads to the clarifications which might be hoped for.

The packed chapters of this book bring out, in a wealth of detail, how often the contribution of churchmen has been no more than to throw into the ring the ideas which are the common currency of the age – perhaps the peculiarity has been to throw them with a slightly awkward ecclesiastical gesture, as if impeded by a cassock or by insufficient knowledge of the wider bearings of what was being said. So we get churchmen in the Victorian period – the more broad-minded of them – doing their bit to promote the *laissez-faire* economics which Walter Bagehot and others were trying to substitute for Holy Writ. We get, at the present time, endless pronouncements from such bodies as the World Council of Churches which merely regurgitate the most widely-held political superstitions of the age. Yet there were wide areas, in education and what are now called the social services, in which the clergy, because of their multifarious contacts with the poor, spoke with a degree of knowledge not easily equalled in the days before the state began to take what has become practically an exclusive hand in these matters. 'Only the "vulgar" Marxists have supposed', the Dean says,

> that the Church ignored social evils and the sufferings of the working classes. Philosophical Marxists know better. They see that churchmen were full of concern for the poor, but they see also that they were the victims of their own class moralism, presenting solutions which comprehended neither the subtleties of working-class social custom nor the possibility of reconstruction.

Yet this is an unsatisfactory obeisance to the direction of the compulsory Marxism of the age. It does nothing to answer the question, which must recur to any reader of this book at more than one point, as to what, if any, were the specifically Christian views on social matters expounded by churchmen during the period, and whether there is any compelling *social* reason why people, whether in the working classes or elsewhere in society, should be Christians. There is no question, for the orthodox, that there are such reasons, but it can hardly be said that the most of the pronouncements alluded to give more than a shadowy notion of them.

If the real defects of the social thinking of the period arise from, or are evidenced in, the lack, among churchmen of original minds applying themselves to these questions, a further difficulty in taking one's bearings is the disorganization of the Church of England which leaves it uncertain what the 'Church's' view is. E.R. Norman quotes an excellent remark of Maurice Reckitt's on this point. 'It is surprising, and a little alarming', Reckitt wrote, 'to observe how easily the Christian social enthusiast will come to claim ecclesiastical authority for his individual convictions, and even be found to declare "the Church teaches", when all he ought to say is "I think".' It is not necessarily a bad thing that there should be a little disorder in these matters. The ramshackle certainly has its place in a spiritual institution, since it is to operate not by the deliberations of men but by the wind which bloweth where it listeth; but slackness does not necessarily bring spiritual virtues with it. E.R. Norman points out that 'For most of the nineteenth century there lacked the means of defining Church teaching – at just the moment in English history, with its huge economic and social changes, when adjustments were necessary.' Still, the successive Church Congresses, Church Assemblies and General Synods have not in fact provided a focus to which the ordinary churchman can turn naturally or with any great expectation of enlightenment. In the Church of England we remain at sea.

In times like these, when 'the adoption of social teaching in the Church' is 'also complicated by the unprecedented acceleration in social change', as Norman says of the nineteenth century, and when, it may be added, there is great uncertainty in our theological formulations, there is probably less to be said for yet one more attempt to give an authoritative (and no doubt more or less democratic) centre for the definition of social principles and objectives than for the formation of natural groups of people who actually want to find out what Christianity could imply in these fields. Maurice Reckitt himself has figured in more than one such group. Because of my own place on the periphery of the Church, as of other manifestations of reality, I have found most useful those places in which Christian and non-Christian minds have been at work together, not with any design on one another but in pursuit of common interest. One such group was the *New English Weekly*, under the editorship of the late Philip Mairet, to which Reckitt contributed extensively, though usually anonymously. The *New English Weekly* was, naturally, a place where nobody said 'The Church teaches' and everybody said 'I think': I cannot help regretting – though I am far from complaining, because it was on the very fringe of his subject – that Norman did not find room so much as to mention the name of Philip Mairet, though there are over thirty references to his collaborators. For Mairet, the most open-minded as well as the most self-effacing of men, a name almost obliterated, could not help himself turning over the issues of the day, in a manner too far-sighted to attract much attention. No one could have been less dogmatic; he merely knew that the natural order was part of the divine order, and had little explicitly to say about the latter. The living, if barely writeable, history of the Church is as likely to be found in such quarters as in the pronouncements of synods. It is part of the merit of *Church and Society in England* that the author, while maintaining a considerable elegance in the ordering of his material, has gone as far as he could towards the unwriteable, finding his matter entwined 'in the mechanics of social class, of communal tradition, or inherited wisdom, or economic fact.' Mairet was surely a manifestation of that purpose which, in Norman's words, hedges 'the ambiguities of present realities with intimations of the eternal'.

It may not be out of place – or, if it is, perhaps it can stand all the same – to end by a word about the current *language* of the Church. Everyone is caught in the decay of our speech, and the Church can only say what it has to say through language it has made its own. It was one of the great conquests of the sixteenth and seventeenth centuries that the Church commanded a language at once profound and familiar. Now, after immense deliberations, it injects trashy and unmeaningful speech even into its liturgy. There is no such thing as passing on profound truths in superficial speech. So, in the field of social exploration, nothing much will be said in the current language of sociology.

Coleridge Revisited

Samuel Taylor Coleridge, *On the Constitution of Church and State*, ed. John Colmer (Vol. 10 of *The Collected Works of Samuel Taylor Coleridge*, Routledge/Princeton, Bollingen Series LXXV)

When I read Coleridge's book again, after a gap of years, I was disappointed. This was a book, as I remembered it, which tied up the nineteenth century, and so ourselves who live in a century made by the nineteenth, to the great English world of the sixteenth and seventeenth centuries, the period in which England defined herself before succumbing, finally, to the poisons, first, of the Scottish intrusion; secondly, of the forces of capital which blew up the homely manor houses of an earlier period into Palladian show-pieces which did not grow out of the ground; and thirdly, of what passed for a new form of English empiricism but was constructed on a scaffolding of ideas and ideology from the *encyclopédistes* and the world of Roman law. My own sympathies went straight back to the older time, not so much leaping over the intervening period as tunnelling under it, partly because my roots went back to the small but durable bourgeoisie of 'parrocks and turbary rights' and immemorial generations of farmers – families which had never been hoisted to the meretricious grandeur of nineteenth-century public schools, or money in excess of what was required to carry on, nor had entered the new world of proletarization created by the Industrial Revolution. Of course these sociological considerations did not much enter my head when it was first full of that Caroline definition of church and state, which in turn goes back to Hooker and what he goes back to. There was a host of nearer considerations, shaped by the impact of France and Germany and India, in which I spent, successively, more or less time in formative years. There was the impact also of Whitehall on a mind entirely unformed for such a career, and indeed ingenuous about the whole notion of a career in a way which put me at a huge distance from my contemporaries from Oxford and Cambridge for whom entry into the cadres of the higher Civil Service was a natural progression in a world taken for granted. Finally, or rather concomitantly, there was the homeliness, if I may so express it, the complete acceptability in the recesses of my mind, of the literature of the seventeenth century, to which I had largely made my own way – set on to it originally by pointers, first, in Lamb, and then, precisely, in Coleridge himself.

So I had reason to suppose that *On the Constitution of Church and State* would still be alive for me. If a conception of the state – and I mean of the modern British state – rooted in the Stuart monarchy took some reaching, from the little world without orientation in which I grew up, so did the conception of the church, in either its Anglican or its millennial role. Such instruction and practice as came my way, as a boy, happened to be mainly that which was furnished by a United Methodist chapel in a working-class suburb of Bristol, and I was very little conscious of the Anglican generations standing behind me on both sides of the family. So it was the bible and hymn-singing, excruciating public prayers which, as I remember them from adolescence, were chaotic, sentimental, and not without topical allusions; Sunday schools with no theology behind them and from which graduation was to a men's discussion group of low vitality at which the unemployed were never unrepresented and of which the orientation, so far as it had one, was indicated by the popularity of the hymn which asks, with, I suppose, long muffled echoes of Tom Paine,

> When wilt Thou save the people,
> O God of battles, when;
> Not kings and thrones, but people,
> Not stocks and stones, but men?

The negative phrase in the last line may not be quite right. I can at least claim to have swum in the back-water of a great historical aspiration.

I suppose all this has a sort of repressed Erastianism about it, certainly an inability to see religion without the predominant element of social preoccupation. Eating comes first, everyone would have said, and that is less revolting than it may sound to people whose main nutritional hazard is eating too much. It is indeed a simple realism. All this fell from me, as it was bound to do for a boy who did well at school, showed early symptoms of a passion for literature, and at seventeen was an undergraduate with the contemporary world opening on all sides before him, if only intellectually. The Christian religion was whisked away like a dirty table-cloth as I sat down to eat. It was many years – as one reckons years when one is young – before I noticed that anything was missing.

This is not the place to attempt to put a date on the rectification of that omission. A date would, in any case, give a false precision to something which was more like a slow change in physical condition. What can be dated is the point at which I formally gave myself up. For some reason – or, more likely, without any special reason – I had never been baptized. So this was something I had to arrange for myself, at the age of thirty-nine, before being admitted to that other sacrament, which I had come to desire. To talk of understanding what one is doing, in such cases, is rather absurd, but I had a sort of apprehension of the creed, beginning with God the Father Almighty, Maker of Heaven and Earth, and pursuing in the bottom of my mind that sequence of propositions that follows from it or, perhaps more exactly, radiates from the Incarnation, the burial of God in Man, so to speak, which implies the rest of the comedy – to use Dante's word. In the years that followed I frequented the Communion, the practice being, in this as in other matters, more important than the theory. I also explored the Prayer Book, in an amateurish way, not only acquainting myself with the earlier versions, of 1549, 1552 and 1604, and the medieval Sarum book from which it was so largely derived and translated. Moreover, I read largely in the various sixteenth- and seventeenth-century books which deviated to left or right of the Anglican middle – the Middleburgh book, the Puritan *Directory*, Laud's Scottish Prayer Book, and pursued the history into the eighteenth century with the non-jurors and the productions of Deacon, Whiston, Henley and Stephens. I must have felt a certain need to find out. The epoch of my baptism was also the time of writing *Christopher Homm*, which was a slightly belated *nel mezzo del cammin*, so these desultory liturgical studies were in a sense also an attempt to find out what that book was about, something which could only be known – obviously – after it had been written.

It all seems a long time ago. It must seem, also, a long way from *On the Constitution of Church and State*. All this is an elaborate way of saying that, however remote these matters might seem from the contemporary world, they were to me matters of here and now, just as my Caroline politics had to accommodate themselves to the modern administrative scene, some manifestations of which struggle are exhibited in *The Spirit of British Administration*.

On the Constitution of Church and State is a curious book, even for Coleridge. It points back to the main scene of Anglican performance, in the seventeenth century. The editor of this new edition, John Colmer, quotes a marginal note Coleridge wrote in 1830: 'God knows my heart! there may be & I trust there are, many among our Clergy who love, prize, and venerate our Church as earnestly and as disinterestedly as I do! But that any man, "on this side idolatry" can love and prize it more, or more sincerely, it is not in my power to believe.' At the same time, there is an element, Germanic rather than Platonic, of pursuing bubbles of ideas away over the horizon, in the manner of the discussion. The long title adds that the constitution of church and state is to be examined 'according to the idea of each'. The pursuit of notions wrapped in words, which came easily to Coleridge and which his German studies did not render any more down to earth, must have puzzled many who bought the book in the hope of the promised enlightenment on the affairs of the day. The second part purported to contain 'aids to a right appreciation of the Bill admitting Catholics to sit in both Houses of Parliament', any objection to which could have sprung only from popular prejudice or from a political memory as long as that of the Roman Church herself; and the whole work was in fact occasioned by reflections on the Bill, or on what Coleridge feared it might contain. But, in true Coleridgean form, the first chapter is devoted to 'prefatory Remarks on the true import of the word, IDEA; and what the author means by "according to the Idea".' What he meant is not so difficult, as emerges after a few pages, when the reader is 'made aware... that the particular form, construction, or model, that may be best fitted to render the idea intelligible, and most effectually serve the purpose of an instructive *diagram*, is not necessarily the mode or form in which it actually arrives at realization'. 'You can say that again!' the coarse, practical observer might have commented. All one can say is that it is better than the sort of confusion of ideas with reality which is the effect of Marxism on so many minds. But it is clean contrary to all good sense to maintain, as Coleridge does, that 'a Constitution is an idea arising out of the idea of a state'. The excess and inflation of the nineteenth century have entered Coleridge's bones as surely as into those of the false empirics who are always talking, after the French fashion, of written constitutions and abstract rights.

It is part of the productiveness of Coleridge's prose that he no sooner starts to say something than he is driven to explain something he should have said before he opened his mouth. Since this is an impossible situation, he leaves us with pointers and provisional ideas which enter into our own minds and there operate to more or less effect, rather than establishes any conclusion we can use either as a raft to cling to or as a battleaxe to hit anyone else over the head with. The second chapter explores 'the idea of a State in the larger sense of the term, introductory to the constitution of the State in the narrower sense, as it exists in this country'. Ah! But by the end of the chapter, we have reached the notion that the constitution, 'in the more enlarged sense of the term', is the constitution of the *nation*, and that to understand that we must also 'have the right idea of the *National Church*'. So the way is cleared for the most original part of the book, which has attracted liberal anarchists such as Herbert Read as well as pillars of Victorian orthodoxy such as Thomas Arnold. The crucial element is the definition of 'the Church of England, or National Clerisy', in a manner which is entirely untheological.

> THE CLERISY of the nation, or national church, in its primary acceptation and original intention comprehended the learned of all denominations; – the sages and professors of the law and jurisdiction; of medicine and physiology; of music; of military and civil architecture; of the physical sciences; with the mathematical as the common *organ* of the preceding; in short, all the so called liberal arts and sciences, the possession of which constitute the civilization of a country, as well as the Theological.

The conception is medieval, so far as it is historical at all. The 'clerisy', in this sense, had in Coleridge's day shrunk to a degree which made the proposition seem paradoxical; in our day it looks frankly ridiculous. Or, to put the matter another way, one would have to think of the clerisy as an overwhelmingly lay phenomenon, and so far as the clergy belonged to it at all, it would be as a relatively insignificant group in a lay *milieu*, to which they would be wholly subdued. In Coleridge's definition, the theological element was 'placed at the head of all'; but, even then, 'not because its members were priests', but because of the predominant position of theology, as 'the root and the trunk of the knowledges that civilized man.' It is still possible to maintain that that is the position of theology, against all appearances to the contrary; but that can be maintained only by a partisan view, not merely because it would evoke massive ridicule, but because theology no longer speaks a language which is in the end intelligible to unprejudiced minds seeking the truth in good faith.

This does not exhaust – it hardly begins to account for – the main themes of Coleridge's remarkable book, which is certainly one of those which every literate Englishman should read. It does bring me almost to the end of my concern with it at the moment. The 'blessed accident' – which is how Coleridge saw 'Christianity, or the Church of Christ' 'in relation to the National Church' – has ceased to exist, in that relationship. It has no intelligibility. What then is the position of the theological rump, in our now lay secularized clerisy? There are three possibilities. They can stay and fight their corner, struggling for an intelligibility which might come again, and will come, if it is the truth they are concerned with. They can sit on pillars, in some recess of the national structure, waiting for better times. Or they can let their taste for having an ecclesiastical club carry them into one or other of those international gangs of opinion – that which has its headquarters in Rome or that which has a shadowy international meeting-place in Canterbury. In any case it will be a *political* choice that is being made.

For my part, I shall prefer those who stay and fight their corner, content to be merely the Church in a place. This is partly because – perhaps it is wholly because – faced with the unintelligibility of the language the church speaks, I am of a religion in which – to adapt Coleridge's phrase – Christianity is an accident; the religion of our fathers, or the *mère patrie*, of the spirits buried in the ground, of the religion of England, I cannot help it. Of course, this in turn conceals a profound cynicism.

A Viewpoint on the Book of Common Prayer

One of the ugliest things about the row which has been set off by the recent petition in favour of the Authorized Version and the Prayer Book is the blind fury, in certain quarters, at the mere notion that six hundred laymen chosen as 'representing aspects of national life, more especially in the arts', should venture to meddle in matters which, these critics said, were no business of theirs. The signatories might be musicians, sculptors, actors, scholars in various disciplines including literature and theology, they might be novelists, soldiers, they might – to sink to the lowest point in the scale of things – even be *poets*. What had the language of the Bible and Prayer Book to do with them? These books, to which generations of English speakers have owed an essential part of their education, were the private property, it was implied, of the bishops and clergy and of those laymen whom a very peculiar series of elections had brought to membership of that patently unsatisfactory body, the Synod of the Church of England.

That there should be a widespread concern for the beauty and homeliness of the Authorized Version was itself an offence. Beauty is the sign of the devil's work! That cry has been heard before. The Bishop of Peterborough, a distinguished witness and apparently one of the few bishops moved by this assault on our heritage, said in a letter to *The Times* (19 November 1979): 'One or two of the speeches in the recent Session of Synod might have come from the lost and unspeakable speeches of Attila the Hun.'

It is not the intention of the bishops and clergy who are mainly responsible for the state of affairs to which the Church of England has been brought to *burn* the offending books. The intention is merely that they should grow dusty in corners, or stay locked in vestries, while their place on the lectern and in the pews is taken by the lucubrations of – as David Martin has said – mid-Atlantic linguistic bureaucracies and their offshoots. Anyone who takes the trouble to look into half-a-dozen churches and inspect the books can confirm this – if he has not already been painfully alerted by what is going on in his own parish.

The methods by which these changes have been brought about have not always been above suspicion, and the Synod itself can hardly be said to have won its way into the hearts of ordinary churchgoers, who in general have been utterly unaware of what they were up to. These questions of Church government have their own importance, not only in what the bishops might regard as the proper places but for all who care for the openness and integrity of our national institutions; but it is the wider implications of what is going on that I wish to consider here.

Can it really be said that the language of the Church is of no concern to anyone but her officials? Such a claim – which is implicit in so much that has been said about the petition – is in reality so monstrous as to be full of the direst consequences for the Church itself. For there are many who are not Christians – people who understandably find that all their patience and intelligence in other fields of inquiry, and even the excursions they have made into the theology of the day, do not bring them to the point of entertaining the kind of belief which is required for even a half-acceptance of the traditional doctrines – who none the less admit the right of others to such belief and would wish to keep open the channels of communication with their Christian contemporaries and – as everyone who understands the point of liberal studies at all must do – with the past.

The impoverishment of the life of the nation, which depends on its *intellectual* life to a degree which the philistines are always unwilling to admit, must be enormous if these channels are not kept open. The fate of the Church – humanly speaking – could in these circumstances only be one of increasing degradation. It must decline into a foolish sect, unable in the end to talk to the simplest intelligence because it has turned aside from its task of convincing the most able or even as much as impinging on their concerns. For a contrary view, one might turn to Augustine or Dante, but what is that to a Church which turns its back on Hooker and Berkeley and Butler?

Of course there are arguments for the use in church of a language 'understanded of the people', but the crass ignorance of many of the apologists of the New English Bible and the Good News Bible and the services known as 'Series 3' is that they suppose that such speech is within the grasp of anyone who chooses to open his mouth, and certainly of the respectable scholars and public relations men who have put the current inferior wares on the market. Of course, to be 'understanded of the people' on any subject is a matter of the greatest difficulty, and on matters so little in the ordinary course of listening and viewing as the Incarnation and its consequences there may perhaps be a little more than the common difficulty.

This is a problem which those who have a cure of souls have always to reckon with, when they are not deflected into the easier task of delivering moral discourses which would sound well at the United Nations. It is perhaps less the lack of receptivity in the congregations – which is no novelty – than an understandable feeling of ineptitude on the part of the clergy, which makes so many of them crave a Bible and liturgy which is not in that funny old language – as it seems to the less literate among them. Here one enters upon a field in which it is insulting for a layman even to open his mouth. But at the risk of being misconstrued, one may say that the clergy will not escape their duty of exposition by degrading the quality of the subject of their exposition. No one is seeking to discourage them from using all the resources of contemporary thought and speech in their sermons or in their discourses with the faithful and the unfaithful. On the contrary, it is precisely those menacing outsiders – less full of malice than seems to be supposed – who *want* such discourse to reach the level of general intelligibility it must reach if there is to be any possibility of a future society with some tincture of Christianity.

So great was the indignation of those who condemned the petition because 'some atheists signed with great fervour, holding that it was a national question', that they gave no weight to the fact that the signatories who might fall within that description were appearing side by side with men in Holy Orders, though for fear of embarrassing them 'very few clergymen were approached', and that the body of petitioners included a great many, perhaps a majority, who were familiar with the life of the Church, and very many who were communicants of more or less regularity. No conclusive statement can be made on this topic because the signatories were – properly, as it seems to many of us – simply not asked what their standing with the Church was. It is surely a bad day for the Church of England when it turns its back on the laity because they are not fully paid-up members. That is a point of view utterly sectarian and un-Anglican. 'What has the Church to do with the national heritage?' some clerics have asked, displaying an utter ignorance of what has been entrusted to them by their great forbears and proving that they have never considered the contents of that Prayer Book which they are busy shuffling out of sight. However, the matter will not be so easily resolved. There is too much life in the old book yet, as in the Authorized Version which will rise and smite them hip and thigh.

What do the furniture-removers suppose the Church of England will look like when they have finished their work? Do they suppose we go to church to listen to *them*? To hear the latest news from Synod? To hear what the World Council of Churches is up to in the way of amateur politics? Or that we shall choose the times of service to admire the buildings, like blundering tourists? Not at all. The Bible and the Prayer Book were what gave the services of the Church of England not only their splendour but their meaning, and some who came into the Church, not lightly and unadvisedly, but after mature reflection and through a desire for the sacraments, now feel so betrayed that the sacraments themselves cannot be taken in this desolation, for a moment must come when ignorance deprives us of their meaning and mystery. I venture thus far beyond what might be thought the proper field of the *Times Literary Supplement* because it has been assumed by many apologists of the new versions that the question of language has nothing to do with the theological functions of the Church. It has. Those to whom these things mean nothing may still be scandalized that a national institution should see fit to declare, through the actions and inaction of its governing body, that literacy and integrity of speech have nothing to do with the concerns which concern them.

That no bishop – that the Archbishop of Canterbury himself – should not have risen in Synod to put in a good word for the volumes entrusted to him at his ordination, that none should have felt obliged, in the face of a petition signed by six hundred persons of good standing in the Commonwealth, to explain to the flock what value was now to be placed upon these treasures, is something so monstrous as to lead some of us to suppose that the Church of England has, in effect, resigned. She no longer speaks to the nation or even attempts to do so, for what has she to do with publicans and sinners, let alone artists who are the worst of the lot?

It is a blind retreat. But human beings will use the difficult art of speech, and a refusal to meet the petitioners on that ground exposes a profound evasion of all the issues, theological and as well as linguistic, which gave and give life to the work of the great Anglican figures of the past. Is that all nothing? Then let the bishops reflect on what Coleridge said of our 'loved and prized' version of the Bible: 'Without this holdfast, our vitiated imaginations would refine away language to mere abstractions'. It is happening now. Let those – whether Christians or not – who have or teach children at least see that they get the Authorized Version.

THE EIGHTIES

The Alternative Service Book

It has long seemed to me that the Book of Common Prayer could do with a little editing. The exhortations, which are never used, in the Communion service might perhaps be relegated to an appendix; there might be some clearer indication of the date of Easter, than the Table to find Easter Day; the Golden Numbers – but no, surely they must be supposed to have charm, in a world which prides itself on its numeracy. Very little would be needed to make the book easier for congregations to handle: for that matter, they have managed to handle it for upwards of three or four hundred years. However, the ecclesiastical authorities have now given us something better – or at any rate bigger. Here, in some thirteen hundred pages, is the result of a labour which has occupied 'first the Convocations and the House of Laity, and latterly the General Synod, for more than fifteen years'. It is with relief that one learns that this publication marks a pause in their 'programme of liturgical business'.

The book looks more like the product of a programme of liturgical business than the kind of simplification one might have hoped for. It is true that the date of Easter, up to the year 2025, can now be determined by a glance at a new table; there is a Table of Transference to amuse learned children during the sermon, and it is simpler than the Prayer Book exercise with Golden Numbers. But the pattern of the services themselves is of bewildering complexity. This book makes too modest a claim, when it calls itself the Alternative Service Book. It is no mere alternative to the Book of Common Prayer, but contains within itself so many varied forms of service that it would be better called the Book of Alternatives. One gathers that those fifteen years of liturgical business did not end in anything that could be called unanimity, unless an exhausted agreement to differ can be called that. It is not that the ancient theological controversies are not muted. They are, although their aged heads pop up here and there. But what the variety of services primarily represents is a variety of tastes; there is certainly no objective principle which could determine the choice of one set of services rather than another. There are alternative blessings and alternative confessions. A bit of what you like does you good – that seems to be the underlying principle: what you like – within limits.

'Unity need no longer be seen to entail strict uniformity of practice', says the Preface. It can hardly be said that *strict* uniformity has been seen within living memory, and indeed the long years of indiscipline among the clergy are an important part of the background to the present disintegrative book. What is new now is that the notion of a standard of practice has in effect been abolished. So we have 'The Order for Holy Communion Rite A' and 'The Order for Holy Communion Rite B', but each of these proves, on examination, to offer a number of variants, to be adopted or not according to the devices and desires of clergy or congregations, or whoever is strong enough among them to get his way. Do you prefer the first, second, third or fourth eucharistic prayer? The first or the second intercession? And so on. Variety is the spice of life, they say; it is less certain that it should spice liturgy to the extent that no one but an expert in Alternative Services can really keep up with it, and that going into a church beyond his own parish boundary no one will know what he is going to find. Indeed, he will be lucky if he knows what he will find in his own parish.

All this is supposed to be good. It has, however, until recently been a predominant part of Christian education for the churchgoer to hear familiar words until he knows many of them by heart. Not for me to say what may happen to souls, under the old dispensation or the new, but under the old, *minds* were actually filled with something. Not only were the words of Mattins and Evensong, the Communion service, and the psalter, so familiar as to be only just below the surface in the memories of ordinary Anglicans; the system provided for the public reading of the Bible in the Authorized Version. This education has, admittedly, long been slipping with the decline in churchgoing and the virtual elimination – by the authorities – of Mattins and Evensong as popular services; but the slipping cannot be taken as an argument for letting it slide altogether. The fruit of excessive variety will certainly be even greater ignorance, for let no one suppose that people will possess anything of the wealth of the Christian tradition unless they learn something first. Even the Lord's Prayer is now on sale in three versions – that of the Book of Common

Prayer, which until recently every decently brought-up child knew; that of Rite A *et passim* and that of Rite B *et passim*. The latter varies from the true English version only by tiny verbal changes so silly that no one but a pedant could have thought of making them at all – changes which, moreover, no one familiar with any range of English as it is spoken today could imagine would be clearer to anybody. So many people must have had a good idea during those laborious fifteen years, and so many people must have preferred their own good ideas to other people's, that there is no way of getting that much-to-be-desired pause in liturgical business except by concluding how right almost everybody was, and making a puzzle book of 1,300 pages.

The width of nefarious agreement over the text of the Alternative Book has been made possible by the fact that the book itself was strictly unnecessary. There was no great theological issue at stake, no anxiety widely and deeply felt which the book in any manner resolved. The difference from the situation in Cranmer's day, which is often invoked as a precedent and excuse, could not have been greater. Cranmer's books represented the resolution of agonizing differences; it is the lack of any comparable predicament at the origin of the new book which makes the latter so frivolous by comparison. Even the Prayer Book as proposed in 1928 was *about* something. Of course the Alternative Book has behind it the Continental liturgical movement and the stream of domestic scholarship for which Gregory Dix's *The Shape of the Liturgy* may stand as an indicator. Dix's bitter pages against Cranmer have had their influence here, as well as those more illuminating parts of his work which have a bearing on the changes in the order of the liturgy now ambiguously promulgated. But, important as these scholarly developments are, they represent a shallow stream compared with the discontents which burst upon Europe in the Reformation. It is the chance confluence of this stream with the real current of the age – a self-assertive humanism the history of which runs from the more extreme Protestantism of the Reformation, through Locke and Voltaire to the current religion of democracy – which has swept the present book into being. To that extent the authors of the Preface are certainly right when they say that 'those who seek to know the mind of the Church of England in the last quarter of the twentieth century will find it in this book'.

But what a mind! It is distressing to those who have known and loved the Church of England, not only in Cranmer but in

Hooker, Herbert, Vaughan, Jeremy Taylor, Swift, Berkeley, Butler, Law and many another, to find to what mouthpieces she is now reduced. It is not those great men of the Anglican tradition who are the mere stylists; it is not even the signatories of David Martin's notorious petition who hanker after that distinction. The authors of the Alternative Service Book are the real literary gents. 'Composed in the very finest modern English', says the press release, 'this new service [*sic*] brings the form of Anglican worship right into the twentieth century.' Whoopee! In fact, there is hardly a page of straight twentieth-century prose in the whole volume. And as for the verses so coyly introduced into what used to be Evensong, they turn out to be by Robert Bridges: 'We see the evening light, / Our wonted hymn outpouring.' You need to be something of a stylist to see that as more in tune with the twentieth century than Bishop Ken.

The pretence of modernity is fundamental to the Alternative Book, and to apologias which have been so widely made for the new services. The practical thought in the mind of the more simple-minded parsons has been that there must be *some* reason why they could not keep their churches full, and that as everything really successful seemed to be *modern*, they had better try a bit of that themselves. That might not make church quite as acceptable as the telly, but they could try. The secret of many things, they had heard, was in good public relations. The Prayer Book and the Bible sounded so unfamiliar to those who were not familiar with them that it would be nice if things were said in such a way that everyone would think that they had encountered just such language in the pages of the *Daily Telegraph* or some other 'quality' paper; so they started using translations of the Bible which sounded like that. (Only in limited circles is thinking yet advanced enough to look rather to the *Daily Mirror* as a model.)

Of course things did not work out exactly as had been hoped. One reason is that the ghosts of the Authorized Version and the Prayer Book were too powerful. It needs more than a prudential decision to speak of the things the Fathers of the sixteenth and seventeenth centuries spoke of, in a language which owes nothing to them. Echoes of the old speech sound through this new book, only the original rhythms have been nicked and chopped here and there and inept words introduced which do not carry conviction.

It may well be that the real difficulty about revising the Prayer

Book at this time is that there is no contemporary theological language which really carries conviction. We have to have some patience in educating ourselves in our ancestors' language in order to know what they meant. I once heard a wretched child set up in church to read the story of the creation of Eve. The only comment one could make on the passage was that no one could believe a word of it. If such stories are not understood with the imagination they are not understood at all. The ordinary language of the twentieth century means by understanding something mainly mechanical and quantitative. Until this primary theological difficulty is faced, there can be no serious beginning of an attempt to restate the traditional matter of the Christian faith. And of course the restatement will be slow, partial, and hesitant – quite unlike the verse of Robert Bridges or the prose of Professor Frost.

It would seem all too simple a game to point to examples of sheer outrageous ineptitude in the language of the Alternative Book, were it not that many people including, it would seem, most of the bishops and a large majority of the other members of Synod, have their perception of language so blunted that they simply do not know the living word, and the living cadence, from the dead. This should not surprise us because the living has to be new and anyone familiar with literary history knows that, since the date of the *Lyrical Ballads* (1798) at the latest, it has taken several decades for any new tone to win public acceptance. That is a phenomenon of the current phase of the language from which the writers of liturgies have no celestial exemption. One might say that the project of an alternative book was doomed from the start, given the many hands that were to meddle with it and the representative approvals which had to be sought at all stages. These difficulties could have been foreseen, but only by people of more literary perspicuousness than, apparently, those who actually had charge of the Church's affairs. At the risk of encountering readers who cannot see what is wrong with the new versions, I will give a few items from a schedule of comparisons which might go on for ever.

Take Morning Prayer. One of the 'sentences' reads:

> In everything make your requests known to God in prayer and petition with thanksgiving. *Philippians* 4:6.

This is preferred to the Authorized Version's

> In everything by prayer and supplication with thanksgiving let your requests be made known to God.

Perhaps only a trained palate would observe the difference here, and markedly prefer the older version. It is also rather hard to see what constitutes the 'modernity' of the later version. Second item: as to rhythm, the Confession drags along like a lump of dead meat; but those who do not see that cannot be made to see it. More will recognize the effrontery of preferring a version of the *Venite* which has

> In his hand are the depths of the earth: and the peaks of the mountains are his also

in place of

> In his hand are all the corners of the earth; and the strength of the hills is his also.

The reader who cannot understand the enormity of the substitution is fit only to be a member of Synod. In the *Benedictus*:

> To shine on those who dwell in darkness and the shadow of death (ASB)

is not 'modern', but sham antique; and compare the rhythm with that of:

> To give light to them that sit in darkness, and in the shadow of death (BCP)

which is every whit as intelligible.

> Bless the Lord all created things: sing his praise and exalt him for ever. (ASB)

'Modern'? No, only mediocre sham religious. The earlier version, which is being pushed aside for this, is breath-taking:

> O all ye Works of the Lord, bless ye the Lord: praise him and magnify him for ever. (BCP)

As if in shame, the authors of the Alternative Book reprint the Prayer Book versions of the Canticles in a sort of appendix to Morning and Evening Prayer. If they had that much shame, where was the courage which should have made them reject the inferior versions altogether?

The case of the psalms is very odd indeed. The psalter did not enjoy the benefit of 'repeated scrutiny by the General Synod', but, desperate to have something worse than Coverdale's (the BCP) version – as one easily might have – they hit on the English text published in 1976 by David L. Frost, John A. Emerton and Andrew A. Mackintosh. Good for them! But bad for the rest of us and an irreparable loss to any congregation that makes the changeover. 'Modern'? No. An insensitive pastiche. There are some good laughs for the student of the bogus contemporary.

Praise him in the blast of the ram's horn:

sing our alternative Davids.

Praise him in the sound of the trumpet:

answers old Coverdale from his tomb. Ah, Coverdale, we must tell him; at least we moderns know it *was* a ram's horn, and do not mix it up with any instrument we have actually heard in the twentieth century.

One can only hope that when the Alternative Book at last falls heavily into the pews, the eyes of priests and congregation will be opened and they will see that this is not a Prayer Book made new for the twentieth century but a compendium of old hat including 500 pages of mutilated collects, sentences and readings from every version of the Bible except the best. They should laugh unsanctimoniously to see that the bishops have promoted themselves above the Queen, in the Church of England's first attempt since the Reformation to set itself apart from the polity in which it lives; and to notice the concurrence of innocent scholarship and political innuendo implied in the odd name of 'President' given to the priest at Holy Communion. I suggest that there should be a competition in every parish for the most striking pair of comparative phrases from the old book and the new. When the congregation has played this game for a week or two, they should hunt round to see where the churchwardens have hidden their real Prayer Books, and blow the dust off them.

Tinkling Symbols

John Coulson is a theologian who has been hob-nobbing with literary critics. He is an authority on Newman; the literary critics with whom he has been hob-nobbing have been, predominantly, academics. The presiding literary figure in his book *Religion and Imagination* is Eliot, whose critical theories – though not his critical judgements, which belong to a more open world altogether – owe much to Newman, as Coulson himself demonstrates. Coleridge and Arnold have their place; then Leavis shows his hand, and we are among the orthodoxies of post-war university teaching, for better or worse.

Why should a theologian turn to literary critics, and is there anything concealed in the great forest of post-war academic theorizing about literature which will help him to explain himself? Theology is a part of literature. It is hardly a popular part, in these days, but it remains true that without some reading of Hooker, Butler and Law – to mention no others – anyone's knowledge of English literature must be sadly incomplete. So far, so good. But whether the more theoretical sort of academic literary criticism, in the last fifty years, has added much to the understanding of literature, is open to doubt. Some are so rude as to say that it has done more to set up a barrier between the student and the texts that matter. Perhaps it might be a last hope for the more abstruse academic theorists to launch themselves upon theology, as they have launched themseves upon several other studies including sociology and politics. But what is there in it for theologians? If they are in search of respectability, on the grounds that the mountain of literary theorizing is more in the public eye than their own unfashionable study, they are probably on to a bad thing, for the lava emitted by the great post-Leavisian eruption is crumbling away fast. Could one find a contemporary poet, novelist, or mere enthusiastic reader, who claimed to have found much help there?

Of course, theologians have to apologize as never before. There is so little general acceptance of their premisses. John Coulson wriggles before the fundamental articles of belief, which he clearly feels cannot be justified by common sense. So he seizes on the notion of metaphor and symbol, which admittedly have been, and are, the basis of much religious language. The Creed itself is a *symbolum* or symbol. Dante was baffled by what he saw in Paradise, as who would not be? But the problem of apologetics has always been to put into the ordinary language of truth, of ordinary truth, the elements of the faith. This language changes with the knowledge of the physical world, for that is where most of us are most conscious of living. The problem has increased in complexity as the complexity of the physical sciences has increased. Still, other analogies can play a part. So John Coulson takes refuge with the analysts of metaphor.

The literary metaphor is dense in Shakespeare, and is thinner in Arnold – so runs the argument. The dense metaphor gives a clue to the nature of fundamental theological statements. All may not be lost – I have to compress the argument – because the dense metaphor is still possible as, it is alleged, in Eliot's religious poems. So we look at the way the professors read poetry or even prose fiction and hope to make the reading of the Creed more plausible. The professors are roused to a sort of disbelief. They understand each metaphor in *Lear* beautifully because they understand them all, keep them all in their minds and so see each part of the play in relation to all the parts and to the whole. That is how the Christian faith should be understood, as witness Newman.

There is a snag. The critic is predisposed 'to believe in the reality' of what the poets and novelists imagine, but 'the theologian goes further.' Too true! 'He seeks imaginative assents which are convertible into certitudes.' In that crux John Coulson has got no further than Newman, so it must be questioned whether the academic company he has kept has done him much good.

John Coulson's argument is subtle, and anyone who is interested should look to his 170 pages rather than to my paragraphs. Newman thought that 'assent to religious objects, as if they were objects of sight... was the privilege of a devout nation only, and "such a faith does not suit the genius of modern England".' Precisely. When it comes to reassuring ourselves that our metaphors correspond to something outside ourselves, we look for moral support to the company we keep. 'The Church completes this authenticating function for Newman. The university, for Leavis, performs the same function.' Clutching at straws! If these indications suggest anything, it is that if the faith is preserved it will be by people who withdraw from the world, as has been done before.

The more socially robust apologist may prefer Dr Johnson, whom Coulson quotes as saying: 'The ideas of Christian theology are too simple for eloquence, too sacred for fiction.' Johnson would not have had much truck with Coulson's argument. But then, he thought Berkeley could be disproved by kicking a stone, and that 'we *know* that we have free will.'

A Gentle Warning

A bill designed to secure that, subject to certain conditions, at least one main service a month, in Church of England parishes, should be in the form prescribed by the Book of Common Prayer, is certainly an absurdity. It is absurd, almost everyone will say, at this time of day that Parliament should be asked to regulate what the parsons get up to on Sunday mornings. Members of Parliament thought they had washed their hands of such things in 1974, and that was late enough in the day. The promoters of the Bill which had its successful first reading on 8 April 1981, and is to have a second reading this week, are, however, by no means so ingenuous as might appear. The first reading of the Bill attracted a degree of attention – and of parliamentary attendance – which few can have expected. The promoters were thus able to demonstrate that, far from being out of touch with the times, they had a real political sense of what is important to people. There was great ecclesiastical indignation, on the grounds that the matter was important only to a *minority* – which would be an odd and unsatisfactory reason for Parliament *not* concerning itself with any subject. It may be added that the assertion that Anglicans who want the Prayer Book are a minority within the Church is – well, just an assertion.

The more solemn reason given for the indignation of Synod-loving Anglicans (*they*, surely, are a minority!) is of course that the regulation of church affairs was put into the hands of the Synod in 1974 and that unsanctified parliamentary hands should no longer touch such matters. One can understand these sentiments on the part of those who thought they had climbed into the Synod as into a space-ship, and pulled up the ladder, but whatever the impression of those inside, such vehicles are controlled from the ground. The privileges Parliament gives, it can certainly take away. It beseems the authorities of the Church of England to remember that in the country at large their membership, however reckoned, is now a minority, and they should not expect from the public a respect they are not prepared to accord to serious elements within their own circles or outside.

It would certainly have surprised the ordinary churchgoer, in 1974, to learn that what was being plotted under the guise of a measure to allow the Church to manage its own affairs, was a complete change in the character of the Church of England. Concern was expressed at the time, by some of the more wary, about the possible fate of the Book of Common Prayer, and even as late as last year, when the Alternative Service Book was going through its final stages in the Synod, assurances were given that the Prayer Book still stood, and that no one therefore should lament its loss. The assurances were, frankly, a pack of lies, and indeed the conduct of the ecclesiastical authorities at large, in relation to the Alternative Service Book, has been of a kind which would have been unsparingly blasted by any political opposition, if anything so disingenuous were practised – as who shall say it has not sometimes been? – by a government. Nothing could have illustrated better the inept and unhealthy cosiness of the Synod than their utter ignoring of the petition presented to them on the initiative of Professor David Martin. No one expected the *fauteurs* of the Alternative Service Book to turn tail at the sight of the petition, but that the petition should have been utterly ignored, that no reply of any kind should have been thought necessary, could only be taken to mark a determination on the part of bishops and clergy, to say nothing of the lay ecclesiastical politicians, to turn their backs on responsible outside opinion and behave as if they were a congregation of saints who had no need to notice the vulgar and the damned. That the petition was largely representative of educated opinion, literate and musical, meant that the Synod were in fact turning their backs on that alliance with learning which was one of the glories of the English Church in better days. No wonder the Alternative Book is what it is.

Now that the Alternative Book has been promulgated and widely distributed and the Prayer Book in most places pushed into corners, it is apparently thought safe to be honest. We find, for example, the *Carlisle Diocesan News* saying: 'Diplomacy may have required the unglamorous definition – "Alternative Service Book" – but the truth is that an alternative liturgy is a contradiction in terms... It is time therefore to abandon political tactics and cover-up titles which suggest that this is no more than an alternative, and that 1662 stands unscathed.' So the people of England have been kidded by these scruffy ecclesiastical politicians, and are now reckoned of so little account, in the Councils of the Church, that the little joke can be admitted. No wonder it was felt, when the petition was presented to the Synod, that the presence of outsiders of any sophistication would be an embarrassment. 'For our health's sake,' says the encyclical from Carlisle, 'the blood must be changed.' (The blood is that contaminated by the Book of Common Prayer.) 'What matters now is that the operation should be swift and complete.'

Time for Parliament to intervene? I think it is. Indeed, one may say that the Church of England has begun its course of synodical government by an affront not only to many of its members but to Parliament itself. For did not the authorities of the Church take on the new form of government well knowing, in their inner councils, what they would get up to, but carefully concealing the drift of their politics? Of course neither the promoters of the present Bill, nor those who support it from a distance, expect it to pass into law, and one can imagine the Government being more than a little worried if it faced that possibility. So far from wanting to meddle in such things, the State is delighted not to have to do so. None the less, in the last resort, if clerics are silly enough, in ordinary political terms, if they are dishonest and reckless, they cannot in the end escape retribution from Parliament. That, be it said, goes for other bodies besides the Church of England; it is *not* a peculiarity of the Establishment. For Parliament can do as it likes, and will do, if sufficiently moved. It may be that people now think that the old conflicts between Church and State are something only to be read about in history books. Not at all, as even a short political memory will show. Perhaps it is only in foreign countries, in France or in Poland, that such conflicts can happen? Not at all. We may be sure that, in the last resort, the country which, of all others, roused itself to throw off a foreign ecclesiastical administration and to work out a series of settlements which gave us, after all, a decent history of political liberty, will not stand more than a certain amount of nonsense in the name of religion, whether from the Moonies or anyone else.

The Prayer Book (Protection) Bill is the gentlest of warnings.

An Abdication by the Church

Having now pushed aside the Book of Common Prayer, the Synod of the Church of England, in its session in March 1981, turned its attention to less important matters. For, although the full consequences are yet to appear, nothing could be more important, to the Church's continuing identity, than the Prayer Book. In their passion for style – a *modern* style, they were ill-informed enough to say – the authorities seem to have forgotten that for the Church to lose her corsets was to lose her shape. I dare say, however, that with their other ruling passion for a hasty ecumenicism, they welcomed this inelegance. The truth none the less is that the Prayer Book contains a whole system for living in the world – in this realm of England for which it is designed – and if one does not have that system one has to have another, and that other has not yet been adumbrated. No wonder so many ordinary Anglicans, men of no vision, are puzzled.

The meetings of Synod throw into uneasy prominence the ordinary corporate problems of the Church – the problems of politics and polity which the Prayer Book, put together under real pressures and not in the frivolous spirit of so many current reforms, solved so deftly that the business of re-defining them in the contemporary context has been funked or perhaps merely ignored. Of course the loosening of ties with the state has long been gleefully welcomed by those who see in the growing dissociation a mark of sanctity as well as of liberty, but the giggling should be suppressed for things are not as simple as that. This church is still called the Church of England and one might have some reservations about the exuberance of the Bishop of Guildford, for whom 'what is becoming important on the world scene is also appropriate in England'. A little more admission of myopia might bring discussions nearer the ground.

The political fallacy which rages most strongly in this recently-liberated – or recently disoriented – Church of England is that there is or might be such a thing as a church without political trammels. One might say, with all deference to Thomas à Becket, that this notion of a possible independence of the church is but a version, writ horribly large, of the extreme liberal fallacy that individual opinion is always right and the state is always wrong. The most ineluctable of political trammels, however, are not those laid upon churches by the state but those they are subject to merely because of their nature as institutions. There is no acting as a body without acting politically. There are the horrors of internal government, exemplified in the Synod itself, and one need do no more than point to a remark of the Bishop of Truro – certainly one of the most clear-headed of the bench of bishops – in the course of the present session: 'The matter before us cannot be settled by the counting of heads.' The counting of heads must always threaten to drive the Church to compromise – a situation which may be well enough for a lay government, which tries merely to get by, but which must raise rather fundamental questions about the real nature of a body which has more august pretensions.

Of course, difficulties of this kind are not peculiar to the Church of England or its Synod, but these institutions are peculiarly vulnerable because they have committed themselves to the absurdity of a largely democratic assembly giving itself the airs of a government – rather as if the House of Commons tried to function without Crown or Ministers or government departments. That such a body is more or less at the mercy of the bureaucrats and committee-men operating in the neighbourhood must be obvious, and no doubt a little plotting with Church House helps on causes whether good or bad. There are also inescapable external complications about the Church of England's position as a political body, and these show up comically in relation to our Big Brother the Pope. For while the Church of England has been busy demoting itself to the status of a sect, the Pope has been exploiting the possibilities the media offer to his far-flung empire in order to strengthen his political impact to a point which would have been sharply contested in the days when there were Catholic monarchies to recognize the power struggle for what it is. Well might *The Times*, a paper not notoriously critical of papal manoeuvres, report that 'there was general agreement' in Synod that the Pope's visit 'was an occasion for warmth rather than for euphoria'.

Of the subjects which engaged the Synod at this session, the most important was, unquestionably, that of the proposals for a covenant with the Methodist, United Reformed and Moravian churches. The Synod's characteristic conclusion was to authorize a further step in the direction proposed, but not by a majority which would have left the final outcome beyond reasonable doubt. An interesting feature of this debate was the appeal by the Bishop of Guildford, in a speech which apparently did not mention the Prayer Book, to the authority of the Alternative Service Book – that mistress who has been introduced into the house doing the honours while the lawful wife was locked in her private sitting-room. The outsider could only gather that the Church of England has abandoned its claim to be the historic Church in this kingdom, and that the social separatism of the Reformed and Methodist bodies has with the passage of time given them a theological justification which would have surprised the Wesleys. It is rather as if the Church of England itself claimed no historical lineage further back than the administrative separation from Rome in the sixteenth century, or as if it were determined in the interests of equality and fraternity to make nothing of it. It all seems very odd, and the scheme bears the marks of opportunist botching, even if that botching now has quite a history of its own. Perhaps at the back of some of the protagonists' minds is a dubious identification of 'visible' with administrative unity, and surely it is strange that, at a time when the Church of England is further than it ever was from making plain to its ordinary members what it believes, it should propose the assimilation of greater uncertainties. The mirage of '1,000 million people of many different races and cultures' said to be 'baptised members of the body of Christ' is perhaps distracting to those engaged in local business. Still, the question of what people here and now actually know and believe is of some importance, if a church is a congregation of faithful people. One cannot but have sympathy for the minority in Synod who cannot accept the separation of questions of order and arrangement from matters of faith.

Apart from the proposals for a covenant with Protestant dissenters, the main subjects discussed at this session of Synod were some matters of ecclesiastical discipline in relation to marriage, and a report of the Church's Board on Homosexual Relations. That neither subject was regarded as ready for definitive treatment need surprise no one. A cynic might say that what the Church is asking itself, in a complicated way, is whether it should follow the drift of the times, and if so how fast. Every precaution is required, for these are concerns in which people are most ready to prefer themselves to the Church. It is not so much what people do, as what they say about it, that has changed with the century. The standard of acceptability in the past could seem to emanate from the Church, but it is now clear to everyone that the real determinant is social practice. Where does that leave the Church? No polite person now refers to extra-marital relations of any stability as fornication, but what exactly is one to make of a service of blessing – as talked of and to some extent actually used – for what must be ranked ecclesiastically as second class cohabitations? It is just kindness, perhaps, and that is something, as those outside the Church would be the first to admit, in their Pelagian way. So conscious of fashion has the Church become, in sexual as in other matters, that many are left wondering whether it is not so much set against the world as following the world's teaching, but at a respectful distance.

The Reverend Member?

There is good reason for thinking that Members of Parliament are not drawn from as wide a circle as they might be. There is no shortage of lawyers, company directors and trade union officials, nor of doctors and teachers of one sort and another. But that still leaves as virtual absentees many classes of persons who collectively know a lot about running what is now usually referred to as the economy. One class of persons who are entirely missing is the clergy of the Church of England. It cannot be said that their absence is the key to our present troubles, or even that it has been widely lamented. The clergy are, however, a special case, for it is against the law of the land for them to sit in the House of Commons.

We are happy to have a Synod always anxious to put things right. On the list of Private Members' Motions for the meeting next week (February 1982) there is one to be moved by the Archdeacon of Derby, which asserts 'That this Synod believes that clergymen of the Church of England should be free, like other citizens, to offer themselves for election as Members of Parliament' and seeks to move the Government 'to amend the relevant Act which forbids them to do so'. One should be astonished at nothing promoted in the Synod, and in this instance the author of the motion can point to the backing of a recommendation in the Church and State Report, 1970. There is a current case, supposed by some to be pathetic, of a clergyman who values his orders so little that he is laying them down, as far as in him lies, in order to circumvent the Act. This gentleman apparently feels that it is more important to be an MP than a parson – a point of view which, to say the least, does not display great unworldliness.

What would be the effect of this change in the law, if it were made? Not, one imagines, the flooding of the House of Commons with clergymen – the electors would see to that. It will be observed that the author of the motion has his eye on the liberty of the individual rather than on the well-being of the Church; what matters is that the clergyman 'should be free like other citizens'. Like most other citizens, it would have been better to say, for if the clergy are excluded by law as others are not, there are many whose employment and careers would be gone if they entered politics. What the Synod ought to be debating, surely, is not how free clergymen should be but whether the Church they serve would benefit from the proposed distractions. The legal exclusion is an oddity and there may be a case for removing it. What seems odder still is that the Synod should busy itself about this rather trivial matter before considering whether the Church needs clergy who are MPs.

The reason for the exclusion of the clergy seems to be lost in the mist. Blackstone thought that not having to serve in Parliament was originally regarded as one of the privileges of the clergy rather than as a restriction. Be that as it may, any question of removing the exclusion now will at once raise other questions of Church and State, notably that of abolishing such vestiges of the Establishment as remain. The political innocence of the reigning authorities of the Church of England, and of a large part of the membership of the Synod, is fabulous. Many who support the forthcoming Private Member's Motion will no doubt be delighted to see how much of the structure of the Establishment falls down when they touch it – and surprised a few years later to see how much harm they have done. There are Anglicans who think it wicked that they should have any privileges not shared by their non-conformist, including Roman, brothers. Rome no doubt agrees, as she proceeds quietly, with the help of the Foreign Office, to extend her own political influence, and for the moment rests on her laurels, having at last achieved a Papal Nuncio at the Court of St James's.

This step, whatever the arguments for it, can hardly be thought of as one towards equalizing the privileges enjoyed by the various ecclesiastical bodies at work in this country. It is, rather, a retrogression. If papal diplomacy were restricted, as on ordinary international proprieties it ought to be, to the affairs of a small Ruritanian state in Italy, there could be no possible cause for objection. But the Pope is a sadly mixed-up functionary, and his diplomats presume to speak on behalf of members of the Roman communion anywhere in the world. This not only amounts to giving the Roman Church an external diplomatic voice, and so an advantage not enjoyed by other ecclesiastical bodies; it goes clean against any democratic notion of government. Any diplomatic action on behalf of citizens of the United Kingdom should surely be taken by Her Majesty's representatives and by no one else. There is not a shred of support in constitutional theory, nor in the prevailing beliefs about the meaning of democracy, for any other view of the matter.

The current vein of self-immolation among Anglicans very likely appears to those concerned as a mark of spiritual purity. It is indeed a mark of Puritanism, which is not quite the same thing, though Puritans have always seen an affinity. An ecclesiastical structure cannot help having some sort of political existence. The Roman Church as the successor of the Roman Empire has always been aware of this, and has never ceased to meddle with the affairs of sovereign states. The post-Reformation English Church, in its heyday, had a delicate internal relationship with the state which kept it clear of the worst meddling; even so its privileges have been inexorably eroded because democracy cannot, in the end, admit any other appeal than to popular opinion. The papacy, like the monarch, is ultimately threatened by these tendencies. Both may survive a period of populism, but neither is founded upon populist principles. The monarchy we may have good hopes of, for it so to speak defines the terms of reference of our democracy and is the embodiment of its territorial reference and of a loyalty which is necessary for our survival.

The papacy can look after itself, and it has on the whole done this, through the ages, by taking the political colour of the moment, as far as its lumbering steps allowed. Its untiring political encroachments have been slapped down time after time in the course of history. At the moment the Roman Church has what is, historically considered, an odd reputation as the champion of democracy in Poland; this must be largely the result of a series of events which has made it a centre of national feeling as it was in its former struggles against the Russian Orthodox Church. Politically, the motive of all Rome's politics may be said, without disrespect, to be its own survival and its own prevalence. The politics of present-day Anglicans have a childish look, in the face of such dignified and long-term objectives. To continue to chip away at the residue of the Establishment which the present arrangements are, without having anything to put in its place but a vague sentiment – that is not enough. No doubt a Church which has made light of the Book of Common Prayer and the Authorized Version must be thought to glory in its intellectual decline, but that sort of foolishness may after all not be a mark of sanctity but merely an insult to the intelligence of the Apostles.

Anyhow, when the Archdeacon of Derby rises to propose his motion in the Synod, he will have an opportunity of demonstrating that he understands that the Church of England does not exist in a political vacuum.

Notes on Church and State

I

The Thirty-nine Articles are rather unfashionable reading, but they are very good reading none the less. They are, of course, much spat upon by Anglicans these days, like other monuments of the English Church. As to their theology, Newman thought he had proved that they were in accordance with the Council of Trent, while generations of more Protestant persons have – shall we say? – taken another view of the matter. It could be argued that their theology is eirenic, if confused. It is not, however, my purpose to engage in polemics in matters so far above my head. What I should like to draw attention to is the politics of the Articles, of which it can be said that, at the least, they are no more inept than some recent inventions in this field.

One has to turn over several theological pages to come to: 'XXXVII. Of the Civil Magistrates.' 'The Queen's Majesty,' we read, 'hath the chief power in this Realm of *England*, and other her Dominions' – and the article goes on to make it clear that that does not let out the clergy, notorious through the centuries for claiming various privileges for themselves, as well worldly as spiritual, it may be said. To drive home the point with a minatory look at the chief contender for such privileges, the article concludes, that the 'chief Government... is not, nor ought to be, subject to any foreign jurisdiction'. It seems a bold claim, in an England continually open to a seepage of regulations from Brussels and elsewhere, but the Articles were conceived in the more youthful and confident days of the National State.

Article XXXVII, which is one of the longest, goes on to explain that what is at issue is not the government meddling with 'God's Word, or... the Sacraments'. No, it is to keep the upper hand on 'all estates and degrees... whether they be Ecclesiastical or Temporal'. And quite right too, one might think, with one's mind on what used to be called the peace of the realm. Or, quite wrong, with one's mind not on old ecclesiastical quarrels but on international courts of Human Rights and such-like fantasies of the contemporary imagination.

These would have been strange new perspectives for the authors of the Thirty-nine Articles, and they would have asked, very reasonably, what powers upheld these non-domestic authorities? Where, they would have said, still thinking ineptly of the Prince of This World in Rome, was the crowned head which nurtured these pretensions against Her Majesty? While this question might not be altogether so foolish as the political circumstances of the present age might at first lead us to suppose, the contemporary answer would have been profoundly shocking to the questioners. If the suspected crowned head was not to be found, were the distributed Powers of Darkness to which such international authorities owed their authority not to be regarded as even more sinister? They had their agents everywhere, worse than the Jesuit priests who, in Elizabeth's reign, were after all deliberately treasonable, like the agents of Moscow in the twentieth century.

This is not the place to examine the immense web of documents and justifications which maintain the human rights industry as a powerful international cartel, more or less beneficial, more or less not so, like most such cartels. What would really have shocked the Tudor politicians would have been to discover that it was not these organizations as such, their princes, directors and judges, which or who, in the last analysis, claimed this superb authority on earth, but that these authorities pointed away from themselves to the voices and consciences of mankind at large. This would have puzzled them because they would not at once have seen how the testimony of all these consciences could have been collected and reconciled – a good question. It would also have worried them because, although themselves passing as the supporters of the individual conscience, up to a point, they had not intended that things should go so far. The Roman authority notoriously and, they thought, erroneously pointed away from itself to a divine commission. No sooner get away from that false claim, they would have said, than we find authorities pointing to a human commission which was hardly distinguishable from a mob.

We who understand the refinements of democratic machinery – or who have accustomed ourselves to behave as if we did – know that there are methods of ordering and civilizing the individual opinions which would otherwise make up a mob and extracting from them something which resembles due process of government. We could laugh at our Tudor forebears and assure them that, rotten though our governments might be, they had many sophistications unknown to earlier ages and indeed managed to avoid some rather rough Tudor habits. We should also have to point out that the Protestant revolution had been so successful – more successful than either the Tudors or the Stuarts intended – that in our sort of state religion itself had become wholly a matter of individual conscience, though some people restricted their consciences in deference to an authority they had chosen for themselves. Humph! the Tudor statesmen might have said, thinking still of that Bishop of Rome who, they declared, had 'no jurisdiction in this realm of England', as well as of sundry tumultuous conventicles with which they had had trouble.

The authors of the Articles did not go too deeply into this question of liberty of conscience, which it would have been difficult to do after thirty-six articles dealing with points of ecclesiastical doctrine. They did, however, treat briefly, in the remaining paragraphs, with one or two matters of conscience which had given some trouble from Anabaptists and the like. 'The laws of the Realm may punish Christian men with death, for heinous and grievous offences', they said, discreetly leaving it to the civil laws to say what offences were so considered. They were not for any interference with the traditional dissuasives from public disorder. Nor would they brook awkward questions of conscience about the defence of the realm: 'It is lawful for Christian men, at the commandment of the Magistrate, to wear weapons, and serve in the wars.' Note, however, the moderation of this claim. They had no need to think of a universal conscription, of the kind familiar to us since the epoch of liberty opened by the French Revolution. They did not assert a positive Christian duty to bear arms, which would have raised intractable questions about the clergy. It must not be assumed that they were thinking of a modern liberalism in relation to the laity, for a very moderate Anglican divine of the Stuart century said that ''tis pity but that his neck should hang in suspence with his Conscience that doubts to fight' when his country is invaded and that 'in offensive war, though the case be harder, the common Soldier is not to dispute, but do his Prince's command.' The contemporary state so far admits the existence of an unprovable conscience as to allow objection on general pacifist grounds – mainly, no doubt, in spite of the patter to the contrary, because there is less trouble that way.

A more ticklish point – though theoretically only, for it has nothing to do with modern economic arguments – is the question of property. The authors of the Articles, concerned no doubt for the propertied classes but also for the only form of public order they could conceive, boldly asserted that 'the Riches and Goods of Christians are not common, as touching the right, title and possession of the same'. That was what 'certain Anabaptists' did 'vainly boast'. With their minds on the same disturbers of the public peace, the authors of the Articles also asserted that, 'when the Magistrate requireth, . . . so it be done . . . in justice, judgement and truth', a man might swear on oath in a court of law – another disputed point. This little difficulty has naturally disappeared as, in deference to conscience, the respectability of mere affirmation has grown.

III

Conscience is a very sophisticated conception, but it can also be a very simple one. A casuist may think condescendingly of a conscience not instructed by himself; some highly instructed persons – Pascal for one – have thought some casuists rather funny and rather dishonest. But what all consciences have in common is that they have been *taught*, more or less. They are a product of our civilization and barbarisms, as well as of the controverted residue which was there 'originally', whatever that might mean. So the conscience of the world, so frequently reported in the media to be 'affronted' by this or that, is a rather suspect article. Who taught it? one must wonder.

Indeed all consciences are suspect, as the Church has been among the first to point out. The mind of man is infinitely devious, and claims to purity of intention are to be taken with a pinch of salt. That of course goes for ecclesiastics as well as for the rest of the world. There is nothing more difficult to impart, surely, than the divine residuum of which they claim to be the exponents. The statement of doctrine has, traditionally, been hedged with many precautions, none of which has given universal and unqualified satisfaction. Be that as it may, the application of doctrine, the appreciation of its consequences in the field of action, has proved a treacherous one for all concerned. There is a vast area of ecclesiastical pronouncements which a reasonable man may regard with suspicion. 'The Church of Rome hath erred,' – the Thirty-nine Articles declare – all particular churches have erred: that is certainly the commonsense of the matter as relating to all ordinary ecclesiastical pronouncements, whatever may be the case as to the ultimate residuum of doctrine. The ordinary victim of ecclesiastical guidance is in an uncertain position, like the rest of us, when it comes to taking a view on the affairs of the world, if only because information has not always been all it might have been.

Whatever may be the quality of the guidance afforded it, no one disputes that the conscience is an individual faculty, to be exercised as best we can in the face of all the evidences and instruction presented to it. How far we should listen to father before we decide – and indeed, who *is* father – are questions at the bottom of all the argument which has gone on on the subject in recent centuries: all that is distinctly at the sophisticated end of the range of conceptions of 'conscience' now prevailing in the world at large. The range extends far outside the world of theological conceptions – or of what is commonly understood by them.

For Machiavelli a mask of religion, on a competent politician, was likely to be – precisely – a mask; and wily men have always been suspicious of eloquence. But the great popular success of 'conscience', from the Reformation, through the vainly boasting Anabaptists and the like to Voltaire, Rousseau, the French Revolution and beyond, has delivered into the hands of politicians an armoury of a more potent kind.

For we have long arrived at Democracy, somewhat fallible in its ordinary practice, as indeed imperfect in its organization, but generally said to be infallible in principle. If anything goes wrong, everyone agrees at once that there wasn't *enough* democracy. Have some more and everything will be all right. We have not been righteous enough, according to current conceptions, so the wrath of God – or some more popular substitute – is upon us. What we used to have, in this country, in the days when foreigners were misguided enough to imitate us, was a *mixed* government, royal, aristocratic and democratic. A mixed government is in fact not only the best sort to have, it is the only sort you *can* have, in the modern world. It is the right recipe for the mixture which is difficult. But the patter put out no longer says that. It says that governments – all decent governments – are 'democratic'; the various mechanisms which make them work in spite of being democratic are more or less ignored, more or less concealed, more or less denied. Yet who does not know that the tiniest organization – let alone a modern government – will not work without one or two hard-bitten people who actually do things and take account of facts, as well as the uncertain number who stand around talking and expressing opinions which may or may not take account of the facts?

The centre of this mystery is the encouragement, by those who are elected, of belief in the magical nature of the process. Who elected you? is their question, which may be counted upon to floor any non-elected person who might come near to winning an argument merely on merits. Of course, in an appropriate constitutional context this is absolutely right, for arguments have to be ended somehow, so that the work can go on. But the constitutional context seems to matter less and less, for beyond the elected person is the individual voter, whose untiring conscience is perpetually to be probed to find an answer more correct than the correct answer that was found last time. Moreover, since elections unhappily do not take place quite *all* the time, even in the most sophisticated democracy, various ways have to be found of discovering what the oracles would be saying if they were asked to speak. And the obvious way is to ask them to speak, out of season as well as in. So we get various collectors of oracles, of varying degrees of professionalism and amateurism; their objective is to launch themselves on properly constituted governments waving documents which prove that on some point or other the official augurs are wrong, as indeed they frequently are, though it does not follow from that that any particular set of unofficial augurs is right.

'Two things fill my mind with ever-increasing wonder,' said Immanual Kant, the highbrow exponent, if anyone ever was, of the Nordic Protestant conscience, 'the starry heavens above and the moral law within.' Kant's wonder might have increased still more if he could have seen the excesses of conscience in our day. What he had in mind was the solitary philosopher taking a dog for a walk. What we have to think of, in the context of contemporary politics, is a variety of persons not all in the same tradition. The old casuists had in mind a patient who would stop and listen to them, but our public will not stop to be instructed. The casuists were certainly right to make the point that the individual might often confuse what he thought was right with what he merely wanted; they omitted, in general, to add that the same might be true of the casuist. We have greatly simplified these matters, so far as politics are concerned. In democratic practice, as well as mythology, what you want and what you think should be done are one and the same thing. A conscience, ultimately, is a vote, and that is all there is to it.

In this historic migration of the conscience from religion to politics a strange metamorphosis has occurred. For the original question of conscience was, What should I do? The political question is, What should someone else do? In spite of some more unobtrusive activities going on here and there the Church, deferential as usual to the drift of the times, shows signs of following this political lead. Once we were invited to pray God 'to save and defend all Christian Kings, Princes and Governors', so that the established authorities could get on with their duties in accordance with *their* consciences. Now we are more likely to be asked to uphold alleged rights against the better judgement of some government or other, it may be that of the Queen's Majesty, over whom the bishops have now given themselves precedence as if they were common Anabaptists. They are making obeisance to the supreme power residing in the conscience of votes.

For the Roman church things are probably a little different. They have a long tradition of meddling in the affairs of lawful governments and take like a duck to water to the business of putting governments to rights. They even – though it is an absurdity – have their own diplomatic representatives.

III

Democracy has in effect dis-infected the individual conscience of its sanctity, at the same time that it has made it the foundation of the state. For the conscience of mankind, that of a nation, of the 'communities' of which, in this country, the nation is allowed to be made up, is a collection of votes and it would be to succumb to the clap-trap of the system to suppose that it is any more. The historical prestige of the truly *individual* conscience – the theological and, to a less extent, the philosophical one – is for the moment enough for politicians to invoke it, but that is a sleight-of-hand. There is no collecting all the determinations people make for themselves, as to their own actions. What can be and is vociferously collected is *opinions* as to what someone else ought to be doing, and politicians of various descriptions offer themselves as instruments for giving effect to all that is finest and noblest, etc, and that can be made out, at a quick look, to be derived from the sacred fountains of individual reflection and individual devotion.

The politicians are by no mean confined to the constitutional machinery, or to what is left of it or has been added to it. Indeed it is arguable that, to an increasing extent, the elected members of political parties, operating at Westminster or in local government, more and more have to fall back into a role formerly occupied by the Civil Service, of responding to political pressures generated by more strident figures. It is as if, between the official politician and the individual opinions of his constituents, which he is supposed in some sort to represent, a whole new army of irresponsible operators has slid. It is to this ghostly and it might be said sinister set of unavowed politicians that the official politician has to bow; it is they who collect individual voices, or who speak directly to the voters. No wonder there is confusion. The situation is of course not entirely new – what social or political situation is? – but there is enough in it that is of relatively recent development for the reality of government to be much farther than before from its constitutional appearance. The influence of the media is much talked about, though certainly far from sufficiently accounted for, as yet. Spasmodic attention has been given to the operation of pressure groups. Our concern here is only with those pressure groups which wear the sheep's clothing of religious opinion.

Can these religious groups, churches, organizations more or less under more or less leaky ecclesiastical umbrellas, prophets invoking more or less clandestinely Divine Powers which are thought still to have a certain voting strength, really be wolves? The BBC runs, at 8.15 on Sunday mornings, an illuminating programme called *Sunday*, an appreciable part of which, each week, is given to statements for or against some currently debated political issue. The members of some church here, or some committee there, or some organization purporting to be of more religious intent than the rest of mankind, is put up to make out that 'Christians' or 'Christian opinion' is in favour of, or against whatever it is in favour of, or against. Occasionally the view is supported by some sketchy argument with, let us say, theological connections. More often than not one is faced with mere assertion or, as they say, faith. It would be an undeserved compliment to the clarity of mind of many of the speakers to say that they are deliberately using a tried rhetoric to advance their particular political opinions, though here and there, no doubt, there are lucid politicians who deliberately use some 'Christian' organization as one more forum for their views. But, motives apart, the nature of the operation is to try to collect listeners who are, or imagine themselves to be, Christians, behind some bit of a programme which will have to be settled by governments or other properly constituted authorities of the state.

Why not? most of them would say, either in genuine astonishment or with the weary air of those accustomed to the prejudices (usually qualified, though with no great historical accuracy, as 'old-fashioned') of those who think 'the Church should not meddle in politics'. There are several theological answers to this question, all more or less debatable in these circles, no doubt. There is also a non-theological answer of some importance. This is, that it is not in terms of their 'Christian' appeal that the matters they raise will be settled. It is even wildly discriminatory (usually held by such speakers to be a damnable thing, in other contexts) to suggest that this or that religious opinion should have any particular weight in settling affairs of state. The arguments have to be in terms of money and interest – held to be universally valid counters – or of 'rights' which, whether imaginary or not, are so abstract as to be equally comprehensible, and of cognate, even identical, meaning for people of all races and cultures – for the 'conscience of mankind', you might say.

The churches themselves, it ought to be made plain, do not really exist for democratic politics. This has of course been clear enough, on that remote continent of Europe, ever since the French Revolution. In this country the survival of certain constitutional arrangements, to say nothing of the lack of clarity in the intellectual atmosphere, has made it possible to contend – though with decreasing conviction – that 'Christian' opinion ought to count for something. In the countries where the social institutions of the Roman Church have survived best it has been necessary for politicians to make various overt arrangements with the Vatican, but that is a political story on its own. For democracy there can be no 'Christian opinion'; there are just opinions, and out of the resolution of these opinions, more or less imperfectly expressed, and the invincible facts so far as they are apprehended by governments, come the decisions which, for good or ill, governments take on our behalf. The opinions must – or we have unfair discrimination! – be valued not on the basis of their quality but of their number; it is that which has to decide. Admittedly most government decisions are in practice taken – perhaps happily – in ignorance of what 'most people', or even most of their party supporters, think about the matter in hand. And there are, to put it mildly, various ways of calculating a majority, so that the skilful operator in government is not as much trammelled as, on pure democratic theory, he should be. But an approach by an archbishop or a cardinal to the seats of power is quite rightly regarded with suspicion. Whom is he trying to kid? The only authority he has a right to invoke is that of his constituents, and their connection with him is, so far as political actions are concerned, a pretty phoney affair. In so far as he is listened to it is because he comes trailing votes, or because it might be worth inquiring whether he does.

The theory of vote-catching is, however, no more than the ultimate concern of politicians, the sanction which determines, for a time, whether they will be there or not, when the next caller comes. A more elusive but, in the end, more powerful consideration is the nature of the discourse in which public discussion of political issues is conducted. This is more and more determined in the melting pot of the media. To that extent no doubt the promoters of 'Christian opinion' (normally meaning that of that sector of the opinion of Christians which comes nearest to the 'Religion of Democracy', of which more hereafter) and 'Catholic opinion' (normally meaning a Roman-Irish mixture) are right in trying to get their voices heard in the confused jumble of broadcasting. Neither having anything to do with the devotions of the people, it perhaps does not matter that the best they can hope for is to leave traces on a process of decision-making which disowns theology altogether.

IV

The pretence that politics is an affair of conscience is very seductive. It enables those who promote it to think well of themselves. It flatters those who support it, for they are told that they are virtuous too. And whatever the changes in manners which result in yesterday's scandals being today's respectabilities, people always like to be thought virtuous, it seems, even though they may shrink from any terminology they believe to be old-fashioned.

This is far from being altogether a bad thing, in political terms, for the survival of some form of collective prejudice is essential, for a society to survive – *any* society. The history of the prejudices now reigning in this country, and beyond, is at least as long as the history of Europe. In their present form these prejudices derive partly from the historical church, partly – and more largely – from post-Christian pagan sources which owe a good deal to ecclesiastical history. It is a commonplace that 'scientific' liberalism has more than a dash of Christianity in it, and that what is called 'humanism' is a post-Christian humanism. This makes the situation of the churches a rather complicated one, when they dabble in public affairs. The weaker heads in the ecclesiastical world are apt to see, in the 'rights' now bandied about so freely everywhere, an expression of what Christianity is 'really' about. More wily and sophisticated persons see a connection which may enable them to interest pagans in the doctrine of the church, which they assert is what the 'rights' are really about. Both are rearguard positions, so far as the historical church is concerned. They are a recognition that the churches are not among the socially or ideologically dominant forces, and that to obtain any sort of hearing in the public world they have to scream aloud – shouting with the best of them, so to speak.

Whether such loud and vulgar talk is possible, without denaturing the message they have to deliver, is for ecclesiastics to determine. If their predecessors spoke more genteelly, it is because they were more assured, socially, than can be the case today. 'A gentleman in every parish,' said Coleridge, singing the glories of the English establishment. That is not what we have nowadays nor, if we have, would the parson be listened to on account of such a social status, now discredited. Popes were – and as far as seems plausible, still are – much given to showing kings and other rulers that they should, in the last analysis, take their orders from the see of Peter – a point of view which Dante, and no doubt many others in that 'age of faith' as well as in less faithful ages, found to be a detestable enormity. The claim is merely the extreme example of the church – or its ecclesiastical establishment – keeping its end up with the world.

It is difficult to discuss these subjects without coming near to theological ground which I should wish to avoid and in particular to the whole range of questions about the nature of the church. Anglicans, as usual, have a disarming and ambiguous answer to begin with: 'The visible Church of Christ is a congregation of faithful men, in which the pure Word of God is preached, and the Sacraments be duly administered...' (Article XIX), but that stops no one arguing and indeed such arguments can be stopped only by Authority – politically an aberrant notion, at least in our time; the notion of an authority defining itself is utterly unacceptable. Be that as it may, the church which 'keeps its end up' in the world, whether Roman, Orthodox or Protestant, does so by the most human of means. The judge in this matter is the world, which makes no bones about *its* own authority, however its constituent elements may bicker among themselves as to their share of it. What matters to the world at large is its prejudices, what matters to the political world is its votes. No doubt the Pope's advertising man, Mark McCormack, is bringing fresh enlightenment to the Vatican on these matters. The antics of men in funny hats, or in funny collars, and the degree to which these men pretend to or actually can influence the views of their constituents, are what matter to the world. The theological subtleties adumbrated in Article XIX are beside the point. And when the authorities of an ecclesiastical institution – whether Papal, Rastafarian or Anglican – speak on a matter of public interest, it matters neither more nor less than the support they can command. So the more long-lived of these institutions tend to take on the social characteristics of the age. The Papacy has been princely and vicious in its time; it now wears an altogether blander look and speaks of rights – a word whose meaning changes with the times. E.J. Delécluse in his *Journal* for 23 February 1826, tells how a young Roman who killed a prelate was *'émancipé'* by Leo XII; he was formally given some extra years (he was only 18) so that he could enjoy the benefits of capital punishment for which the lower age-limit in the Papal State was then 21. Emancipation in this sense has no doubt gone out of fashion in the Vatican.

The point is that a church, whatever its theology, must when it acts on the public scene take on the role of a political institution. The fewer practical responsibilities of its own it has, in any political field, the more respectable it will look. In the twentieth-century world, there has been a tendency for churches to confuse playing a sort of game with opinion with the prophetic role which they must be supposed to exercise without violence to their more intimate nature. Anyhow, even a genuine prophecy is only an opinion, when it comes on to the modern political scene. In emitting opinions churches are in some sort playing a political role; they are bodies elbowing around in the state and trying –

like how many others! – to give events a twist which the unassisted electoral processes have failed to give them. Institutions engaged in such manoeuvres are a normal part of our society. The most notable are the TUC and its constituent unions, and if general secretaries have an election at some point in their career to give them democratic legitimacy, they may in time come to speak with as much remoteness as any archbishop or cardinal.

With the Christian denominations which are now, so to speak, part of the advisory crowd on the public scene there are also Jews, Muslims, and Hindus to be considered. The Jews have been long established socially, so it is most often as a voice of conscience that they are heard, like the various Christian bodies. Because Muslims and Hindus – as groups, though of course by no means always as individuals, many of whom know all anyone need know about British ways – are still in the process of assimilation, they tend to appear in the public mind rather as racial than as religious groups. As far as they are public voices of conscience, they naturally couch their appeal in the vague generalities of 'world opinion' rather than in the traditional (near-Christian) language of this country. Muslims and Hindus have a delicate problem they in a manner share with Jews and Roman Catholics; that is the temptation to invoke the help of their brothers across the seas. While no one would wish to suppress this activity entirely, it has its dangers, for those who use it are helping themselves to an extra weapon not available to the ordinary irreligious, or even Protestant, native. This tends to direct attention away from the channels available to all citizens, and to encourage thoughtless people to represent the ordinary difficulties of social life as intolerable oppressions that call for the intervention of outsiders.

There is a danger that groups with what might be called allies of conscience in other countries will exercise a disruptive influence by claiming to be not merely a domestic body seeking political influence but the representatives of a collectivity which can assail the elected government waving the banner of a foreign power, however discreetly. We are so used to this sort of thing that the impropriety of it, in democratic terms, easily escapes people. Things were clearer on the less crowded stage of the nineteenth century. The first Roman Catholic peer to take his seat in the House of Lords delivered himself of a defence of drinking the Pope's health before the Queen's. Surely this is a piece of ill-manners, or a mild sedition? It was certainly in contradiction with Lord Arundell's main thesis that the Pope's authority was of a wholly different *kind* from the Queen's.

V

The Anglicans view of politics, which has been so inconsiderately overturned by the authorities of the Church of England without their putting anything in its place or, to all appearances, having any idea what they were doing, is one of great depth. The product of much conflict, it is characterized by a great – some might say excessive – serenity. The Church of England has always been 'unquestionably loyal', as Bishop Ken said, and I cannot, myself, see anything wrong with that.

The Church of England is the Church in England – that is the basis of the Elizabethan settlement which, admittedly, is too *geographical* in conception for the modern world, to say nothing of its being too undemocratic. The claim is essentially the same as that which the Roman church still makes, when it refuses – as at critical points it always does – anything like full recognition to other churches. There has been an immense Roman propaganda, since the sixteenth century, to deny the historical continuity of the English church, and this is no place to continue the brawls which this has occasioned. In any ordinary sense of the word 'truth', the detail of all historical claims to continuity, from wheresoever promulgated, is riddled with lies anyway, which is not to say that there are not degrees of truth in this matter. Be that as it may, the old Anglican conception, like that of the wider medieval church, was that everyone was a member of the church and of the commonwealth, of the spiritual and the temporal communities. The difference is that before the Reformation there was an appeal to Rome, supposed to be upon spiritual matters, though most often the differences were on political and economic matters in which it was handy for the ecclesiastic concerned to call in a European authority who was as much a prince as any of them, whatever else he was or wasn't.

After the Reformation, the appeal stopped with the sovereign, and in course of time the control of the sovereign was taken over by constitutional processes – ultimately by the democratic controls we know. Throughout this process the Church of England had its ups and downs, including the years 1645-60 when it was an illegal, underground organization. As it chugged on after the Restoration, with more or less absurdity and decreasingly general acceptability, it remained, theological niceties apart, *the* Church in this land. It occupied the historic buildings; it baptized, married and buried most of our ancestors; for years it doled out the social security and in very recent times it was the rag-bag to which all ordinary soldiers not claiming some special dispensation were presumed to belong. Its ordinary members did not have the feeling of belonging to something special, but to something ordinary; they were the non-peculiar people. As such, they vaguely supported the establishment and were faintly bolshie about it. They were far from feeling any special duty to agree with the vicar, still less the bishop, and as for clinging together in a gang, in the way that non-conformists of various kinds, including Roman Catholics, might do, that never entered their heads. The slightly flabby tentacles of the church stretched out into the ordinary population, and it was by no means clear where they stopped. Of course this state of affairs has at various times been regarded as theologically scandalous by more than one party in the church, but they have only been parties and the ordinary untheological Englishman did not think a lot of them. With the sharp decline in the intellectual calibre of the clergy, which I am afraid must be admitted, its mere failure to recruit any sort of reasonable share of ordinarily able people, the strong intellectual case for the soggy middle – the historical case – fell by the wayside. It began to be thought that all intelligent people would be content with a new mixture made up largely of the follies and vanities of opposed and vocal ecclesiastical parties. This is, roughly speaking, the rubbish now enshrined in the Alternative Services Book.

What we have now, instead of a *via media*, is a sort of canting conspiracy of the more superficial elements in both ecclesiastical wings, a church of *opinion* rather than of fact and history. The bishops were careful to put themselves before the Queen, in The Alternative Service Book, for the first time publicly showing their jealousy of their Roman brothers. The political implications of this have been passed over in complete silence. Might it not call in question the propriety of the establishment? When at the last Synod a back-bench cleric put down a motion in favour of disestablishment, the bishops and whatever other authorities manipulate the strange body shuffled it to the end of the agenda, so that it should not be discussed. But of course the issue is there, and not only in the queer little display of pique over precedence. The whole tone of the Church of England is now that of a sect; we hear that 'the church thinks this' or 'churchmen think that' – news indeed to most ordinary members of the church, who did not think they had handed their opinions on public affairs over to those to whom God had no doubt given a special authority but not always, alas, a sense of the limits of their competence. The proper Anglican view of these matters, it cannot be often enough said, is that the church instructs its man, makes what it can of him in the circle of its devotions, and then leaves him to go out and play his part in the commonwealth as best he can and as his own peculiar knowledge and experience, whatever they may be, suggest.

Ecclesiastical authorities who think they can upset this sober and realistic arrangement without raising the question of disestablishment have got another think coming. They are claiming to be *a group with an opinion*, like any other, and like any other they will become. Why should Anglican bishops sit in the House of Lords, and not the Chief Rabbi? Is it certain that the religion of democracy most of them now favour – I mean that sentimentality about vulgar opinion which has come to be regarded as a sacred principle – will leave them in the House of Lords or in residences anachronistically called palaces? It is fortunate indeed that circumstances are such that the central question of the religion of the sovereign does not arise at the present time – as some enemies of the Church of England would certainly wish it to have done – for in the present utter disarray the Anglican contribution to the discussion would certainly be a pitiful one.

One hardly likes to suggest it, but perhaps the Anglican authorities should encourage some thought to be given to the political position of the church. They should start with the study of the not very trendy literature of passive obedience, to which some of the greatest names in the English church have contributed. It is the counterpart of the classic attitude of the English layman – the man who goes to church but forms his own opinions on public affairs including, of course, the public affairs of the church. George Berkeley was not a silly man, and what he had to say on the subject would make a good starting point. Was he not Bishop of Cloyne as well as being one of the greatest of English philosophers – in the older sense of the word English, no doubt? It would certainly sound strange, in a committee of Synod, to hear it maintained 'that there is an absolute unlimited non-resistance or passive obedience due to the supreme civil power, wherever placed in any nation'; or 'that loyalty is a Moral Duty, and disloyalty or rebellion, in the most strict and proper sense, a Vice, or breach of the Law of Nature'. Still, the experiment should be tried, and would surely do something for the sloppy intellectual atmosphere of the parent body.

The great refinement of the old Anglican system, in the matter of politics, is that it neutralizes entirely the position of the church as an organ of opinion, and any disposition of its members to form a gang, leaving it to the individual subject and citizen, oriented as far as may be by historical Christianity, to play his part in the commonwealth as seems good to him. No man can do more, and a man who takes a certain view of public affairs *because* a bishop or any other ecclesiastical authority so suggests, is doing less.

VI

It was asserted by Blackstone that Christianity is part of the laws of England, but it has to be admitted that things have changed since 1765. Nor is it true, as was suggested in the correspondence columns of the *Spectator* (11 July 1981), that it is 'far simpler... for civil authorities to consider the truth of any religious teaching rather than pretend they are all of equal worth'. The subject is not simple at all. Macchiavelli may be consulted as to some of the difficulties of past practice. In a modern democratic state, it is not the truth that matters, but the number of people who share any particular beliefs, whether deluded or not. And the *suprema lex*, whether in despotism or democracy, is the *salus reipublicae*, the mere continuation of the state, a matter rarely mentioned in decent society, like some other matters, but there all the same.

The practical problem, in England today, is how things should be arranged in a society which is residually Christian and which still has the church built into its non-representative institutions, but in which the representative institutions, where the effective power lies, are bound to ignore religion except as an element in opinion. As an element of opinion, Christianity, in a variety of forms, is still dominant, but there are Jews, Muslims and Hindus to be considered. There is also the vast mass of the population who now understand that religion no longer confers respectability and who therefore do not mind what happens to it, as well as the active minority who, following Karl Marx or Voltaire, or some other modern figure, think it should be abolished. All these opinions are equal, as far as our political institutions are concerned; even bishops, in their constitutional capacity, have to take account of this fact. The sovereign is not the sovereign only of Christians, still less only of Anglicans. Indeed while in the sixteenth century it was said that the religion of the people follows that of the prince, in the twentieth century we may take it that the religion of the prince, so far as it means anything constitutionally, will have to follow that of the people. If the whole population of this country were converted to Hinduism, the sovereign would certainly have to be a Hindu. In the present Babel, and the present atmosphere of (at least theoretical) religious tolerance, the natural arrangement is for the Queen to follow the historically appropriate branch of Christianity, as long as she does not make too much of it.

One aspect of the problem which is now commonly overlooked is the primitive role of religion as a means of binding a society together. Societies are bound by what they are bound by, not by what they ought to be bound by, and once there is serious competition between religious conceptions, none of them has a chance of being the binding force. One can understand why the deification of the Roman emperors, so absurd from our point of view, was proposed and finally accepted in a government which had extended itself to cover too many races and religions; and why when Christianity began to look like a winner, there was nothing for it but for the reigning emperor to take it over and make it the imperial religion. No form of this imperial solution is open to us. If there is, or is to be, a common religion, it can only be the religion of democracy, to which everyone more or less gives assent, and if it is not altogether understood by those who profess it, that is something it has in common with other religions. It has profound inadequacies – like the worship of the emperor – but like the worship of the emperor it can be practised side by side with another religion, except by persons of some scrupulosity or too much given to logic.

In a dim way, the Church of England perhaps understands this. But it is in a dim way. The Church has conceived the notion of re-modelling itself in accordance with the more recent religion. An awful matiness is to replace Christian charity. A vulgar expression, designed not to add to the hearer's understanding, but to limit the Church's message to what the hearer already knows, has replaced the traditional language of Anglicanism, and with it both the rigour and the subtlety of its whole historical heritage. The aim evidently is to *substitute* the religion of democracy for the Christian religion. This naturally will not work, or if it does, people will no longer be Christians, whatever they call themselves. Even if success goes only so far as infiltrating the religion of democracy and attempting to overlay it with Christian meanings – rather as the Church in the early imperial centuries treated various pagan practices, giving them a Christian excuse – that will not work either. The religion of democracy is not a pre-Christian thing into which posterior meanings can be injected, but a post-Christian thing which is made up of Christian-derived elements gone slightly askew; it is a form of heresy, however amiable.

The only possibility is to accept the religion of democracy as the state religion in which Jews, Muslims, Hindus and others can also participate. This is not without its dangers for the state, as the uncivilized form of Christianity – Christianity, that is, before it had received its Roman education – was dangerous. Since the fundamental tenets of the democratic religion cannot be denied one should leave them as they are and content oneself with the *de facto* accretion of other elements, the most necessary of which is a profound respect for our local institutions and in particular for the government by the Queen in Parliament. Respect for the operations of this system has been eroded by the proliferation of international institutions which have their importance in their place but which are not to be regarded as alternative authorities.

The notion of a national religion, to which newcomers of all kinds can accede and which the native population more or less alienated from Christianity can recognize, is bound to be regarded as rather scandalous, and I do not propose to continue the argument beyond this point at the moment. I will however venture an Anglican comment. It is that the Church of England would in this conception of things, be free to be true to its historical mission as an 'unquestionably loyal' religious body which did not seek to influence governments except by bringing up Christians who would then exercise their own judgement in the affairs of the commonwealth. It would be free also to use the full measure of its riches – not least the Authorized Version and the Book of Common Prayer – to make a critical impact on the blowsy world of the late twentieth century, instead of aping the manners of that world as it seeks now to do. As for its traditional politics, they are not merely innocuous, they are manifestly favourable to the well-being of every man, woman and child in the country, whether of immemorial English stock or recently arrived from Central Europe or from Central Africa. Do they not centre – so far as this world is concerned, and this world is the world of politics – on the wish that the sovereign – the Queen in Parliament – should be granted 'in health and wealth long to live' and that she should be strengthened so as to 'vanquish and overcome all her enemies'? What citizen of the United Kingdom, with the minimum of benevolence towards the country, can wish for less?

*Overheard by God**

That an omniscient God should hear what we say is perhaps not a very novel or striking idea. We thought it was so. To be 'overheard by God', however, suggests something more – or perhaps something less. For it implies that God has no right to listen, as if he were some eavesdropper like Mercury, rather than the God of Judaeo-Christian tradition. It is certainly some sort of comic figure that A.D. Nuttall starts off with – a reading spirit, it seems, for

> this study begins with an intuition that for much of our older literature one may suppose the presence of an extra (inhuman) reader: that which is written for man is always and necessarily read by God. The bourgeois marriage of poet and reader which now dominates literature and criticism was once infiltrated by a third party.

– a curious way of putting the matter: most said he was there all the time. In any case, the ability to read must be so small a part of omniscience that the sally gives a false orientation at once. For the God of George Herbert was not a textual critic but the one to whom 'all hearts are open, all desires known, and from whom no secrets are hid'. Though Professor Nuttall imagines that Herbert 'would fight like a tiger against every word' he has written about him, my own view of the matter is that though he might not have agreed, he would have been benign.

Nuttall helpfully tells us, on the penultimate page of his book, that he writes 'as one brought up by unbelieving parents in an unbelieving culture', and 'true to that nurture and that culture by mature conviction'. A conservative of unbelief, evidently, and a chip off the two old blocks. This shows: indeed the book illustrates at many points the fact that while those with some Christian training come without difficulty to share in our sceptical

* A.D. Nuttall: *Overheard by God: Fiction and Prayer in Herbert, Milton, Dante & St John.*

tradition, which is after all post-Christian, those who have been shielded from the Christian faith find it hard to know what they have missed. It is not that Nuttall has not read big books on the subject: he has read in particular some of Calvin. But it is clear that he thinks of the Christian religion as a series of propositions to be assented to (or not) rather than as a reading of the facts of life. He makes all too much, in considering Herbert, of a few propositions of Calvin, and all too little of Herbert's way of life and his ordinary devotions. To put it no higher, the Book of Common Prayer and Herbert's own *Country Parson* throw as much light on the poems of *The Temple* as *The Institutes* could do.

Whereas Nuttall's mind tends to work like a computer, of two alternatives accepting one and sending the other into limbo, that is not the case with Herbert's or indeed Dante's. (There is a chapter on the third canto of the *Paradiso*.) Herbert cannot be caught out by the paradox of 'Nay, even to trust in him was also his' because that paradox is at the heart of the Christian religion. Nuttall says 'it paralyses both poetry and prayer'. But the facts, however disconcerting, are that prayers invoking the same sort of trust have been used through centuries and that Herbert, paralysed though he is said to have been, did write *The Temple*. It would be unkind to take up Nuttall's suggestion, elsewhere in the book, that his own 'line of thought... is that of a fairly bright schoolboy of sixteen', but perhaps he is sometimes a little too smart. He has an interesting discussion of polite plural-for-singular pronouns ('they' as well as 'you'), and illustrates it from Wyatt's marvellous 'They fle from me that sometyme did me seke'. We are asked to believe categorically that 'the reference throughout is... to one girl': which is perhaps pushing a good theory a little too hard. When we find that a reading of St John's gospel has led Nuttall to the conclusion 'that Jesus was mad', perhaps we are entitled to think that he is too full of his own fleas to be a very good critic.

However that may be, this book, which is careful up to a point and clever to a point somewhere beyond that, does raise important questions as to how far a lack of contact with the historical church is already making it difficult for people to read the older literature – and it is of course the whole fibre of the literature that is threatened, not just the overtly religious parts. One would, for example, hardly begin to get the feel of Swift if one did not understand something of his roots in the church, and Chaucer and Shakespeare themselves must lose some colours for those quite outside the frontiers of historical Christianity. The cultural depravity of the churches themselves is, of course, doing much to encourage the dissociation between them and literature. If only the Authorized Version of the Bible could be read in all schools, as it was until recently, that would be something; it ought, indeed, to provide the basic education in English. For those who are studying English literature in sixth forms or in universities, some acquaintance with the Book of Common Prayer should be compulsory. This is bound to raise hackles among those for whom the book is to be classed as reactionary reading, but they should be encouraged by the fact that the Church of England apparently now hates it.

Martin Browne and Religious Drama

To a young man who had known the earlier work of Eliot as a revelation, of a kind which is hardly possible after the age of twenty, the publication of *The Rock*, in 1934, brought a puzzling impact. Any new work from this august hand could not be received without a respect not free from awe. On the other hand a first reading of the new text displayed the demi-god walking with a more ordinary allure than one had thought possible. My predisposition in favour of Eliot was so great that this fact itself passed for a minor revelation, as I suppose it was. There was that awful prose dialogue, and I hardly noticed that in the 'Prefatory Note' Eliot had tried hard to dissociate himself from some of it. My reaction anyhow was astonishment, then puzzlement, that the exponent of a magisterial discrimination had allowed such talk in his neighbourhood. I was sufficiently apprised, from *Ash Wednesday* and the pages of *The Criterion*, of Eliot's ecclesiastical interests, and was perhaps more prepared than some of my contemporaries to think that these were not in themselves a subject for derision. I knew nothing, however, of 'Anglican circles' of any kind. Eliot's Christianity was an intellectual possibility, merely, seen without the supporting social network. Some of the choruses of *The Rock* yielded their own rhetorical intoxication, even if it was a less acute pleasure than was to be had from *The Waste Land* or even *The Hollow Men*. There was the novelty – to me – of the choral speaking, and here and there verses which seemed proper enough from the lips of the London poet:

> I journeyed to London, to the timekept city,
> Where the River flows, with foreign flotations.

Too many things were happening at that time for me to consider the new techniques and the new tone – or the new preachments – very coherently, and the greater polish of *Murder in the Cathedral* (1935) must have been vaguely reassuring. In retrospect one might say that, despite all the polish, despite all the literary accomplishment – which Eliot's verse never lost – *The Rock* and *Murder in the Cathedral* represented a coarsening in the mind of their author, and a coarsening of his versification.

What was supposed to be happening – and this no doubt deflected the reader's mind, as such generalities do – was the revivification of the poetic drama. In the events which were supposed to constitute this process, the late E. Martin Browne played an important part. The 'Prefatory Note' says that the scenario of *The Rock* was written by Browne, 'under whose direction . . . and submissive to whose expert criticism', Eliot had written the choruses and dialogues. That was a beginning for Eliot. He had been brought in, at Browne's suggestion, to write a 'play' (his own inverted commas) to raise money for the Bishop of London's Forty-Five Churches Fund – a request which his long-standing interest in the drama must have disposed him to comply with. No doubt his enthusiasm for his relatively new-found Anglicanism was also a motive; it was as if he had been asked to open a bazaar. George Bell, the Bishop of Chichester, who did more than anyone to make drama respectable in church, already had his eye on Eliot.

Martin Browne's book is enlightening on such matters as well as on his own background and that of Henzie, who contributes to the book though she died in 1973. Martin himself died while the book was being prepared for publication. Henzie may well have been the real theatrical motive force in the 'Two in One' the couple were. 'If Martin had married another woman', she says, 'he would, I believe, have had an utterly other career. Dog-collars and gaiters . . .' Martin himself says: 'I had always taken it for granted that I should ultimately be ordained.' He was at Eton. At Oxford his 'centre for both instruction and worship became Pusey House'; there was also the OUDS. Then there was a period – with Henzie – of 'workers' education' centring on the Folkhouse in Doncaster, followed by years in the Carnegie Institute of Technology in Pittsburgh, before 'George Bell's call' came for him to be Director of Religious Drama in Chichester.

The poetic drama had been revived before; indeed one might say that it had been intermittently revived ever since it actually existed, in the days of Shakespeare and Jonson. The success and novelty of the Restoration was really the comedy in prose, which had its own succession. The nineteenth century left a dead weight of more or less un-produceable poetic plays to fill the less-read pages of the collected works of respectable poets. If we now consider that there was no poetic drama in the earlier twentieth century – unless you allow Yeats – this is not because no plays were written then; they were written in plenty. Gilbert Murray's translations of Greek plays were even a success at the box-office. The peculiarity of the new movement was its association with religion: and religious drama had, to all intents and purposes, existed only in the Middle Ages. If Eliot had not been enrolled, the new squib would have been as damp as any of the others. If Eliot's appetite had not been whetted by *The Rock*, the impetus he gave the movement would have had no great force. But he had written a religious 'play' and wanted to write a play. It was Bell who invited him to write for the Canterbury Festival of Music and Drama, and so we have *Murder in the Cathedral* which, Eliot stipulated, Martin Browne was to direct. A success of a kind the play certainly was, and the role of the chorus was developed dramatically, in every sense of the term. If there was more of design than instinct in the management of the plot, as indeed in all Eliot's plays, that is hardly surprising in view of his lack of training in the theatre. A more radical difficulty, which affected the whole movement to promote a religious drama, was the lack of any widely and profoundly shared view of what the Christian religion was about. Eliot was certainly acutely aware of this, and that must account for the element of didacticism which is traceable not only in the *Murder* but in *The Family Reunion* and the later plays.

Eliot had long ago (in 1926) propounded the view that 'dramatic form may occur at various points along a line the termini of which are liturgy and realism'; the practical implication was that one should get away from Archer and Pinero. The difficulty about this theory was that the nature of the liturgical end of the line was obscure. A liturgy must have a public reference and a publicly apprehended, if not entirely explicit, meaning. This the Christian liturgy could hardly be said to have had, even in the 1930s. The most widely diffused conception of religion was that it was a matter of individual conscience. It is doubtful whether George Bell reflected profoundly on these matters, or even on the fact that, when the mystery plays were performed, they were the most appealing form of entertainment within reach. The subjectivity of religion, and the availability of other forms of public amusement, meant that the conditions for a religious drama, in the old sense, were simply not there. There had in fact been no such drama for four hundred years. A 'revival' there could not be; what was in question was the invention of a drama which could attract a demure middle-class audience, a few intellectuals who still had some notion what the Church was about, and ultimately parish parties. For Eliot his recruitment to the cause must have meant that his first incursions into major theatre took place under somewhat protected conditions.

Bell's initiative is said to have led to a 'great outburst of poetry and religion mingled in drama' in the 1930s and 1940s. Certainly some work was produced which would not have been produced without him. As an attempt to find a new way for the Church to address the world at large, the movement was a failure. 'Drama is still on the periphery of the Church's work, and no doubt will stay there', Martin Browne concludes. 'But the last half-century has seen them come together, for each other's good.' It would be nice to think so, and there may be something in it; certainly drama might affect the *presentation* of religion. Browne points to *Waiting for Godot* (1955-6) as a watershed for the theatre. This success was not merely a matter of technique. The bleakness of the play corresponded to something in the audience's apprehension of the world in a way that Eliot's re-hashes of sainthood and martyrdom did not. It was after this that the Church began that messing about with its liturgy of which we now have the disastrous results. In 1932 Bell, Browne and others agreed that 'the Authorized Version of the Bible was especially suitable for text as well as subject of religious plays'. *Autre temps, autres meours*? The real change is slight. The principle to which Bell subscribed shows no more understanding of style than has been shown by the authors of the Alternative Service Book, who thought that an alleged 'modern style' would bring home the bacon. The weakness is the mark of a profound intellectual fault. The defect, in 1932 as more recently, is in the Church's exposition of its meaning; if it could recover in that respect, style would look after itself. A liturgical drama requires a basis of common apprehension in author and audience, which means a bond of a kind we should be as likely to call political as religious. Such a bond cannot have a Christian character in a society in which theology does not speak a language which is intelligible to the secular world. Nor, in this state of things, can a liturgy be rewritten: to talk of making it 'intelligible' is either a laugh or a lie. Pending a new clarification of meanings, better try to understand what our ancestors were saying. And perhaps, meanwhile, we had better rely on such occasional insights into the truth as we may get from the odd dramatist incidentally, rather than look for a bishop who will again revive 'religious drama'.

Religion and Public Doctrine

'People are fully alive to the danger of superstition in priests', wrote Lord Salisbury in 1876; '... in course of time they will find out that... professors may be just as bad.' They have found out; that much progress must be allowed to the past hundred years. The question whose prejudice is bigger than whose, of course, remains, not only as between professors and priests, but between members of these classes severally. It is revealed by Maurice Cowling in *Religion and Public Doctrine in Modern England* that this 'profoundly normative' back-biting goes on even among professional historians, however much we may have been inclined to believe in the objectivity of their studies and the evenness of their tempers. Beneath the 'placid malice' of professional history, we are told, 'conflict is continual, in magazines, lectures, supervisions, appointments committees and books, between four or five world-views which are not compatible with one another'. So much for our illusions, if we had them.

It cannot be often, however, that in embarking on 'an extensive work' of history the author gives us four hundred and fifty pages designed to elucidate the point of view from which he will be writing. That is what we get here. For this volume is 'preliminary' only. The main work – in how many volumes, we are not told – will be a history of 'the public doctrines which have been propagated in England in the last century and a half'. It cannot be said that the notion of 'a public doctrine' has yet emerged with utter clarity. We are told it is something which 'adumbrates the assumptions that constitute the framework' – rather on the lines of the House that Jack built – 'within which teaching, writing and public action are conducted'. More explicitly: 'In England all participants in the public realm have had a doctrine, whether they have known it or not. Almost all of them have had a doctrine about England, whether the subjects they have written or talked about have been English or not.' That more limited notion I begin to understand, or I think I do, though it does not achieve articulation in the present volume. And although what we have here is 'an examination of the author's relation to the events of which the main work will provide a history', it is a little difficult, in the absence of that main work, to have more than an impression of what events are indicated. They lie, clearly, in the field of those changes of which one aspect is the replacement of Christianity, in greater or less degree, by doctrines which are potentially or actually anti-Christian. What is before the reader is 'a discussion of thinkers who have helped' the author to understand the significance of the history with which he proposes to deal.

A curious bunch they are, these thinkers who have influenced him – curious as a bunch rather than as individuals. The first is A.N. Whitehead, whose conception of religion was everything that might be expected from a man of his generation who was the son of an Anglican clergyman, educated at a public school and Trinity College, Cambridge, and who as mathematician and philosopher collaborated with Bertrand Russell. It is a good touch of Maurice Cowling's to comment that 'Whitehead's respect for religion was spoken of with respect'. Cowling's second influential thinker is Toynbee, one of those boring minds which must be employed somehow – a man who chose a subject so vast that he evaporated into it, taking the world with him as he thought, though fortunately a few myopic people were left carrying on below. Toynbee was against any such notion as 'the exclusive nature of Christian claims', and may be said to have provided the theoretical basis for the Archbishop of Canterbury to approach the Ayatollah Khomeini as one religious leader to another, as well as for much more that eminent clerics get up to these days. Whitehead and Toynbee, we are told, were the baggage Cowling took to Cambridge as an undergraduate in 1943 with – rather oddly, it seems to me, for the time of day – scrapings of 'Belloc, Bergson, Shaw, Wordsworth, Macaulay and Carlyle'.

In his undergraduate period, which was split by three and a half years of army service, Cowling underwent the wholesome influence of 'Three Anglican Reactionaries' – Canon Charles Smyth, Kenneth Pickthorn, and the Edward Welbourne who became Master of Emmanuel – then of Eliot and David Knowles. The next phase of Cowling's opinions is represented in a third part of the book by Butterfield, Oakeshott, Collingwood and Churchill, all regarded as more or less subversive. The final phase and the fourth part of the book present us with Kedourie, Waugh, Salisbury and Enoch Powell, together with some fifty academics

– from Stubbs to Edward Norman – whose biographies provide a rich fringe of footnotes.

It is an extraordinary performance, and surely a laborious and somewhat inelegant way of establishing 'the existence, and the importance of a field of study'. I cannot but wish that Cowling had instead introduced his forthcoming history with a single essay in which he would have drawn the various strands from his authors into a statement of his own conclusions. What he is concerned with is 'a reaction to the realization that a post- or anti-Christian doctrine not only exists but has gained ascendancy'. There must be people for whom this realization is a matter of astonishment but they represent a somewhat modest level of sophistication, given the intellectual history of the past four hundred years. The bite is in Cowling's qualification that the ascendancy has been achieved in the era of 'universal suffrage and universal education'.

These developments have of course changed the operation of public doctrine in every field, and in every field that is a matter of scandal to some. There is no reason to quarrel with Cowling's assertion that 'Christian Conservation is... an instrument of investigation, a tool with which to approach the foundations of modern thought and the limitations of modern thinking', but it must be added that it is a useful tool just in so far as it manages to say something about these matters in terms which mean something to those who do not share the general view of the world it implies. This has, presumably, always been the problem of Christian apologetics.

The doubt which assails one, at this stage of Maurice Cowling's exercise, is whether he has that degree of openness of mind which successful apologetics require. The vulgar *will* believe that if they are to subscribe to Christianity it ought to be true in some sense of what they ordinarily mean by saying that things are true, and there is a huge task to be undertaken by theologians before that can widely be the case. Meanwhile, many of those who 'profess and call themselves Christians' – in the modest phrase of the now discarded Prayer Book – naturally stretch out their hands to supports they believe to be publicly recognized as valid, including some of those which Edward Norman and others think they have the best of reasons for denouncing. For public recognition is one of the most powerful criteria of the truth, the ability to see a church by daylight being something, after all. In a profound sense, the truth is what we would all agree about if only we could be made to see it. Cowling's collection of mentors leaves one uneasy. It is not only the disproportion of academics, one might say of Cambridge men; it is also the curiously hedged sensibility, and in particular of social sensibility, suggested by the prominence of figures more or less acceptable in a fairly closed middle-class world, who in spite of their worthiness and abilities, must be classed as less than first-rate by any wider standards, though there are, admittedly, also such people as Oakeshott and Kedourie. And what are we to make of a man who finds in Waugh illumination on the relationship between religion and society? Or who finds that Enoch Powell demands attention in this first volume as he will undoubtedly demand it later? What strange orientation makes Cowling see Churchill's influence on what the English 'wished to believe about themselves' as brought about 'to a far greater extent through his books' than 'by his public presence'?

There is a certain bookishness about Cowling's approach to subjects which call for a wider sensibility; in the case of Eliot, his understanding of his subject is defective not only through lack of sympathy but through lack of information. It cannot be the case that Eliot 'had begun to pick up Maurras' in the 1920s, as 'in the thirties he picked up Christopher Dawson, Demant, Mairet, Maurice Reckitt and Karl Mannheim'. The influence of Maurras was incomparably more radical than that of the others, and it must date from the year Eliot spent in Paris around 1910. The reference to the 'Rev.' Maurice Reckitt and the casual allusion to Philip Mairet suggest that Cowling has some more work to do, before his second volume, on the later Eliot's connections with the world of Anglican sociology. The real trouble, however, seems to be that, in seeing Eliot primarily as 'an influential variant' of a 'type of Anglicanism' – that represented by the 'Three Anglican Reactionaries' – Cowling has missed most of the man, as a curious piece of pontification about the poems shows that he has entirely missed the poet. (The poet he really warms to seems to be the pre-war Enoch Powell whose work 'registered the resigned, masculine gloom of the Trinity ethos'. Perhaps that is unfair, but clumsiness about poetry is significant in the elusive studies Cowling is attempting.)

That the Christian religion, at any rate in its public manifestations, is in decline in England as in other Western countries is hardly deniable. There are those who manage to see improved private devotions as counter-balancing the overt decline, but they are rather like those who saw an increase in 'moral influence' which was to follow the demise of the Empire. It is certain that, unless Christianity has its own flourishing institutions, fewer and fewer people will find themselves in a position to know what that religion is. Not only have many individual pieties found a place within institutions of a certain worldliness, but the most recessed and fugitive devotions are strictly unthinkable without such institutions. Someone has to do the dirty work. So the question of public doctrine is very much a question of institutions, and of 'a doctrine about England' much more explicit than anything that emerges from Cowling's first volume. The recession from Christianity which Salisbury witnessed, not without a thought for 'the holders of accumulated capital', has gone far since his day and has been widely welcomed. The universities and most schools have been completely secularized, or carry residual traces so faint as not to affect their general character. The rate of dissolution has been much accelerated by the media, now really the *only* institutions which have massive public influence, and which convert religion as well as political events, 'the arts', and all particular knowledge and expertise to the purposes of a power-ridden entertainment world.

Edward Norman has spoken of the 'withering away of the ecclesiastical parts of the constitution', which is evident enough; the question now is rather whether, under the influence of pseudo-populist conceptions (all populist conceptions are inevitably pseudo), the whole constitution is now being dissolved. The processes involved in that, too, may be sure of a wide welcome, though it does not follow that they will bring in an age of contentment.

There is a sense in which those well-established middle-class university gents, Toynbee and Collingwood, may be said to have been prophets of the dissolution now being effected by the media, which are really superseding universal suffrage as a solvent. Toynbee's whole conception of a 'unified world' and 'superseding nationalism' were such as to distract attention from the actual problems of now and above all of here, and one may regret that he did not choose some field of operation less malleable than history. Perhaps – as he might easily have done – he should have become a civil servant, when he could have used his industry on no worse objective than plans even more grandiose than those of the late Lord Armstrong for the inflation of Whitehall. Collingwood's 'infinite world", in which every fact was included,' is merely an unrestrained version of the media-man's lie about bringing the world to your doorstep. As Cowling says, 'the claim that universal history was essential in theory and impossible in practice raised important difficulties'. Well, it would. Similar difficulties have been encountered by more practical post-Hegelians, who have by sleight of hand managed to read the universe in the light of their local and immediate interests, and indeed the universality claimed for Christianity poses comparable problems.

A local habitation and a name are, however, of the essence of Christianity, though its exponents are always rushing off into more or less wild abstractions, and 'a doctrine of England' is not necessarily an absurdity. Such a doctrine was expressed in the Book of Common Prayer, which saw 'this realm of England' as a sovereign place which admitted the wiles of no foreign administration. As regards the general affairs of the kingdom, this did not need to be spelt out; as regards ecclesiastical affairs, it was thought necessary to make the point that 'the Bishop of Rome hath no jurisdiction'. Religion being merely the truth, as revealed, there seemed no reason to suppose that it would be better understood across the Channel or across the Alps, and indeed there was thought to be some evidence to the contrary. This did not mean that the King or the Archbishop had replaced the Pope; it meant simply that the Pope had not been replaced and was a superfluity. Of course various worldly matters which Rome had dealt with had to be dealt with somehow. The Church of England seems to have lost confidence in the arrangements that were then made, and many of her more innocent clergy and laity even talk as if Louis XIV did not meddle with ecclesiastical appointments and as if Rome itself was not a political institution.

The assumption of the Book of Common Prayer was the medieval one that members of the state were also members of the Church – a point which it was not unreasonable to reinforce at a time when the Reformation was bringing bloodshed into every country in Europe, through circumstances of which the affairs of Ireland are a late and lamentable example. A subject might 'wear weapons, and serve in the wars' – as Christians had always done – but only 'at the commandment of the Magistrate', and that meant under the English Crown. There were prayers for the King, as there had been before the Reformation, and as elsewhere Roman Catholics prayed for the Emperor. By the time of the slightly florid additions to the book in 1662, the prayer was that the King might 'vanquish and overcome all his enemies', and no nonsense.

A notable peculiarity of Prayer Book Anglicanism, as compared with what goes on at the present, is that it provided a milieu for the devotions of Englishmen, and for their instruction in the Christian faith, without providing a forum for anything that could be called 'Christian opinion'. The Englishman was expected to go out from the Church and play his part in the commonwealth as seemed best to him. We now have a Synod cackling on about this and that and pretending to give the opinion of the Church on various political issues – an unedifying display, though I am happy to say that I never met an Anglican who felt himself bound by what is said there.

There were, of course, some noises in Convocations and Church Assemblies in the past, but with the establishment of the Synod the Church of England has wilfully demoted itself from the station of a national Church, to which it is perhaps no longer called. Its voice has acquired a sectarian stridency. It is now only vestigially more in the commonwealth than one more organ of opinion, and a badly briefed one at that.

Having thus stepped down – out of deference, it must be supposed, to democratic opinion – the Church of England must find itself at a disadvantage as compared with more practised agitators, and it has failed to achieve the status of a dissident, without which much pressure cannot be exerted. Given the folly of many Anglican counsels, this may be as well; still, the advices of the authenticated dissidents are not always of the wisest either. The major ecclesiastical operator of this kind is the Roman Church, which has long practice in that role in this country and has long been fortified by an influx of Irish clergy. Its peculiarity is that it combines the role with a relatively authoritarian structure, and has a directorate outside the country and engaged in world-wide politics.

The politics have been given a new lease of life by a world in which the media favour the voices which address not so much *urbem* as *orbem*. No doubt the Papacy will burn its fingers with the democratic states as formerly with the Christian monarchies, and the media will in time make more use of their opportunities for destructive criticism in that quarter. Meanwhile, however, the Roman Church in this country is sitting relatively pretty. There are, of course, also the traditional English Protestant nonconformists, whose position is now much that of their parent

Church of England, if rather less confused. Then there is a host of more or less Christian sects of different ancestry, for the most part relatively undisciplined socially as well as theologically. There are the Jews who have a long and complicated relationship, not always the happiest, with the historical Christian churches, and who also dispose of international aids, though without formal organization. There are Hindus and Muslims, again with more or less informal relations overseas, with complicated social problems but with undoubted potential status as minority groups to be listened to.

It is difficult, in these circumstances, to see how a 'Christian conservatism', as adumbrated in this volume, can arrive unaided at 'a doctrine of England', however will it may be fitted to expose 'the limits of modern thinking' – by which appears to be meant that congeries of liberal prejudices which is the nearest thing we have to a consensus. A state which cannot pick and choose among the religions practised by its members is already in search of another religion, and ours may be said to have found one already, in democracy. As a system of belief – or of self-evident public doctrine – this at least has the advantage of being held by most of the population, including the vast majority who practise none of the traditional religions and know or care almost nothing about any of them. That the religion of democracy is neither more scientific than any other, nor guarantees the continuance of democratic institutions, must afford opportunities to discredit it, though they have been little used at present by Christian bodies. However, the prospect of an ideological battle for the control of the state cannot be said to be attractive, whether the assault comes from nominal Christians or from nominal atheists. The examples of charity offered by the Russian Revolution as by the Reformation and Counter-Reformation are discouraging. Better, it might be thought, to hang on to an erroneous public doctrine which has just happened, or not to have too much public doctrine of any kind, if that were possible.

It is perhaps not possible, for no political balance was ever held for long. But those who do not believe in the encouragement of rage may well hold that concern for public doctrine should, so far as may be, give way to an examination of the facts. If the Christian religion is true, then the creed is among the facts; if it is not, not. The Johnsonian Tory, in an age of demoted Anglicanism, should be content to exercise a more than Roman patience in waiting for the facts to be recognized and the Church in this realm re-integrated. There is some explaining to do before that can happen. Politically, this quite imaginary Tory will ignore democracy as a faith and give his attention to the facts of the constitution. In a world in which slipshod discussion of affairs has become a primary form of entertainment, there can be few grounds for optimism. None the less, the fact that all government is in its nature monarchic, and that it is modified and informed, not *per*formed, by representative institutions, might surely become more patent than it is. And for 'a doctrine of England' it would be better to substitute 'the facts of England' – complex and confusing, like all facts, but of their nature less hard to seize than those of universal history or 'one world', and so offering better hope of a realistic perspective.

The Archbishop's Travels

One could almost find it in one's heart to leave the Archbishop of Canterbury alone with his sorrows, as he awaits the Pope's visit. This little ecumenical occasion cannot be quite what he imagined. It may perhaps have the healthy result of bringing out the differences which the authorities of the Church of England have been trying to smudge ever since they were given their head in 1974. However that may be, a church of so many alternatives should not be altogether surprised if some people are unable to see that a multiplicity of differences points infallibly to unanimity. Not all have been sanctified in the coffee-bars of Synod. But, however it may be with these high theological matters, there are more sordid considerations.

That the Pope should pay a pastoral visit to his followers in England is clearly something he may do if he wishes. One might think that he risks confusing himself as well as other people by his taste for travel, and that he might be better employed at home in the Vatican, but that is for him to judge. That he should, while he is here, exchange some civilities with the Archbishop of Canterbury, even with the Governor of the Church of England, is reasonable enough. That the visit should be made the occasion for meeting leaders of other denominations, in order, in his flying visit, to get a slightly less misleading picture of ecclesiastical dispositions in these islands, is also no bad thing.

It is surely rather puzzling, however, that the Archbishop should lay on simultaneous visits by heads of the Anglican communion overseas, as if he should wish to say, not exactly, 'My church is bigger than yours' – which he cannot say – but that he is not just the Archbishop of Canterbury but a bit of a traveller himself, with friends he can visit in other countries, and so cuts quite a figure in the world-wide Church of his aspirations.

Hasn't it all got rather out of hand? A disintegrated church at home is not healed by fixing its gaze on distant shores and the residual politics of post-imperial times. And the Pope surely, for all his talents, will have his work cut out to get even a plausible tourist's picture of this country during his short stay. He has been to Africa, he has been to South America, to the United States, to Ireland; he is always keen to pop home to see how things are going on in Poland. No doubt he has other jaunts in mind. Surely on this occasion he had better concentrate on the United Kingdom? It is a puzzling enough place for those of us who live here, and the airborne businessman, in less exalted lines of business, does not always take in all that he needs to be able to listen critically to the propositions of his branch managers.

If the Pope knocks over the furniture when he is here we shall have to pretend, out of courtesy to a distinguished foreign visitor, that he has not done so, or that it doesn't matter. We could even forgive our own archbishop if, in the heady atmosphere of a clerical get-together, he injudiciously laid on too large and too miscellaneous a party. It is a big occasion and it is not likely to happen again, in his time. But the truth is that this confusion between local and international affairs has become part and parcel of the office of Archbishop of Canterbury, as at present conceived. It is not too much to say that, as things are, the executive head of the Church of England is so preoccupied with his more far-flung collaborators that the Queen's realm of the United Kingdom is small beer to him. This natural preoccupation with the widest dimensions of Anglicanism is understandable enough, for what is more flattering than to be a World Figure? But it is a drawback for the Church of England, the historic entity to which the see of Canterbury has been related since the days of Augustine.

All the most notable developments in the Church of England, in recent years, have been coloured, one might think excessively, by these international preoccupations. Of course there *are* international preoccupations, and someone has to attend to them, but even a good Foreign Secretary is not a substitute for a Prime Minister. The local sheep look up and are frankly puzzled. We like to hear about foreign parts, but we have our own parts. They have been left to wither. That is not how the Archbishop and those who aid and abet him would put the matter. But in fact, we have seen our Prayer Book thrown away, our superb version of the Bible demoted to a position of no importance, and a new sectarianism, which looks only to its own members, sweep over the parishes. Of course it is all in the name of holiness, like every other iniquity carried out in the name of the Church over the centuries – including the centuries before the sixteenth.

Let us pay no attention to holiness – or none to claims to it. It is, really, not the Anglican way. But now, one might say in all churches, not only in our own, the folly of sanctimonious claims knows no bounds. The degradation of current conceptions may be compendiously studied on the BBC's Sunday programme (at 8.15 am every week on Radio 4). In this ramshackle collection of what passes for religious news, not a week passes but some more or less ill-informed person is put up to say, with no authority whatever, that 'the church' thinks this or that about some fashionable event of the day. Politicians may be worried but, bless my soul, Christians know the answers! It is no sillier than some other programmes but it takes all the prizes for pretentiousness – unless, of course, one treats theological pretensions with complete contempt. One might suppose this to be the object of the organizers of the programme, but in fact one hardly believes them capable of such duplicity.

What is the local shepherd doing? Encouraging all this, as far as one can make out. It is, in fact, a natural outcome of the deliquescence of the Church of England, of which the abandonment of the Prayer Book has been more than a symptom. Bandaging their eyes and holding out their flabby hands far as they would go, the leaders of the Church of England have exhorted its poor browbeaten members to avert their eyes from their duty in the commonwealth of the United Kingdom and to join in whatever wild-goose chases are proposed for the improvement of other people. It is not that some of these causes are not as deserving of support as political causes are likely to be, but that the miscellaneous spokesmen who claim our adherence to them because we are supposed to be Christians have no special competence to judge of these matters. The largest element of competence required is generally to be well-informed, which in a world buzzing more than ever with half-baked rumours it is extremely hard to be. Another element is that members of the Church of England have a duty of loyalty no less than other people; if our leaders think otherwise, they have changed the character of our church without authority and without telling us.

It has long seemed to me that, with the loosening of constitutional ties which has followed the dissolution of the Empire and entry into the Common Market, England stands at a disadvantage as compared with other components of the United Kingdom – with Scotland, Wales, even Ulster, though that is a more dubious case. I prefer England to the late Empire, and I should like it to survive. But whereas the other components expect to be reckoned with separately, England has to make do not only with the institutions but the personality of the United Kingdom. We are supposed to like to be smothered. With the Church of England it is even worse. We are blotted out under the Anglican robes of the Archbishop. Why not promote him to the role of Pope (new style) in the Anglican International, and give us an archbishop who could keep his mind on England?

Admittedly this proposition has become more difficult now, with the publication of the report of the Anglo-Roman Commission. A 'universal primacy' sits better with a notion of national churches, holding all Christians in a particular territory, than with a gaggle of churches of opinion each scattered across the world and making for more or less disruption. But that would mean a universal diminution of the authority of Rome, and the assertion of the primacy of Canterbury over the see of Westminster.

Priests' Lib

'Few people,' said the *Mothers' Union Journal*, speaking of Harry Williams, 'can make being human more thrilling, more worthwhile, and more fun.' It is something to live down. It might be thought that a former lecturer in theology, now a member of a religious order, would have a better chance than most of doing so. The matter hangs in the balance, however, when one opens *Some Day I'll Find You: an Autobiography* at random to find that one is in that delicate territory in which saints have fun. The vicar of St Barnabas, Pimlico, here characterized as one of that exalted order, had it – loved it, in fact. When one learns that this vicar, on his birthday, 'used to give us all a lavish dinner at Kettner's', one may, without being a great connoisseur of the clergy, think that one begins to have some clue as to the sort of priest he was. It was in this parish that Williams elected to serve his first curacy. Open the book again, however, and one finds: 'I believe that the Religious (monastic) Life can be lived fruitfully only if those who enter it are constantly aware that they have done so, not because they are more spiritual than others, but because they are less so.' Perhaps the *Mothers' Union Journal* has not got the whole story. At any rate, one would have to read the book to find out.

The story that unfolds is a complicated one. Not that the narrative is at all intricate in design – it is, indeed, all bits and pieces – but the intended range of reference is wide. On the one hand, the book is, as the author says, 'a description of people and places' he has known. On the other hand, he has had troubles not of an ordinary kind, and this 'transposes the book into another key and makes it more like a pilgrim's progress'. The combination is not made any easier by the fact that the pilgrim has not only 'been lucky in often finding people amusing' but has – to judge by some of the trivial or even inane remarks which have somehow stuck in his memory – often been rather easily amused. That is no doubt a winning characteristic, within limits, in ordinary life, but it has dangers for the autobiographer. 'As a boy at home and at school people were not so amusing.' It is the way of the world, and it must be said that the ways of the world at large have had rather a small part in Williams's life, as recorded. For some years of his childhood his family were members of the English colony at St Malo, in the days when 'servants, food and drink were all cheap for English people.' 'But it was Cambridge without doubt that was the richest soil for amusement, since dons' – and Williams was one himself for a good many years – 'for all their intelligence, can frequently be possessed by folly, some of it positively sublime, some with an edge on it which the uninitiated might mistake for malice; while the *naïveté* of undergraduates can on occasion seem very funny if also very touching.' There were also those years at London churches which, to put the matter no more strongly, seem to have had rather special relationships with the world in which they were planted. Indeed it struck me, reading Williams's story, that in some respects the sober and workaday life at Mirfield, where he finally became a monk, was more like the ordinary laborious world than anything he tells us of his life before he went there. 'In Community you have to live at close quarters with people some at least of whom you will find temperamentally incompatible. You must be prepared to associate constantly with at least a few people who get on your nerves.' Just like the office or the Army, one might say.

Williams's father does not appear very vividly in his son's narrative: he seems to have been a sensible, perhaps slightly humdrum, naval officer who retired earlier than he would have liked, having failed to get his promotion. Mother is the dramatic figure of these early years. She seems to have been a pleasant, rather scatty lady who became less pleasant and more scatty after falling in love with a neighbour's son considerably younger than herself. In those far-off days the affair did not immediately – or indeed at all – lead to fornication, but there were inevitable domestic tensions which the naval officer bore with some stoicism. Mother, however, hardly had the temperament for philosophy, and she took to a militant form of Evangelical churchmanship: she became 'a keen Christian out and out for Jesus'. It was, no doubt, as her son suggests, a complication resulting from her feelings of guilt about the young man. She concentrated on this Clifford 'to make him, like herself, out and out for Jesus. Not only did he become a keen Christian but, before many months had passed, said he wanted to be a clergyman,' much to the annoyance of his parents who, however, in the end made the best of it and said that at least he should do it properly and go to Oxford. There was a Christmas party for local children at which Mother, unable to 'trust her French to give a religious discourse', instead 'stood silent and still like a *tableau vivant* of Britannia, except that, instead of holding a trident, her arm pointed to, and her hand touched, the crib in the most melodramatic of gestures. It didn't matter. The French children were clearly prepared for anything from people who were bourgeois, English and Protestant.' Harry records his mother's symptoms with what I suppose must count as filial piety. 'When praying her eyelids covered her pupils, but an area of white below remained uncovered. In this posture she would hold half an aspirin in a glass eyebath with a stem and call down upon it the divine blessing.' It was, Harry says, 'all very far from being unattractive'.

The family moved to Cranleigh where Harry went to school. Hardly surprising that, after the ravages of 'out and out for Jesus' Christianity, between the ages of ten and twelve he became very High Church. He invented an imaginary church of St Joseph's and All Saints, and a parish magazine to go with it: for this he wrote 'Vicar's Letters urging people to go to sacramental confession... to pray through the Virgin' and to recite Compline. He pored over a catalogue from Mowbray's which had pictures of 'candle-sticks and candles of all sizes, censers and incense containers, tabernacles, aumbries, pyxes, bottles with holy corks and holy spoons for holy oil, chalices, patens, crosses, crucifixes, statues of the Virgin, pries-dieux, copes, chasubles, albs, girdles, cottas, birettas, soutanes – the lot'. In a revealing and I think discerning phrase Williams describes these things as having 'a compulsive attraction as if they were a kind of ecclesiastical pornography'. Religion in the Senior School at Cranleigh seems to have been free of the excesses alike of Mowbray's catalogue and Mother's Evangelicism. Harry felt 'the sweet and attractive reasonableness of sober Anglican piety' by the time he left school, but somewhere inside him he had still 'a sneaking feeling that only people out and out for Jesus were really Christians.' No wonder he says he was 'in a religiously divided state'. One learns with relief that when he went to Cambridge he decided that he would go to college chapel on Sundays and that would be that: he would not have 'anything whatever to do with any religious concern – be it groups of pious people or of ordinands, or societies, or missions, or talks or anything'.

This precaution worked, in the sense that Williams's religious anxieties were put into what he rather aptly calls 'hibernation' and his undergraduate years were the happiest of his life. These must have been the immediate pre-war years, but there is no word at this point about the political anxieties of the period. It may be merely that the terms of reference Williams has chosen for his autobiography preclude any mention of them, but one wonders whether there was not an element of moral isolation about the author. How not notice the armies preparing on the other side of the Rhine? Surely this might imply a certain retraction from the world, a turn of mind which tended to excessive preoccupation with what went on inside the mind itself? When the war came Williams was declared to be medically C3 because of bad eyesight, and he was told that he would be called up only for home duties. So he reasonably enough availed himself of 'the permission given to ordinands by the Government to continue their training'. Wanting to get away from Cambridge, he went to the theological college at Cuddesdon, eight miles from Oxford. The last words from the Master of Trinity, then G.M. Trevelyan, were to the effect that as a clergyman it would be his duty to be 'a guardian of British culture and civilisation'. One can understand the author getting 'a great deal of amusement' from this, though one cannot but wish that the clergy of the Church of England had done a little better than they have lately done in this direction.

'Cuddesdon was Anglo-Catholic, but in a sober, restrained Anglican way.' They did not buy much from Mowbray's catalogue. They did, however, 'bludgeon' people – the word is Williams's – 'into the practice of sacramental confession' and encourage various forms of scrupulosity. Later reflections are so mixed up with the narrative, as elsewhere in this book, that it is hard to be clear how Williams viewed the place at the time. There is perhaps a hint in a curious story which exudes a horrible atmosphere of clerical fun. Three ordinands were in a bathroom, preparing for bed. One of the number was a future overseas bishop who was 'extremely self-conscious about keeping the rule of silence after Compline'. The third man indicated that he had an important message for this spiritually superior person, then loudly whispered 'Balls!' in his ear. There is a peculiar tone in Williams's comment: 'It was a supreme moment for which the only possible sequel was the recital of the Nunc dimittis.'

The next stop was St Barnabas, Pimlico, one of those Anglo-

Catholic town parishes where the clergy seem to be not so much from another world as from an altogether different part of this one. The vicar was not only a saint, as already reported, but 'a tremendous dear', and the social atmosphere must have had more than a touch of nineteenth-century Oxford and Cambridge clerical slumming. It is true that the vicar was so disillusioned with Anglo-Catholic frolics that he once threw a lace alb across the vestry floor, but the local 'dustmen, charwomen, roadsweepers and so on' – everyone seems to have been employed by Westminster City Council – would hardly have grasped the import of such a gesture. There was a certain wartime matiness to make contacts easier, but they cannot have been very easy for a curate 'stuffed full of ideas learned at Oxford and Cambridge' and temperamentally needing more shelter than most. Williams had even to be a scoutmaster, which must have been agony for him. He once took the boys camping in Berkshire, but was granted some respite from the burnt potatoes or whatever it was the scouts ate, for the vicar of this rural parish had been a chef at Claridge's. But then, it was a Trinity living.

Williams's second curacy was at All Saints, Margaret Street, near Oxford Circus. The congregation was 'entirely eclectic' – that's to say, All Saints wasn't really a parish at all. People came to listen to the music, odd ones popped in for confession. There seem to have been lots of jokes about religion, pulling the legs of the 'nauseatingly religious', and so on, while the clergy congratulated themselves that they were Cambridge men. You have to be a specialist to care for this sort of thing, or not to have some sympathy with the dull people who thought that to say that 'the only way to get through Holy Week was on champagne' was hardly becoming for a clergyman. It is surely a silly thing to say? Whatever it may indicate about the speaker's spiritual condition, it certainly indicates a lack of public reference. That such a place as All Saints is reported to have been should ever have been thought a proper place to train a young clergyman is grotesque. What has happened to that 'sober Anglican piety'? What has happened to the Church of England? But this, of course, is an institution that silly ecclesiastical clubmen are dogmatically *not* interested in, so long as they can giggle among the ruins.

Anyway, matured by these experiences, the young Harry Williams is offered posts at two theological colleges. These he turned down, but he did in the end accept an appointment at Westcott

House, a theological college in Cambridge, headed by Ken Carey who was no use at all 'if a young man was not particularly attractive physically and came from a lower middle-class background'. Here the aroma of clerical homosexuality begins to assert itself, with the complication of snobbery or at any rate a lack of the social sense which should be among the minimum requirements for the head of a theological or any other sort of college. After three years Williams was offered, and accepted, a fellowship at Trinity. He was home again. He found 'this friendly and congenial atmosphere almost painfully enjoyable', but – and here we are approaching the psychological difficulties which are crucial to the book – 'it often overexcited' him. He found that his feelings 'became too hectic for them to be unwound properly'. It is impossible to follow the subsequent course of events more than superficially. There was 'an increasing load of guilt', life was so 'pleasant', and fits of 'apparently uncaused terror'. There was a crisis of homosexuality: he 'fell in love with a colleague; totally, hopelessly and catastrophically in love'. His phobias mounted alarmingly. There was a complete breakdown, which left him under the hands of an analyst for some years.

What Williams says of the behaviour of the clergy towards him at this juncture is not reassuring from any point of view. 'They felt that they must be able to do something for me,' he records. 'So they wheeled out various pieces of ecclesiastical apparatus with the intention of using them for my good. They wanted to choke me with Holy Communion, to persuade me to make a good confession, to have me anointed with oil. When the clergy had tried out all these devices and saw that the effect was nil, they began to get shirty.' The Bishop of Ely anointed him in his private chapel, and celebrated Holy Communion, but all he got from this 'combined operation was severe ear-ache'. He reserved his confidence for his more or less non-Christian and certainly non-church-going analyst. Yet he says: 'if I never went to church or said my prayers' – as became the case with him for some time – 'there remained in me none the less a Christian insight without which I don't think I could have passed through the worst period of pain, when everything was a black nothing.' No doubt this is true, but it cannot be said that, as the story is told, any reader who is not already some kind of Christian is likely to feel that he should put himself to school.

When he was, by whatever means, 'raised from the dead', Williams began to consider 'what to do about sex' and during the next few years he 'slept with several men, in each case fairly regularly'. This was 'one central area' of his life in which he 'told all babbling churchmen to go to hell'. He 'fell deeply in love' twice after the disastrous affair that ended in his breakdown. He says: 'I longed desperately to share my life with another person, which for me had to mean another man.' In this he never succeeded. None the less, his last twelve years at Trinity were 'a very happy period indeed'. He was tutor and Dean of Chapel. This meant, as he says, that he 'was never entirely certain' what his position was 'in terms of ecclesiastical law'. At least he was not under the jurisdiction of any bishop, as apparently college chaplains in general are not: this is one of the curiosities of the Establishment, and presumably where there are no ecclesiastical superiors there can be no indiscipline. There is a good deal more about these Cambridge years, parties, fun with ginny clerics at a folk mass, the arrival of Rab Butler from the great world outside. Butler could be felt, it seems, as 'a bit of a threat' to the assumption that 'the scene to which you yourself belong is superior to all others'.

What does it all amount to? A mass of anecdotes, swirling around a figure who is perceived rather dimly making his way through them. One has, so to speak, to eat a lot of superbly served cucumber sandwiches at Trinity, to admire more than one wants to the moral superiority of the English community in Tangier and smile with a lot of liberated clerics, as well as read one's way through a number of re-statements of Christian belief which amount to precious little in the end. Williams makes great play throughout of being the enemy of every kind of churchiness, but really this can keep you going only if you have a large stock of churchiness – as he had – to begin with.

Richard Baxter

Richard Baxter wrote a lot of books; 'very sad ones', Swift said, in a marginal note in Burnet's *History of my own Times* (1724-34). Burnet had computed the number of Baxter's books at 'near 200'; Baxter himself admitted to 128; there was much besides these volumes, including 'more Prefaces to the Works of others, than any Man of his time' had blessed the world with. N.H. Keeble, who has probably by now read as much of this author as anybody, concludes that 'even a sober judgment might claim not only that Baxter was the most voluminous theological writer in the English language, but that there can have been very few people who have ever written more in English than he' (*Richard Baxter: Puritan Man of Letters*). That is something for *The Guinness Book of Records* but it does not in itself promise great happiness to the reader. One might ask, as with other records, whether such perseverance was really necessary.

Dr Keeble does not go so far as to assert that it was, but he gives us Baxter's apologia: 'Truly I have no Excuse or Argument but those of the Times, *Necessity and Providence.*' This of course had a suitable scriptural basis (1 Cor. 9:16), but the necessity laid upon Baxter 'to preach the gospel' hardly proves that he *had* to write 128 or 200 books; there might have been other ways of preaching, less tedious to posterity? To Baxter's credit, posterity was not what he was thinking about. He was concerned, like other practical men, with what seemed to him the needs of the moment; his accounting for his many books by the 'sudden occasions' that 'made them seem necessary at the time' suggests a sort of pious journalism. The ordinary comedy of authorship is not far away, when we find him complaining that 'every ignorant, empty braine (which usually hath the highest esteem of its selfe) hath the liberty of the Presse', and his critics a few years later sneering at the 'multitudes of books, which he *voides* continually', or saying, as Bramhall did, that 'Mr Baxter's happiness is, only by turning the cock to spout out whole pages in an instant'.

Whether or not the proliferation of Baxter's books is attributable to a divine necessity, there was certainly a market for them. Keeble points out that 'religious publications comprise nearly half the total of all books published in England at least until 1640' and they formed a large part of publishers' lists for long after that. Moreover, for most of the seventeenth century discourse about politics tended to take the form of discourse about religion, and indeed the affairs of the day were religious affairs, whatever other elements they comported.

Baxter was the son of a yeoman, a Shropshire lad of the most authentic kind, and he had a largely country education, not finished off at a university; he carried this native milieu around with him, rather prominently, till the end of his days. He is 'an elusive figure', as Keeble says, but only in the sense that he cannot be pinned down, that he does not fit readily into any of the main categories in terms of which we are accustomed to think of the controversial history of the seventeenth century. As a person, he is not so much elusive as invincible, solid, pious, homely, peaceable, stubborn – a large, sensible man who was a pain in the neck to many but a vaguely reassuring presence to more, wherever he went, and reassuring because in a manner he was vague, in spite of all his attention to details. Towards the end of his life he attained a beautiful complacency, having learned, after emitting so many millions of words in preaching, counsel and in writing, that men are 'loth to be drenched with the truth', which was of course what he had always offered them. He had learned that 'in controversies it is fierce opposition which is the bellows to kindle a resisting zeal', so he became apt, he claims, to keep his judgment to himself: 'never', he says, 'to mention anything wherein I differ from another, or anything which I think I know more than he; or at least, if he receive it not presently, to silence it, and leave him to his own opinion'. He had become like some wise old general secretary of a trade union, of the old school, who has had his battles in his time and is capable of more, but would rather leave fools to talk, and get on quietly with the job.

But what was the job, as Baxter saw it? He lived from 1615 to 1691, and so on the inside of the seventeenth century, and if 'necessity' is a strong word to use by way of apology for all his voluminous discourses, what he saw as the needs of those around him certainly determined the main course of his life, as far as he could himself direct it. There is something profoundly characteristic about what he tells us of his domestic arrangements, which his wife ordered with 'so great skill and decency':

> I had been bred among plain, mean people, and I thought that so much washing of Stairs and Rooms, to keep them as clean as their Trenchers and Dishes, and so much ado about cleanliness and trifles, was a sinful curiosity, and expence of servants time, who might that while have been reading some good Book. But she that was otherwise bred, has somewhat other thoughts.

No doubt it would have been better if the servants had been reading *The Saint's Everlasting Rest* instead of scrubbing floors, and no doubt Baxter was too well looked after to know much about such things. There is indeed, about the immense theological discursiveness of the seventeenth century, more than a suggestion of sober entertainment, of filling in vast tracts of time which would otherwise have been empty. There was after all no television, and respectable people did not go to ale-houses or join in the sports of what Baxter, as freely as any college-bred divine, called 'the rabble'. He was every inch a man of the godly middle sort, moderate in respect of everything except his passion for writing. Not a man of wild prophecies or sudden conversions, he was above all social and conciliatory, and wanted to go to heaven in as numerous a company as might be. He had a 'public mind'; thought much of 'the excellency and necessity of self-denial' and of 'loving our neighbour as ourselves', and hated 'the radical, universal, odious sin of selfishness'. He was at least as much concerned with the well-being of the commonwealth as with his own sanctity.

With such concerns, he worked out a conception of Christianity which was suited to those 'divers obscure persons, not noted for any extraordinary profession, or forwardness in religion, but only to live a quiet, blameless life'. Such people will live under any institutional form, it may be under any religion, and perhaps Philemon and Baucis are as near the mark as the unobtrusive members of English congregations. But for Baxter, in his place and time, what they seemed to need was a religion of 'The Creed, the Lord's Prayer, the Ten Commandments', and he came to feel that he 'had rather read or hear of them, than of any of the school niceties, which once so pleased' him.

And, for all his reflections about speaking Turkish and going to convert the Turks, it was the Church of England, if there could be such a thing, which seemed to him the centre of the commonwealth. This meant for him all the Christians in the kingdom, united in the merest Christianity or in what they could swallow. 'It is nothing but a Christian Kingdom consisting of a Christian supreme Power, and combined Christians as Churches governed by that Power.' As to Papists, it was not their 'errors in the doctrines of faith' that 'were their most dangerous mistakes'; the 'great and unreconcileable differences' lay 'in their Church tyranny and usurpations' – a point of view worth thinking about, though apparently little in the mind of the masters of the present incomprehensive Church of England. Baxter laid it down that 'all coercive power about religion', the settling of the privileges of the several churches, and keeping the peace between them, should be a matter for the ordinary government of the country, which he was still able to think of as 'all Christian princes and governors'.

Baxter, so full of good ideas and of the will to conciliate in particular situations, did not perform with great distinction at the Savoy Conference which settled the Prayer Book of 1662, though the same might be said of other participants, on both sides. Busy as ever, and one might say full of his own fleas, he arrived with his own version, naturally of enormous length, the 'Confession of Sin', said not by the people but for them by the minister, who no doubt could say it better, it being three and a half pages. Even with a more conciliatory bench of bishops, this would hardly have been the way to make progress. (The idea of an *Alternative Service Book*, with something for – nearly – every taste, had not yet been thought of.) An admittedly unsympathetic historian, Jeremy Collier (1650-1726), says of Baxter at the Conference: 'His talent lay in retiring to foreign distinctions, and misapplications of the rules of logic. But whether this involving the argument, and raising a mist, was art, or infirmity, is hard to determine.' However that might be, Baxter's view, as summarized by Keeble, was that 'by the will of God, the Savoy Conference failed: but to mortal eyes the prejudice and policy of the bishops ensured its failure'.

Baxter was convinced that he spoke for 'the greatest number of the godly' in England; in a sense he did, and not least in their muddles, their moderation, their pigheadedness, their dislike of ecclesiastical fripperies and theological refinements. Whether so much good sense is compatible either with full orthodoxy or with radical innovation, may be doubted, but it would be tolerant of both. It is, really, a political virtue, the essential virtue of a modern democracy, in which complacency has its part. It is perfect within established orders, and Baxter himself would have lived peaceably in any order that was incontrovertibly established. In the division of his times, he was thrown back on this notion of 'the greatest number of the godly', which in the real world raises questions as to who are the godly, and whether the greatest number of them are so godly as to be right. This makes problems of church order almost insoluble.

Keeble sums up Baxter's attitude by saying that he 'did not choose between rival positions because he "could not" but because he "would not"', which is convincing until one asks whether we can choose to be otherwise than we are. Anyhow the words indicate the diversity of Baxter's approaches to the problems of his day, and a 'rejection of partisanship' which is supposed to be more the temper of our own times than it was of his. What emerges from this study of him as a man of letters is not a writer who can be recommended, as such, to any but the most pertinacious, but a patient and practical man whose patience and practicality demanded a great deal of the same qualities in other people. Baxter was, after all, a man of more words than it takes to convince those who are willing to be convinced, and the others, as he came to see for himself, never will be. If this is the 'Puritan man of letters', as indeed it is, then, worthy though the model was, we need some other. 'To omit one warning, argument, reason, incentive, or illustration, or to neglect to counter a single error, temptation, or misunderstanding' was, for Baxter, as Keeble puts it, 'to run too grave a risk of failing the reader on the very point where he might need guidance'. The risk for such a writer is that the reader might fail him, as has happened to Baxter: 'Perhaps you may think I Digress from the matter in hand: But as long as I speak but for my Lord Christ, and for *Doing Good*, I cannot think I am quite out of my way.' But these are large claims, and Good is a dangerous thing to be sure you are Doing. Moreover, good writing has its own necessity, a humble one no doubt, but even a divine should think carefully before he asserts that he is excused from it.

Richard Hooker and the Ecclesiastical Polity

It is the temper of Hooker, more than any particular doctrine expounded in *Of the Laws of Ecclesiastical Polity*, which gives him his place as the wisest among the Fathers of the post-Reformation English Church. His gentleness, his reasonableness as against all the exclusiveness of fanaticism, his determination not 'loosely through silence' to allow things 'to pass away as in a dream' but to carry the past with him into the future – these are the qualities which, until recently, marked the course of the central stream of Anglicanism. Without closing his mind to what had happened, or was happening, in other times and places, Hooker was intent on what he saw as the needs of the England of his own time, and it was this comprehensiveness, combined with his acute consciousness of local affairs, which made him the classic apologist of *the* Church of *England*: not a sect, but the historic heir of the medieval church; not a world-wide federation of theological opinion, like contemporary Anglicanism, but the one Sun seen, as it were, through the mists of this island – the only way it can in truth be seen, from this perspective. Not for nothing was he accused, by a contemporary of his own, of preaching 'that the assurance of what we believe by the word of God is not so certain as that which we perceive by sense' – an accusation which he characteristically sought to explain rather than to deny.

Hooker was born in 1553 or 1554 in Devon, a county which, as Izaak Walton appropriately reminds readers of the *Life* (1665), 'furnished this nation with Bishop Jewel, Sir Francis Drake, Sir Walter Raleigh, and many others, memorable for their valour and learning'. He was thus a small child while, during Mary's reign, Protestants were being roasted at Smithfield and elsewhere. These horrors had, certainly, a profound effect on the attitudes of the rising generation, and contributed greatly to the popular impetus of Elizabeth's reign. A curious document of 1559 is Thomas Bryce's *Compendious Register in Metre* of those 'tormented and cruelly burnt within England, since the death of our famous Kyng of immortall memory Edwarde the Sixte' – a production which preceded Foxe's prose *Book of Martyrs* by several years. Month by month, from June 1555, through the terrible years 1555, 1556, 1557, 1558, to November of that last year when relief came in the form of the young Queen Elizabeth, Bryce records by name and place those who died, often ending his six-line stanzas with the name of a martyr, and always with the name of the Queen, as

> When Jone Polley was put to death...

or

> When Wade at Dartford died the death...

or

> When Jone Beche, widow, was done to death
> We wisht for our Elizabeth.

They had her at last, six days after the last of these Marian victims died. No wonder Bryce concludes:

> Pray we, therefore, both night and day,
> For her highnes, as we be bounde:
> Oh Lorde, preserve this branch of bay,
> And all her foes with force confounde;
> Here long to lyve, and after death
> Receyve our Queene Elisabeth.

The practical moral was the need for unity of religion, for the whole kingdom, under what could not fail to be, comparatively speaking, a benign monarch; and this, after all, is the subject of Hooker's great work, as it was one of the main domestic concerns of Elizabeth's reign. If the cloud of heresy charges was removed by the advent of Elizabeth, the political threat implicit in religious differences remained. It was in 1570 that the Pope excommunicated Elizabeth and released her subjects from their allegiance as far as in him lay – which was happily not very far. If this were not enough, Protestant fears were revived by 'the Massacre at Paris', as Marlowe called it – the murder of five or ten thousand Huguenots in Paris and other French cities on St Bartholomew's Day, 1572.

At this time Hooker was a young man of eighteen or nineteen, an age when he is unlikely to have been unimpressed by such events. The defeat of the Armada came when he was in his mid-thirties, and it removed the fear of foreign invasion, so giving solidity to Hooker's vision of an England in which Church and State lived as one, without either yielding to the other any part of its proper authority. There was not to be 'any man of the Church of England but the same man is also a member of the commonwealth; nor any man a member of the commonwealth, which is not also of the Church of England'. That was a version of medieval theory, brought up to date in a manner which implicitly discarded the Pope's pretensions to determine whether the Queen's subjects should be loyal to her, and in effect cut off from the commonwealth those who toyed with such errors. It is this disposition of things, and not any assertion about theological errors in the Roman Church, which has formed the basis of the various restrictions on the civil status of members of the Roman communion. The removal of these disqualifications by the series of Catholic Emancipation Acts had to await a time when the Pope's power to dispense people of their civil duties had become less widely credible.

To a generation which had faced the threat from Spain the need for loyalty to the crown needed no elaboration. In his discussion of the relations of Church and State, Hooker is largely preoccupied with a domestic problem, that of justifying the Royal Supremacy in ecclesiastical matters as against Puritans who thought themselves too holy to be meddled with. These apologetics were, however, in their nature also part of the argument for the validity of the English Church as against the Romans who continued to advance whatever objections they could think of. The Church in Hooker's view was not vitiated by the fact that every sort of ecclesiastical regulation was not in the hands of clerics. With a Christian monarch in a Christian commonwealth, how could that be? The Church was not only the clergy. The contention that supreme power in ecclesiastical causes must rest with the domestic clergy was merely a variant of the superstition that it must rest with the Bishop of Rome. Hooker's view of this matter rests fundamentally on his belief in reason and reasonableness, in 'the benefit of keeping the Law which reason teacheth' and 'the natural finding out of Laws by the light of Reason' which he had to advance against the crude inspirationalism of the more extreme Puritans, and the assertions of those who imagined that all light was to be extracted from the Scriptures. This reasonableness extended to and was one of the foundations of Hooker's view of kingship. He was as little appalled as Proudhon by the thought that a right may be established by conquest: 'For it is God who giveth victory in the day of war'; the facts spoke for themselves, one might say. Without order there is no public society; so, 'unto kings by human right, honour by very divine right, is due', as tribute was due to the Emperor Tiberius. The claim to a moral superiority over governments, made from their different points of view by Rome and by extreme Puritans, is not one that Hooker could entertain. In a Christian country, the civil and religious body were one, as the same man might be both schoolmaster and physician. 'When we oppose the Church therefore and the commonwealth in a Christian society, we mean by the commonwealth that society with relation to all the public affairs thereof, only the matter of true religion excepted; by the Church, the same society with only reference unto the matter of true religion, without any other affair besides.'

The problem Hooker poses, in relation to the affairs of our own time, is how such a view may be relevant in a state in which it can no wise be claimed that every member of the commonwealth is a member of the Church, and vice versa. It is not to be supposed that, in medieval societies, the mass of the population was any more *christianized* than they are in England at present; if one takes as a criterion contemporary pronouncements, whether Papal or Protestant, on public affairs, they were in many respects less so. Still one cannot deny the growing dissociation, from the eighteenth century onwards, between Christian dogmatics and public institutions. Hooker had considered the position of the Church in relation to pagan society; there was the example of the Roman Empire before Constantine. Indeed he distinguished three positions: the first, 'under the dominions of infidels', where Church and State were, he said, 'two societies independent'. The second position was that of 'those commonwealths where the bishop of Rome holdeth sway'; there, church and commonwealth were one but the Pope divided them 'into two diverse bodies' and claimed the upper hand over 'any civil prince'. 'Thirdly... within this realm of England' the case was different again; the pattern was 'God's own ancient elect people' – the Old Testament pattern – where 'the self-same people' were 'whole and entire... under one chief Governor, on whose supreme authority they did all depend'.

Such a pattern is bound to be offensive in our present society – to our modern Puritans, who think the state unsanctified; to Jews, who regard the pattern as their copyright; to Roman

Catholics, who want to give part of their allegiance abroad; in general, to all who believe in the sovereignty of public opinion, however mysteriously ascertained. A constitutional democracy does go some way to providing a solution, for it ensures the dissolution of any theocratic pattern of government. The adjustments are less than perfect, and the problem of relations between Church and State remains. The Roman Church's claims to civil supremacy – already more than distasteful to Dante – remain, though now much muted, and operating not directly on governments but on the opinions of voters. The notion of the Pope's power to divide the *de facto* society into 'two diverse bodies' is strictly intolerable; it contradicts the assumptions of democracy. So is the notion of the right of any national church to regard itself as irresponsible in relation to the state; like the Roman Church, it can only assemble opinions. Moreover, since the post-Christian society is not identical with 'the dominion of infidels', but is indeed a society in which Christians and non- or post-Christians have to get on side by side, as part of the same political body. supremacy in all practical matters has in the last analysis to be accorded to the state. There is a strong argument for saying that all collective opinions by churches on political matters are out of place, and that the only proper role left to them is to instruct their own members so that those members can exercise their several judgements in accordance with their consciences, and so play their individual parts in the state. There should be no question of special rights or privileges for churches – no rights, that is to say, which may not be accorded to non-religious organizations within the state. Some in the Church of England have lately been dreaming that if they withdrew from the historic position of the Establishment, they could be recognized as a special and sanctified body, with prophetic functions. This is a delusion. What would happen would be claiming, within the less protected area of the national authority, the kind of disruptive power Rome has traditionally claimed from a safer distance and its own temporal territory.

One can see new variants of Rome's ancient political game being played for an indefinite time to come, but the character of the game was changed entirely once she could no longer speak authoritatively to princes but seek only to influence opinion. The delusion of grandeur remains, but the many-headed people has become the master, in relation to such practical matters as the Pope could hope to influence outside his own geographical dominion. It may take a long time for this change to be effectively understood in the Vatican, but from the point of view of the national state the perspectives are clearer. The revolution which emerged at the Reformation is irreversible; there may in some future be a world government, but it will not be that of Rome. It could only be a political government which would accept the division of its authority with no better grace than have the national governments which have followed the destruction of the old Catholic monarchies. Meanwhile the national governments all base their claims to authority – in such terms as suit their several situations – on the whole body of their people. Individuals, to be sure, are free to consult their deity or his accredited agents, but governments no longer do so. In this matter as in so many others Hooker was remarkably long-sighted. That is not to say that he thought at all in terms acceptable in a modern democracy, but he understood that, whatever the constitutional arrangements in a state, it was 'a thing most true, that kings, even inheritors, do hold their right to the power of dominion, with dependency upon the whole entire body politic over which they have rule as kings'. The king is greater than the individual, but less than the whole society, *major singulis, universis minor*. As Bracton had said in the thirteenth century, the king should not be subject to any man, but to God and the law. The language is hardly of our time, but the radical meaning, as to the ultimate responsibility, and the limitations, of government, is much what we now approve, whatever developments it has undergone at the hands of Locke and his successors.

There are aspects of Hooker's reading of politics which are less generally understood, and which have been less taken up by those who have come after him. We should be apt to say that 'everyone has some religion' – for since Rousseau we have thought of such things very much in personal terms, as a matter of private thoughts and sentiments. For Hooker, 'every *body politic* hath some religion' – as was evident enough in his time; 'the Church that religion which is only true'. He was concerned with the society which was broadly Christian, which had 'true religion in the gross', and never mind the refinements. Such a society was the church – at once church and state, if one is to distinguish what he regarded as its two aspects; 'first united in some public form of regiment, and secondly distinguished from other societies by the exercise of the Christian religion'. For us churches are, politically, collections of private consciences, and we admit differences between them as between individuals, even though this is in contradiction with both the Church's and ordinary non-religious notions as to the universality of truth. It is arguable that no society can live long on such terms. It may be said that it involves a sleight of hand. For in such a situation, what are we to say of the religion of the body politic? That Hooker was wrong, and that the body politic has no religion? Or that it has a religion which is no longer that of the churches? If the former supposition is more plausible, in terms of contemporary prejudice, the latter is more likely, historically. Hooker looked back to the Old Testament world in which only Israel 'had the truth of religion, and was in that respect the Church of God', and in which other kingdoms had other religions. We look around on a world in which the governments of even 'Christian' countries discreetly make no appeal to the Christian religion, but to a system of 'rights' which they hope will prove more eirenic.

The Church of England, it sometimes appears, cannot too quickly get rid of the traces of Christendom still extant in our Constitution – a Christian monarchy and the two ecclesiastical establishments. It appears to have lost all faith in its mission as *the* historic church in this land, capable of infusing the whole society with the truth, yet that is its *raison d'être*. It makes loving signals to other ecclesiastical groups, but for the *res publica* it prefers that uncertain and as yet not fully formulated religion which the state has adopted as of necessity. The tendency towards disestablishment, which has been so marked in the Church of England in recent years, is a recession not only from the state but, so far as public affairs are concerned, from Christianity. One could understand a Church of England which aimed at reconciliation with dissenters, including Romans, in order to reconstitute, no doubt in some far future, a portion of Christendom. The abandonment of England, in favour of a retreat into individual quietism and participation in international gangs of opinion on this and that, is surely a betrayal. Such a point of view has always been that of those sects for whom the public welfare, and publicly acknowledged reason, meant nothing, and a sectarian future in a pagan state is all that we are now asked to look forward to.

The present generation of ecclesiastical conspirators do not, assuredly, hear the voice of George Herbert addressing *The British Church*:

I joy, deare Mother, when I view
Thy perfect lineaments and hue
    Both sweet and bright.
Beautie in thee takes up her place,
And dates her letters from thy face,
    When she doth write.

Neither, apparently, do they hear the voice of Richard Hooker.

Hensley Henson

Anyone confused by the goings-on in the Church of England in the last few years might turn with relief to *Hensley Henson*, Owen Chadwick's biography of a prelate born in 1863, who retired from his diocese of Durham in 1938 to spend the marginal years of old age brooding over a long career, and made his final exit in 1947. *Retrospect of an Unimportant Life* is what Henson called the memoir over which he spent so much time in those years, and no man in his right mind is likely to claim much more for himself at an age when all ambitions should have receded. There was a flicker of what might have been a glorious sunset, in 1940, when Churchill recalled Henson to a canonry at Westminster, but when he arrived at the Abbey it was to find 'that he could hardly read the lessons properly, even with a magnifying glass as well as spectacles; that his sermons were to tiny congregations and in the blackened church he could hardly see his notes.' Before the end of the month he had resigned, 'realising that it was time to go back to his quiet corner and wait the release of death.'

There is a certain panache – even though it was a failed panache – about this final scene of public life, and Henson was a man who had been much in the public eye, at various times in his life, a large figure, small though he was physically. Such figures are made by circumstances as well as by intrinsic qualities and Henson, who had the sturdiness and plain-spokenness, not to say sometimes the recklessness, to make him noticeable in any walk of life, operated in a world in which a bishop could still attract a certain attention because he was a figure in the Commonwealth and in which ecclesiastical controversies still had a certain scandalous interest. Things are different now that the notion that England is a Christian country has become so attenuated that prominent churchmen themselves seem more anxious to justify themselves in post-Christian terms than to enlighten the world at large by reference to the dogma to which they are supposed to be attached. The public career of Henson illustrates some phases of this change, and it is an exceptional good fortune that the task of writing this biography has fallen into the hands of so scrupulous and learned an historian as Owen Chadwick. The subtitle 'A Study in the Friction between Church and State' indicates – if indication were needed – the biographer's sense of the general importance of his subject, but his eye is on the man in all his quirkiness and complexity so that the authenticity of the portrait is nowhere threatened by any attempt to prove a thesis.

That Professor Chadwick did not rush to take up the invitation of the Dean and Chapter of Durham to write a life of Henson may be gathered from what he says in the preface to this volume. He seems to have had serious reservations about his subject. For him the author of *Retrospect of an Unimportant Life* was 'many things – cantankerous, decisive, courageous, difficult, clear-headed, truculent – but not lovable'. Chadwick was particularly put off by what looked like Henson's folly and vanity in including in the third volume a letter from Lloyd George telling him that 'nothing in his' – Lloyd George's – 'life gave him more satisfaction, than his making Henson into a bishop.' The scruple shows something of the quality of the biographer. 'Did Henson really believe,' he asks, 'that Lloyd George, who invented the welfare state and won a Great War and created modern Ireland, put the making of a single bishop at the top of his list of achievements?' It is the voice of sober realism. Canon Charles Pattinson, who had been Henson's chaplain, finally persuaded Chadwick to take on the at first rather repugnant task of spending so long with the Henson papers and writing the bishop's life. Pattinson told him that 'Henson's autobiography, seemingly so frank, seemingly so devoid of reticence, was not what it looked.' It was indeed 'all nonsense', in Pattinson's view, and he had himself begged Henson to 'throw it away and not to print it'. So there was still a mystery to be solved, and this book no doubt comes as near as anyone ever will to solving it.

Chadwick begins his story by telling us what he has been able to establish about Henson's father and grandfather. There is a certain pattern in this, for Henson *père* had quarrelled with his father and left his home on the Somerset-Devon border in his teens and worked his way up to some prosperity in business. That Henson *fils* was uneasy with *his* father, reacted against him and later began to adopt some of the old man's prejudices is evident as the story of his life unfolds. There were emotional strains on the female side also, for Henson's mother died when he was six and three years later his father married again – a fortunate eventuality, however, for Emma Theodora Parker, a German by origin and 30 years younger than her husband, was a benign influence in this not altogether benign circle. There were other children, including an elder brother who escaped to business early and 'won the repute of being the rudest man in Calcutta' – quite a distinction, one imagines – 'collected a large fortune, and retired to Minehead in Somerset where he lived several years unhappily, with no interests, and no friends, and no conversation, and no religion except prejudice against Roman Catholicism and Anglo-Catholicism. He inherited his father's hatred of Catholics.' Father had been a follower of a desperado called Baptist Noel who marched out of the Church of England following the Gorham case, which was the occasion of a great dust-up in 1849 about the powers of the Privy Council in ecclesiastical cases. The air Henson breathed in his childhood must have been fairly discouraging, one way and another. In his determination to 'keep his motherless family unspotted from a corrupt world' Henson senior decided that the children must not go to school and the future bishop was 'deprived of school companions, deprived of games, deprived of holidays, deprived of everything but religion, brothers, sisters and a good library'. At thirteen he seemed about to get away from all this to business in London, in accordance with his father's plans, but at the last moment the plans fell through, to his own great distress. It was this turn of events which led to Henson's going to school after all, at the age of fourteen, to his being an 'usher' in another school at the age of sixteen, and finally, against his father's better judgement, to his getting permission to go to Oxford as a non-collegiate student. He had no money and as little society as he could have had in such circumstances, but he emerged as a fellow of All Souls, which he regarded as the beginning of his Oxford life. That was in 1884. Hardly surprising if he turned his back on his earlier years. 'The fellows discovered,' Chadwick says, 'that in electing this unusual creature, they elected not only a fellow unlike any they ever met, but a friendly affectionate youth with a gift of sparkling talk and witty repartee.' Henson found himself not only sipping port but, in a modest way, laying bets. He was assimilated by a new world in which it was a not unnatural thing that his abilities should take him to the palace in Bishop Auckland and the the House of Lords. It was a kind of metamorphosis Oxford could achieve, in a more élitist society, and it cannot be said that in the twentieth century that university has altogether lost its power of effecting such changes of fortune – now more numerous and less dramatic perhaps, but still sufficiently rewarding.

There is a certain superficial incoherence about Henson's ecclesiastical career, but in setting out the facts Chadwick leaves one with the impression that his subject was more of a piece than most men. Though it can be shown that he blundered on from one massive conviction to another, one has a sense that the underlying mass was somehow as constant as a human being is likely to be – which perhaps amounts to saying that vows, dogmas and statements of principle are less than they seem, and certainly less than they claim to be at the time of utterance. Henson might have been a businessman; he might have been a lawyer; in fact he became a priest. It was hardly a remarkable outcome, given his background and the general social and psychological conditions of the 1880s. The first move was towards something not incompatible with his final resolution but a little different from it. He vowed himself to a single life for the sake of the poor – which did not stop him, sixteen years later and a canon of Westminster, proposing to the daughter of a Scottish squire four days after meeting her and finding her 'a very charming companion'. In 1886 he considered becoming a Roman Catholic – though 'assuredly not because I believe in Roman Catholicism,' he said. It was at least partly through the persuasions of Gore, then reigning in Pusey House, that he was ordained in the Church of England. In 1888 he accept the living of Barking.

He was full of energy, and Chadwick gives a fascinating account of this episode, in which Henson ably fulfilled the fashionable Oxford dream of the role of a slum priest. In 1894 he wanted to go back to Oxford, but, we are told, 'Oxford would not have him back.'

There followed a curious interlude as chaplain of an almshouse at Ilford. During these years there blew up one of those ecclesiastical rows which then had more importance for the world at large than is ever likely to be the case with such things now. Much passion was spilt on what used to count as Romanising practices such as the reservation of the Sacrament and the ritual displays which appear to have had a disproportionate fascination for some Anglo-Catholics; there were complications also about the behaviour of Lord Halifax in Rome and of Bishop Creighton in the cathedral in the Kremlin. All this brought to life once more the question of how far Parliament was empowered to regulate the Church. 'The crisis in the National Church,' says Chadwick, 'changed Henson's life. It made him think out his Anglo-Catholicism. It revived his strenuous contention for establishment, and made him think further his notion of a national Church. And it made him famous, and so opened the door to the longed-for departure from Ilford.' So confused, in real life, are spiritual and temporal concerns and perhaps motives.

Henson's next twelve years were spent as a canon of Westminster and as rector of St Margaret's. It was during these years that Henson got used to the idea of being a public figure. It could hardly be otherwise, and his sharp and ready tongue, in the service of a life-long determination to say what he thought whether people liked it or not – and perhaps especially when they did not – made him a striking one. No doubt Henson enjoyed the use of his gifts, but it is one of the graces of his character that he prepared his sermons with care and, in so doing, often made them less telling, but also less rash, than they might have been. During these years, too, the former Anglo-Catholic and passionate denouncer of sectaries began to think more of the essential unity of Protestants, and looked to the Nonconformists to 'come and help the Church instead of undermining what good it could do'. He also acquired a taste, which seems to come easily to the clergy, for irrupting upon the issues of the day as if holding an ecclesiastical appointment somehow gave him the right to an outsize voice in affairs. Perhaps his notion of establishment was a little too much the notion that this was required of him. However, he followed the same course in later years, as Bishop of Durham, when he had, by one of those volte-faces which were part of his style, suddenly and, as it were, casually thrown overboard the case for establishment. He was not only loud and frequent in his denunciation of dictators but full of advice as to how the government should conduct its relations with them. 'Come storm or hail, you must speak.' He enjoyed crying for justice whether it did any good or not; perhaps he thought such interventions more efficacious than prayer. It would be more charitable to say that that is how prophets operate. But it must be said that, to the unenlightened eye, the behaviour of Henson, or of Headlam or Bell for that matter, in the face of Hitler and Mussolini looks no different from and no wiser than the ordinary bewildered talk of middle-class English people of the time.

Chadwick's tact and scepticism in the use of what must have

been a large mass of material, including Henson's own diary in many volumes, backed by a wide and deep knowledge of Church history in other times and places, enables him to present simultaneously several levels of his subject's reaction to events, so that what we are left with is not an interpretation but a living figure, uncertain and unsatisfactory – the dominant traits are never offered as the man himself. Henson may rest in peace: the Church of England assuredly does not.

Did Henson leave any pointers as to what her future course should be? It is difficult to see any, for if Henson was not infrequently convinced that he saw with clarity what should or should not be done, the subsequent history usually shows that he did not see very far. He addressed himself always to what he saw as the needs of his time, and the times were always changing.

There is a sense in which all Henson's reactions were fashionable reactions, and even when he – as they say – courted unpopularity he was drifting with the times. It was just that, being so plain-spoken, he was apt to say what many more would be saying shortly afterwards – a recipe for a successful career, whether in the Church or elsewhere. If he faced horrid scandal when he was appointed Bishop of Worcester at the invitation of Lloyd George, it was because he 'had proclaimed, in lecture, in sermon and in print, the right of other men to *deny* the two miracles of the creed and still hold office as priests': it was soon to become difficult to see what degree of disbelief was not allowable, or what exactly was meant by those who claimed to believe.

When, in the crisis over the Prayer Book of 1928, Henson suddenly changed course to deny the right of Parliament to have a say in such matters, he was moving no further than to claim for the Church a freedom which was quickly to become identified with the ordinary notions of democracy. His difficulty in both junctures was that he stood for conscience, and conscience, on the public stage, is hardly to be distinguished from mere opinion. In the political world, opinion is the supreme governor, or so it is popularly believed. The Pope can preach democracy in Poland and monarchy in Rome, but no such duplicity is possible in the Church of England, which has been a part – or it might be said an aspect – of the body politic and not a separate polity with its own designs and ambitions. Through all his changes, Henson was deep in this English tradition which sees the common honesty of the citizen as no different in temper from that which the Christian should exercise when he puzzles over his dogma. The duty of a preacher such as he was to instruct consciences. There was a certain sleight-of-hand about this, for he emerged in a world in which a gentleman with an Oxford accent, living in a large vicarage or even a palace, would customarily be listened to with respect. What happens when one opinion really is as good as another? Is a nation imbued with the findings of the Christian conscience even thinkable in such circumstances? Or must the Church retreat behind its own battlements and become the enemy of civil society? Or at best a pressure group among how many others, differently motivated?

The creeds themselves have a political history, in the Roman Empire, the feudal world and the residual monarchies: the politics of disintegration will not leave them untouched, any more than it will the institutions in which they have been transmitted. For all its turbulence, in our perspective the career of Hensley Henson looks bland, as that of a churchman hardly aware of the gathering storm.

George Herbert

It says something about current academic practice that Routledge and Kegan Paul succeed in marketing, under the title of the Critical Heritage Series, bundles of criticism of writers who have hardly had time to collect a heritage of any kind. However useful it may be to have compendia of what has been said about Eliot, Pound, Joyce, Forster, William Carlos Williams, Beckett, Nabokov or even George Orwell – and here, if not before, one's confidence begins to sag a bit – all they can contain is near-contemporary appreciations on which the irony of time has barely begun to play. With George Herbert (1593-1633) the case is quite different. C.A. Patrides has had four centuries to draw on, and he has wisely restricted the twentieth century to less than eighty pages and the nineteenth century to little over a hundred, so enabling himself to give almost comprehensive coverage to what comes before that. We thus have matter for a study not only of the ups and downs of a reputation but of changes in approach to the poetry and indeed in critical habits at large.

The matter from the seventeenth century is hardly literary-critical at all, in any of the ways in which that term is now understood. It starts with a mere exchange of verses between friends – Donne's lines to Herbert, sent with one of his seals 'of the Anchor and Christ', and Herbert's reply. Next comes Bacon's dedication of his *Psalmes*, a polite return for Herbert's share in translating *The Advancement of Learning* into Latin and perhaps with the *arrière-pensée* that Herbert's would be a good name to invoke as he ventured into the fields of poetry and piety, for neither of which the former Lord Chancellor was himself famous. Then we come to Nicholas Ferrar and with him to the point which has exercised Professor Patrides most, in making his collection, that of an 'ulterior motive' standing in the way of what he regards as the proper appreciation of the 'poetry as poetry'. People will regard Mr Herbert as holy, and *The Temple* as an aid to devotion. It is no good expecting anything better from Nicholas

Ferrar, who was busy at Little Gidding with similar concerns and since it was to Ferrar that Herbert delivered his manuscript, on his death-bed, with instructions to publish or destroy as he thought best, he must be regarded as being as close to Herbert's mind as anybody. Is that a critical consideration? It might be. Admittedly it is dangerous ground. Patrides calls attention to Vaughan's regrettable emphasis on Herbert's 'holy *life* and *verse*' as if a *life* could equal a *verse*, he seems to say – or perhaps only, 'as if a life should be taken account of, in reading a verse!' Of course it often is, in the case of lives which make a point of being rather unholy – no more popular subject, in fact.

But of course Patrides is right to feel anxious. We have seen the name of Rimbaud swept along on a tide of notions as to what constitutes the good life to thousands who do not care for his exacting poetry. Such figures get caught in political currents and the sale of *The Temple* – 20,000 copies in the years to 1670 – must owe a lot to the banning of Anglican worship and the suppression of episcopacy, to say nothing of the death of the king in 1649. Patrides gives us at length Barnabas Oley's *Prefatory View of the Life of Mr Geo. Herbert*, 'only too justly', as he balefully says, 'later acknowledged by Walton as indispensable for "some of those Truths" he himself was to extend'. Walton's *Life* of course dominates the 'heritage' of the seventeenth century, and the biographer is so little 'critical'. We are given an interesting extract from Ralph Knevet, not published until 1966. Knevet, though anxious to follow Herbert 'in His Devotions' must count as a man of letters for he attempted to complete *The Faerie Queene* as well as to imitate Herbert. He is well read and tells us that 'Dante affordes us better matter then words' – which shows how greater poets than Herbert have sunk from critical comprehension in their time; he also makes the good point that the *matter* of the *The Temple* is better than that of the 'sublimated Wittes of our Nation' whose one notion is 'to idolize some silly scornfull woman into a fooles Paradise of self admiration'. Seventeenth-century criticism comes alive for Patrides with what he calls Dryden's 'explicitly pejorative allusion to Herbert's mode of articulation' when he banishes Shadwell to 'some peacefull Province in Acrostick Land', but too much should not be made of this, which merely tells us that Dryden was heading in another direction, as we knew already. More significant evidence of the reception of Herbert's verse towards the end of the century is the collection of thirty-two poems into a hymn-book, in 1697, and the charming 'Youth's Alphabet: or, Herbert's Morals', which Patrides calls 'doggerel'.

The eighteenth century opens with a flourish with Joseph Addison, that merely fashionable man, explaining in the *Spectator* that the taste of the best people has changed in a way that the town may not yet appreciate. It is thirty years after Dryden's crack, and that is about the time that such things still take. 'This fashion of false Wit...in particular may be met with among Mr *Herbert*'s Poems.' Then comes an awful exhibit in the form of an extract from a 'considerable manuscript', happily unpublished, by one George Ryley, of whom nothing is known except this melancholy monument, which comprises 'elaborate annotations' on *The Temple*, the 'actual meaning' of which 'was deemed to require explication in depth'. I recommend a posthumous PhD for this author. In 1725 there are still some verses from John Reynolds, 'a moderate dissenting minister', celebrating the 'seraphic singer' in eighteenth-century style and incidentally distinguishing sharply between Herbert and the opportunist Christopher Harvey who had long ago managed to get his verse bound up with Herbert's. That seems to me evidence of continuing life of a kind, even though Reynolds regrettably regarded Herbert as a saint. Patrides makes an interesting allusion to Dr Johnson and in the same breath that he tells us that there are seventy-eight references to Herbert in the *Dictionary* exclaims: 'How fortunate for Johnson that no second hand reports of *his* views exist!' He would have made a fool of himself, Patrides implies. I do not think so, though Johnson would, of course, have shared the fatal weakness of so many others for Herbert's piety. Wesley – a tainted source again – loved Herbert and setting himself boldly against the tastes of the day asserted that his poems were 'scarce inferior either in sense or language to most compositions of the present age' – a masterly understatement. Cowper at twenty-one 'pored upon' Herbert's poems all day long and his malady 'never seems to much alleviated' as while he was reading him. These may not be the tributes of literary critics, but they demonstrate that, if *The Temple* was less well known than in the previous century, it continued to attract the sort of readers its author would have wished to have.

It is in the nineteenth century – to which, after all, Patrides's conception of 'poetry as poetry' really belongs – that what he sees as the critical dilemma in relation to Herbert really surfaces. Coleridge, with whom this section of the volume properly begins, speaks of Herbert as 'comparatively little known' and praises him as an 'exquisite master' of 'the most correct and natural language' but adds that he is 'a poet *sui generis*, the merits of whose poems will never be felt without a sympathy with the mind and character of the man'. Emerson, though already far from the forms of thought of seventeenth-century Anglicanism as Coleridge was not, clearly felt this sympathy; only his religion was a vaguer one and for him 'criticism is silent in the exercise of higher faculties'. Ruskin saw in Herbert 'the purest unsectarian Christianity' and claimed to owe to him 'whatever has been wisest or happiest in the course' of his own life. We are moving into an aura of nineteenth-century religiosity. George Eliot misquotes Herbert and spoils the rhythm. James Montgomery, a prolific writer of verse among which only the odd hymn has escaped oblivion, saw 'devotion turned into a masquerade' throughout Herbert's writings; no doubt he could not stomach the familiar style and the unfamiliar ideas. *The Temple* of the nineteenth century is really *The Christian Year*, and the difference between the two books marks the decline in theological intelligence and sensibility, as well as in the general *use* of theological conceptions. Keble puts in a good word for himself by suggesting that Herbert is one of those who 'appear rather to fall in ... incidentally' with 'the deepest subjects' instead of having 'sought them purposely' – a good point, if one understands the implications in a sense the opposite of Keble's; for him the result of Herbert's method was 'inappropriate, not to say chilling and repellent'. Patrides is right to see ecclesiastical designs in the frequent republication of Herbert in the nineteenth century, but he does not indicate that the theological revival of the period was accompanied by a massive reprinting of older literature – the Parker Society's reprints, the works of Hooker, Cranmer, Andrewes, Bramhall and many more, to the enrichment of the sensibility of the twentieth as well as of the nineteenth century. Pickering, to whose edition of Herbert Patrides draws attention, also brought out editions of Jeremy Taylor and Fuller. There is no separating the revival of *The Temple* from the theological movements. The danger, as Patrides points out, was that to many readers 'Herbert emerged as a proper Victorian' – though it is rather odd to talk of *The Temple* being 'converted into a collection of poems replete with edifying matter'. A.C. Benson, towards the end of the century, is surprisingly good in his distinction between Herbert's 'curious elaboration of expression, an intenity of compression' and Keble's 'indefinite garrulity, a tendency to diverge on side issues, a vapid displacement of language'.

Patrides limits himself to the first third of the twentieth century; the last extract is dated 1936. It cannot be said that much enlightenment emerges from the early entries – from Dowden, William Alexander or H.C. Beeching, though Dowden does quote Sir John Coleridge's sensible remark that 'if Herbert's words are sometimes hard, you may at least be sure that they always *have a meaning*' – which is really the discovery, if you call it a discovery, of the twentieth century. Clutton-Brock comes up with the observation that Herbert's thought 'is less old-fashioned than that of most of the poets of the eighteenth or even the nineteenth century'. We are in the world of Grierson and ultimately of Eliot, though we have still the bumbling Basil de Selincourt in, I am afraid, this very journal (*TLS*, 2 March 1933). The selection concludes with an excellent extract from Austin Warren in the *American Review*. Warren invokes William Law, showing a sense of the traditions essential for an understanding of Herbert. He notes Herbert's fondness for 'homely analogies and illustrations' and that 'when writing for himself, not for "labouring people", he used such analogies as they would understand'. He remarks that 'his sentence structure is that of the English Bible... His syntax rarely admits inversion or any other mode of poetic dislocation; his sentence structure is that of good conversation – though firm, yet supple and easy.' It is the best of critical summaries.

Throughout the centuries of the 'heritage', Herbert refuses to disappear behind his poems, perhaps because he moves so small a distance from the centre of his own mind. The general question this volume raises is indeed whether there is such a thing as 'poetry as poetry'. What would that be? If poets *say* anything, if in fact they have human speech, like the rest of the world, there is no unwinding Herbert from the cocoon of meaning wrapped about him, or of understanding him except as part of the literature of Anglicanism, now treated with contempt by those who are supposed to be its guardians. There is a sense in which a religion *is* a literature, or at least cannot exist without one. For the literary critic – and for that more important character, the reader – our older literature can survive only so far as the past remains alive, and that means having some sense of its religion. What was said about Herbert in the seventeenth century, however injudicious in the light of modern critical theory, is more important than what our own century has managed to say about him, and Walton's *Life* is still the best introduction to *The Temple*.

The Prayer Book Controversy: an insular view

The circumstances which have led the authorities of the Church of England to encourage the progressive dereliction of the Book of Common Prayer and the Authorized Version of the Bible are of so much complexity that any statement of them is likely to be challenged in one quarter or another. It is hardly for me, who have a modest notoriety as a defender of the old books, to attempt to explain the matter to an American audience. The bare facts, as regards the Prayer Book, are that in 1974/5 the Parliament at Westminster, which had bothered its head little enough with such matters for the last forty or fifty years, relaxed its grip on the national church. It did so in such a manner that the Church has since been able to manage its own liturgical affairs without the risk of being overruled as happened in 1928, when a revised Prayer Book proposed by the Church, after much study and discussion, was rejected by Parliament. Lest anyone unacquainted with the habits of the island should imagine that this meant that no one ventured to use the new book for fear of inquisitorial interventions by the state, it must be said that many parish priests went their own way and that variations from the Book of Common Prayer, including material from the 1928 book, have been used with impunity ever since. It would probably be uncontroversial to say that the clergy of the Church of England have for many years been an undisciplined lot. In 1955 the Church set up its own Liturgical Commission and in 1965 authorized new services 'for experimental use'. 'Since then the Commission has prepared revised forms, sometimes as many as three distinct series, for almost every aspect of the Church's worship.' That is a quotation from the preface to the Alternative Service Book, 1980, an inconvenient volume which has been authorized, without reference to Parliament, in the manner which has been legal since 1975, 'for use in the Church of England in conjunction with *The Book of Common Prayer*.' Parliament did not leave the Church free to abolish the latter book, and the 'in conjunction with' is in recognition of that fact. The whole weight of ecclesiastical authority has, however, been put behind the Alternative Service Book and the Book of Common Prayer has rapidly fallen from use and even from sight, in most places. At the same time, and in accordance with what appears to be the conviction of the ecclesiastical authorities that people can no longer understand the English of the seventeenth century, a variety of contemporary translations of the Bible has largely replaced the Authorized Version, which is the King James Bible.

It is not my purpose to inquire into the theological significance of these events. Whatever it may be – and there is more to be said than that 'new forms of worship do not erode the historical foundations of the Church's faith', which is how the Preface to the Alternative Service Book puts it – these changes mark a change in the cultural, and it may be political, history of England, none the less important because it has not been generally understood. The politics are a subject in themselves, perhaps a rather insular one and, except to the extent indicated below, hardly relevant here. The cultural consequences of the dereliction may themselves be only of secondary interest outside the United Kingdom; they are however of such a nature as to offer, if not parallels, then at least matter for reflection, to people with different political and historical perspectives. Cranmer's books of 1549 and 1552 were the outcome of theological and political developments – the general European phenomena of the Reformation and the emergence of national states. They were the outcome also of the related pressures for a diminution of clerical exclusiveness and for a Bible and liturgy in the vernacular. Cranmer's books and the revision of 1662 drew on earlier matter in English as well as on the Latin service-books; the King James Bible drew on versions from Tyndale's onward. Both Prayer Book and Bible were in response to a popular demand to know what was going on. From repeated and uniform use in parish churches, their phrases went home to generations of English people, illiterate as well as literate, and they became the first and sometimes the only reading matter of those who could read. In the sixteenth century the Church of England was conceived of as the successor, more or less contested, of the medieval Church and the sole heir, in England, of the purer faith imputed to earlier times. At all the subsequent stages of dissent and emancipation from these conceptions, the Authorized Version of the Bible retained its central position, expounded in every tabernacle and read or read at by everyone who knew his letters. Jonathan Swift attributed the continuity of ordinary language to these central books: 'if it were not for the *Bible* and *Common-Prayer-Book* in the vulgar Tongue,' he said in 1712, 'we should hardly be able to understand anything that was written among us an Hundred Years ago...: For those books being perpetually read in Churches, have proved a Kind of Standard for Language, especially for the Common People.' The language of the books was a common possession, an aid to understanding backward and forward in time and, at any given time, to understanding between different classes and localities. The extent to which it has entered into the texture of the literary language, to Hardy and Kipling and indeed beyond, is well understood, even though there are assuredly every year fewer people who recognize the sources. It is not too much to say that the diminishing familiarity with the Bible and Prayer Book – which, of course, did not start with the antics of the Synod after 1975 – has brought with it an impoverishment of the common language and a diminution of common understandings.

In the towns in particular, the reach of the Prayer Book and the Bible has long not been what it was. One can easily exaggerate the attachments of the past, yet until a few decades ago the Authorized Version was regularly used in state elementary schools for Scripture lessons which were an ordinary part of the curriculum, and there were still, for Church of England children and dissenters alike, a large number of Sunday schools. Since the Second World War, there has been a rapid collapse. Now the main source of popular superstition is the radio and television, both using for the most part a language debased beyond anything publicly available in the past. These developments give what plausibility there is in the plea that the older language is no longer a general medium of communication, though they do not, as they are usually supposed to do, give any ground for supposing that the listless and lifeless language of the Alternative Service Book and of the inferior translations of the Bible has any general intelligibility. In fact, very little that is apposite has been said, by the apologists of the new books, about the real problems of understanding which face the historic religions at the present time. The situation has been complicated by issues which carry one far beyond the domestic English scene. There has been an aspiration, on the part of some of the clergy, for an approximation of the liturgy to that used by Roman Catholics, a pressure which has naturally increased since Rome took up the fashion of vernacular liturgies and the Roman Church in the United Kingdom acquired its own depressing and inept English forms. More important is the pressure on the language of England which comes from all sides, in a world in which many more millions speak some version of it, either as a first or a second language, than there are inhabitants in the whole of what used to be called the British Isles. A certain disorientation, as compared with even recent times, is inescapable, the more since the ethos of the age, and the steep political decline of England itself, have led to a loss of confidence in the superiority of the mother tongue; and the process has been assisted by the decline in the domestic prestige of the language of the upper classes.

Seen in this context, the problems presented by the Bible and Prayer Book are closely related to those of literature as a whole. Is the authority of lateral comparisons to be greater or less than that of the local tradition? It has to be remembered that the local tradition is far from being exclusively local; it is rather the funnel through which foreign influences, Latin, Greek, Hebrew, French, Spanish, Italian and German, have played upon those who have written in English in these islands. Each generation continues to assimilate more or less matter from abroad including, of course, that of other English-speaking traditions – which, however, on this view of things, fall into place as something less than major influences. Those who seek to make the most of the lateral influences are emphasizing the value of the contemporaneous. There is a strong political and ideological element in this view of the matter; what is most in evidence is the desirability of understanding between societies scattered across the world. In ecclesiastical terms, this means that the Anglican communion uses English almost as the old Roman communion used Latin, as a *lingua franca*, with the difference that Canterbury lacks the political authority which the Pope's Rome inherited. The former imperial authority of England is a debit, not a credit, in the contemporary world, so that the Church of England itself, so far as it thinks of itself as a member of the Anglican communion, has to be endlessly apologetic and defensive. The favouring of translations of the Bible in what has been called a 'mid-Atlantic dialect' is certainly not uninfluenced by this situation and so – though to a less degree – are the bolder flights of the Alternative Service Book, though in fact those flights are not very bold and there are some odd provincial relics, such as the borrowing from the Church of South India of a hymn which turns out to be by a British Poet Laureate (Robert Bridges, 1844-1930). All this is a distraction from what will be 'understanded of the people', here and now. As against this, attention to the local tradition should mean to the whole recognizable past through that tradition – which surely must be right as a matter of theology as well as from the point of view of making that tradition intelligible to contemporaries. Had the authors of the A.S.B. worked in that way, they would have been content with a very conservative revision of the Book of Common Prayer, realizing that their chances of adding material which *contained as much* as Cranmer's words were – to put it no higher – limited.

The issue – significant for literature at large as well as for biblical and liturgical studies – is that of the centrality of the master texts, the recognition that they *are* master texts. No one but a fool would set about rewriting Shakespeare, or would pretend that a translation of Dante superseded the original. The Authorized Version does not supersede earlier texts of the biblical books; it enhances the importance of those texts for us to the extent to which it effectively assimilates them to our local tradition. The politics of the day assert that Jack is as good as his master, and there are some who will have it that theology asserts the same. These doctrines are wholesome in their proper context. However that may be, those who consider that the day's newspaper or the winner of the latest poetry prize is more to be considered than the master texts should reflect soberly upon Dante's submission to Virgil. So should those who think that the most exalted matter can be dressed up in the language of journalism and of the contemporary poetry trade.

Christian Sobriety

The near extinction of the Church of England, between the parliamentary ordinance for taking away the Book of Common Prayer in 1645 and the Restoration of 1660, had several important consequences. It profoundly affected the character of the settlement of 1662, and made for the touch of intolerance which troubled church and state for long enough after that date. There are two sides to this. There are the theological considerations, which make it inevitable that catholicity in theory should result in a certain exclusiveness in practice, and there are the considerations of civil peace, which must result in a pressure for a comprehensiveness possible only with a minimal dogmatic. To speak of the difficulties encountered by Roman and domestic non-conformists as a 'touch of intolerance' only may seem an outrage, but if one thinks of the Revocation of the Edict of Nantes, or the position of Protestants in Spain or Italy, it was no more. England in the late seventeenth century, and in the eighteenth century, was relatively 'the land of the free', in ecclesiastical as in other matters, as was recognized by other visitors besides Voltaire.

Even before the execution of Archbishop Laud, in 1645, there was a solid opinion in favour of comprehension and tolerance and with an eye on civil peace. Yet in 1642, when *The Holy State* was first published, Thomas Fuller was still too near the administrative unity of the medieval church, and its successor the national church, to think of 'voluntary private meetings' for religious purposes as being other than suspect. He was 'not peremptory but conjectural in doubtful matters. Not forcing others to his own opinions but leaving them to their own liberty'. But what are 'doubtful matters'? The field has extended since then beyond anything even the most liberal could have thought possible. By the time Fuller had had occasion for his *Good Thoughts in Bad Times* (1645) and *Good Thoughts in Worse Times* (1647) and had come to his *Mixt Contemplations in Better Times* (1660), he thought that the sects should 'have a toleration... and be permitted peaceably and privately to enjoy their consciences both in opinions and practices'; he hoped that so they would 'blush themselves out of their former follies, and by degrees cordially reconcile themselves to the Church of England'. For the Old Testament parallel remained: 'England hath but one Isaac or legitimate religion of the church, namely the protestant, as the doctrine thereof is established in the Thirty-nine Articles.' It was an aspiration rather than a practical programme, yet it was practical enough for the Church of England, with all its internal differences, to maintain its predominance until recent time, when the predominance has gone, not to any other form of Christianity, but to a lay conscience which may be half-Christian or post-Christian, but is anyway civic rather than ecclesiastical.

The truth is, that any articulated creed is widely acceptable only at the instance of a political authority, and indeed the basic Nicene creed (AD 325) owed its existence to the Emperor Constantine. The continuance in succeeding centuries of a Roman administration claiming to be distinguished in kind from the less educated polities with which it overlapped, has obscured this fact, but the maintenance of anything like theological uniformity has always depended on political power in the crudest sense of the term. The burning of heretics was a lay function, and the handing over of misbelievers to the civil arm while the Church washed her hands, is a ruse which takes nobody in once the right of the civil power to commit such outrages has been questioned. Once that stage has been passed, all closely-defined religion becomes sectarian, and the more liberty of conscience is allowed the more this becomes evident, for religion becomes in effect a matter of choice. The language of absolutism remains, above all in the Roman church, the most conservative, the most bureaucratic, and politically the most wary, with many features of a type of monarchy so long forgotten that people hardly recognize it for what it is. But for Romans as for the rest of the world, any degree of democratic sophistication in the civil state threatens the discipline of the Church, and brings the status of belief nearer to that of opinion.

Already, in the seventeenth century, the refinements of religious belief, the matters of doctrine which separate the churches, were losing their status as matters of fact. The internalization of religion accelerated by the Reformation meant the approximation of religious to political liberty, if not indeed the identification of the two forms. There is a sense in which martyrdom is a political rather than a religious phenomenon. The Protestant martyrs under Mary died because the state maintained its right to determine what people thought about religious matters. The Roman priests who were hanged under Elizabeth died as the agents of a foreign power, in effect for treason, a crime unlikely to be widespread under any ordinarily satisfactory government. This was an advance, so far as the internal peace of the kingdom was concerned, and saved innumerable lives. The claim for freedom of conscience in religious matters had still to be made, but it became less serious, in the ordinary sense of the term, once it was perceived not to be a matter of life and death. That is not to say that it was not the subject of noisy claims and counter-claims, but the noise and the extent of the dissidence is a phenomenon of psychological relief at the removal of intolerable pressures. The threat of hell-fire was less intimidating than that of the fires of Smithfield. The battles of persuasion and counter-persuasion themselves then became something peaceable persons sought to mitigate.

The many egotistical follies enacted in the name of religion could not be argued into submission, or even into reasonableness, nor could they be laughed out of existence, though this relatively new remedy was attempted, mainly by people whose opinions were more or less set and superficial, and who already looked upon the relatively recently established national church as the good old cause no one should meddle with. After the disaster sealed by the death of the king in 1649, more subtle and more religious minds took another turn, prompted by what they saw as the necessities of the times and partly no doubt by their own necessities. Thomas Fuller, whose temperament was benign and practical and who was more given to common sense than to refinements of argument, and Jeremy Taylor who was possessed of much greater flexibility of mind and, it must be supposed, a much more intense internal religious life, turned their attention away from the public brawls, whether theological or political, towards the pacification of individual conduct. Amidst the welter of arguments, what is called practical Christianity, then as now, was no doubt the only thing which seemed convincing to the ordinary parishioner, however inadequate it might seem to more refined spirits. The great classic of Anglicanism produced by this new orientation is the *Holy Living* of Jeremy Taylor, with its sequel, *Holy Dying* (1650-51).

Although *Holy Living* was intended for ordinary Christians

and was widely read by people who made no special profession of devotion, it contains sections on fasting, keeping festivals and prayer which supposes an attention to these practices which would probably seem fastidious, in our day, to all but a few. Yet the tone even in these sections is of an uncontroversial practicality. 'Fasting, if it be considered in itself... is a duty nowhere enjoined or counselled...' There is no scrupulosity; 'the help which fasting gives to prayer, cannot be served by changing flesh into fish, or milk meats into dry diet; but by turning much into little, or little into none at all...' Of prayer: 'nothing is lost, while words are changed into matter, and length of time into fervency of devotion'. 'Of Christian Religion' – in general – forms only the fourth and final chapter of the book, the first three being given respectively to 'Consideration of the general instruments and means serving to a a holy life', 'Of Christian sobriety' and 'Of Christian Justice'. There is no escaping the ordinary business of life and making up for it in religion. Conduct is the first matter for attention. The fourth chapter itself begins thus: 'Religion in a large sense doth signify the whole duty of man, comprehending in it justice, charity and sobriety: because all these being commanded by God they become a part of that honour and worship which we are bound to pay him.' It is, and rigorously, the religion of common life, from which one is not to be excused on any higher pretext; and it is for this reason, no doubt, that the book was taken so much to heart by generations of English people.

Section I of chapter 1 is on 'The first general Instrument of Holy Living, Care of our Time'. Taylor, as a priest of the Caroline church, was in effect the representative of a prohibited and persecuted form of religion, but he speaks in language which might be that of any sober Puritan: 'For we must remember that we have a great work to do, many enemies to conquer, many evils to prevent, much danger to run through, many difficulties to be mastered, many necessities to serve, and much good to do, many children to provide for, or many friends to support, or many poor to relieve, or many diseases to cure, besides the needs of nature and of relation, our private and our public cares, and duties of the world, which necessity and the providence of God hath adopted into the family of religion.'

The 'Twenty-three Rules for employing our Time' contain much that would recommend itself to any tradesman or farmer: 'Let every man that hath a calling, be *diligent* in the pursuit of its employments, so as not lightly or without reasonable occasion to neglect it in any of those times which are usually and by the custom of prudent persons and good husbands, employed in it.' 'It is better to plough upon holy days than to do nothing.' 'Let all persons of *all conditions* avoid delicacy and niceness in their *clothing* or *diet*, because such softness engages them upon great mis-spendings of their time...' The second chapter, 'Of Christian Sobriety', is no less near the bone: 'Accustom thyself to cut off all superfluity in the provisions of thy life; for our desires will enlarge beyond the present possession so long as all the things of the world are unsatisfying.' 'A temperate man is not curious of fancies and deliciousness. He thinks not much, and speaks not often, of meat and drink.' 'He that is proud of riches is a fool.' 'If a man be exalted by reason of any excellence in his soul, he may please to remember that all souls are equal.' The chapter 'Of Christian Justice' begins with 'Obedience to our Superiors', not the first thing that comes to mind with most purveyors of Christian opinion, in these days, when they hear the word 'justice'. 'That part of justice which is due from Superiors to Inferiors' comes next. Then contracts: 'Religiously keep all promises and covenants, though made to your disadvantage, though afterwards you perceive you might have done better.' Then restitution. The chapter is addressed to the individual conscience, seen in relation to a man's own actions and to matters within his power; the contemporary vulgarity, from which prominent churchmen are far from free, of seeing 'justice' in terms of what other men, and other people's governments, ought to be doing, is not even thought of; let a man search his own conscience, Taylor would have said.

If the disarray of the English church from 1645 to 1660 accounts for Taylor's retreat from public life and his preoccupation with the relatively eirenic questions of private conduct, it was a conscientious disqualification for office in the restored church which sent William Law (1686-1761) in a similar direction. Law was a brilliant controversialist, as the *Three Letters to the Bishop of Bangor* show. But though caught by his scruples in the toils of the Non-Juring movement, he came too late to contribute to its more public phase. He was moreover of a quietist temperament, as shown in the *Serious Call to a Devout and Holy Life* (1729), and he was even more concerned than Taylor with 'Showing how great devotion, fills our lives with the greatest peace and happiness that can be enjoyed in this life.' One is conscious of the existence of an extensive middle class with time on their hands. There is, anyhow, a certain lack of robustness about the Non-Jurors, as of men who enjoyed their consciences in quiet rather than face the ordinary rumbustious world. This is the case with Thomas Ken (1637-1711), in the first generation of what threatened in time to become a sort of ecclesiastical club, frequented by men of scholarly tastes, and surely Edward Stillingfleet (1635-99) was right to argue against his position, that a political schism was not free from blame and that Christians in the first centuries prayed for whatever emperor providence might send them. Law, however, though disqualified for ecclesiastical office, seems to have communicated in his parish church without scruple, and his writings show him, for all his quietism, to have a vivid sense of social appearances. Living contrary to the spirit of the world – the spirit which pursues wealth, fine houses, dignity, power, greedy or delicate eating or drinking – is what the book teaches: 'The history of the Gospel, is chiefly the history of Christ's *conquest* over this spirit of the world.' Devotion for him 'implies not any *form of Prayer*, but a certain form of life, that is offered to God not at any particular *times*, or *places*, but everywhere and in everything.' A man whose intention is to please God, can be 'a saint in his *shop*; his everyday business will be a course of wise and reasonable actions, made holy to God, by being done in obedience to his will and pleasure.' Once again, as with Jeremy Taylor, it is the world of the ordinary Christian which is in view, demanding though his notion of 'the Christian' is. It is for this reason, as well as because of Law's easy and pleasing style, that the *Serious Call* became and long remained one of the most popular of religious books, and for the same reason it should be read by all literate Anglicans now.

The tension between the world of conduct and the world of theology, between *mere* good conduct, which for the Christian includes prayer, and *mere* theology, is an irreducible part of institutional Christianity. Theological refinements, once outside the control of authoritarian government, whether ecclesiastical or lay, tend to divide; mere neighbourliness, as all history shows, tends not to succeed. No solution is attainable in this world, in spite of all the talk of ecumenicism. The shadow of politics cannot be removed from religion, for it is an essential element in religious and in other organization. The question is only how the shadow is to fall, and one may wonder how the prospects for the future are improved by aspirations towards administrative unity.

The Church as Sect

'I have long given up all hope of Church or Christianity.' So the Dean of St Patrick's, a more truthful man than most, wrote 250 years ago to his friend Charles Ford. He added that he had heard of a book – which he would like to see – in which the author asserted that 'the Christian Religion will not last above 300 and odd years'. Time is now running out. Swift explained that his author meant, 'there will always be Christians, as there are Jews; but it will no longer be a National Religion;' and that 'this is enough to justify the Scripture; that, the Gates of Hell shall not prevayl against it. As for the Church, it is equally the Aversion of both Kingdoms' – that is of Ireland and England.

Decidedly, Swift was not a man of the 'balanced liberal style' admired and it must be said exemplified by Dr John Habgood, Archbishop of York. Nor do his works on ecclesiastical or other matters entirely bear out the thesis propounded by the Archbishop in the introduction to *Church and Nation*, that such a style is the hallmark of 'leaders in touch with the more educated elements in society' – as if the author of *Gulliver's Travels, A Modest Proposal* and *The Drapier's Letters* was not so in touch, or was not himself educated, or as if he were, like the Archbishop, an adept of the 'two-sided presentation of a case'. Yet Swift is to be taken seriously. The decline he foresaw has gone on, of late very rapidly, to the point at which the inhabitants of this kingdom show not so much an aversion from the Church as a disregard for it, as an institution, while claims to be more Christian than the Church, or merely more honest, are heard on all sides.

There are all kinds of reasons for this, many of them certainly not the fault of the Church. Hardly surprising then that when the Archbishop comes before the world, trying with painful sincerity to say what he thinks of church and nation in a secular age, he should look so naked. It is certainly very odd, in any historical perspective, that he should appear before the public – even with the many apologies and qualifications he makes – primarily as a sociologist. Is that what bishops are for? Something has been made of his being a scientist; was he not Demonstrator in Pharmacology at Cambridge? However, science is an elusive conception, and Habgood is well aware of the dubious status of sociology. So far as the approach he has chosen means that he is prepared to look at the facts, one hopes that other, methodologically less precise enquirers, will do the same. What it means primarily would seem to be that he is speaking not as a bishop but as an observer, and that he reports on what he observes in terms of such conceptions as 'the pluralist society' rather in the terms proper to what should matter to him most. One cannot help thinking it odd, too, that a bishop should have six months sabbatical leave for such a purpose. One does not readily imagine St Paul doing the same.

In spite of his susceptibility to fashion, one finds that the Archbishop has dedicated his book to his four children 'in the hope that when they are ready to play their full part in Church and Nation, they will find both worthy of their glad allegiance'. Those are words that are worthy of sturdier times and there is recurrent evidence in this book that the author cares deeply about the Church of England and even about the Crown, in a manner which is certainly not now to be taken for granted. Is he perhaps haunted by the church of the Book of Common Prayer, which as chairman of the committee which produced the Alternative Service Book he has done as much as anyone to destroy? He would probably admit that he is; he is creditably uneasy about his work, but with that persistence in wrong-doing which reasonable men like himself always find ways to justify. His argument in relation to the politics of the Prayer Book might be that he has followed them as far as he dared; that in a 'pluralistic society' it is necessary to flatter that imaginary monster, the people, as in other times it was necessary to flatter perfectly real monarchs. He would like to stop the slide to disestablishment, but he offers nothing that could impede it for more than a moment and merely records conservatively the present state of play, like a committee chairman preparing to show that the next downward move is inevitable and will not be fatal. He takes his stand on the fact that 'it is difficult to know what a purely secular monarchy would look like' and that 'at the very least secularisation would result in a drastic loss of symbolic overtones' and 'would also remove a unique point of contact between secular and religious authority'. But what strength can there be in those reservations in a secular society which is said to be a congeries of traditions?

For all his moderation, the Archbishop has virtually given up hope of Church and Christianity as Swift did. For him the time when the Church 'could build on the residues of inarticulate religion, and gradually aim to incorporate once more the whole nation' are long gone by. One sees what he means, but what are the consequences of this position for those who hold it? Only the Archbishop's natural optimism, or his *après-moi-le-déluge* resignation, enable him to take refuge in a theory of relativism which really says no more than that none of us knows it all. Of course nobody does know it all, but if the *Church* in spite of its absurdities does not in some sense know it all, *in posse* at least, it is not the divine institution our forefathers used to suppose. And if it is as open-minded as the author and I hope all of us would have it be, then it will admit truth when it finds it, whatever source it may come from. What then is the meaning of this contenting itself with less than all truth, and less than the truth for all? If every 'tradition', every sect, is to be thought of as on terms of equality, then the Church of England is no more than a club of Christians, with as much right to its democratic opinion as another in the British Council of Churches, but it is not the historical church any more. Multicultural politeness indeed demands that not merely other sects but other religions should be admitted on the same basis, and there is an end to Christianity altogether. Perhaps the best hope for religion is for us all to be absorbed into a sort of extended Hinduism. This must be some way off.

Meanwhile, our position is a rather delicate one and the most likely outcome for most people will be to a non-religious or even an anti-religious ground. The Archbishop himself observes that the increasing sectarianism of the Church of England has led to an anti-clericalism new in this country and, as he says, still much less virulent than that which is known elsewhere in Europe. In fact, of course, there is a lot of cant in the pretence that we live in a new sort of society called 'pluralist', as if people all thought alike before mosques and the temples of other religions started popping up everywhere. Certainly, on account of the transfers of populations, and, more generally, of the new ease of communication between various parts of the world, the differences look a little more blatant than before. The creed and its significance were never, so to speak, the natural habitat of everyone in this country or of any other – as, of course, the Archbishop fully realizes. Were they never true or, if they were – what makes them less true now? And if they are true – in whatever sense we understand that historically difficult word – must not the Church aim at including within its fold everyone in this country, however remote, not to say offensive, such a proposition must now seem? Everybody now talks of understanding other people's traditions, or cultures if the word is preferred. This may be good talk for the purpose of keeping civil peace, which heaven knows is a more serious objective than most of those proposed to itself by the Synod – an institution of whose operations the Archbishop has, understandably, a low opinion. But alas, very little attempt is made to ensure that English children know anything of their own traditions, civil or religious, so it is not clear how this exercise is to be understood. And even with great churchmen, is it really true that they can pick up one 'culture' after another? That they have learned so much that they have got to the end of their own? Or does it make sense to talk of 'separate' traditions at all? Everyone starts from somewhere, and the question is how far he can carry with him the depth of understanding that is given to him in his early years.

That people should be unwilling as they now often are to admit the limitations of their own understanding or to see their centre where it is – in their own country – is an aspect of that emphasis on personality and individuality which plays so large a part in our superstitions. The Archbishop, though as becomes his role as a sociologist he is not unaware of the religious significance of the Sunderland football team, sees the primary function of religion as having 'nothing to do with being the cement of society' but as being about 'the search for personal meaning'. The distinction is surely a false one. Where but in the society we live in are we to find any significance for ourselves? Any meaning of any kind? Any language, without which certainly there is no awareness of meaning? It might be said that the very existence of religion depends upon more than one person believing in it. Certainly the existence of religious institutions, or religious prescriptions of any kind, depends on religion *not* being primarily individual. Within the protected group, of course, the individual begins to conceive of himself by differentiation. But a religion is a group, as a political society is a group and the historic position of the Church of England is that they should be and are in fact aspects of one and the same group, the people living together in one place. In its most general form, this proposition is surely a matter of fact, not just one among a number of possible democratic opinions. That the matter is particularly apt to be misunderstood in our sort of society, and can be presented and worked for only with the greatest caution and forbearance – of which the Archbishop certainly has his share – goes without saying. A possible criticism of his approach is that he is so concerned with the practical fixing of things from moment to moment that the absolute necessity of this general orientation is lost sight of. That he has some general sense of the direction the Church must go in appears, under all the qualifications he makes, from his evident disappointment at the failure of any scheme to re-incorporate Protestant nonconformists, which need not and should not imply anything in the way of premature or even ultimate administrative unity, at any rate as such things are at present conceived. The comprehension of Papists is politically if not doctrinally more difficult, but no less necessary; as is, in the last resort, the conversion of citizens of other faiths. Of course that is to look into a perspective almost infinitely remote. But is there any other perspective for a Christian? Or for an Englishman who sets any value on our local traditions?

That brings me to the question as to what Toryism in the historical sense in which Swift and Johnson were Tories, could mean at the present time. It is certainly a point of view so remote from that of the party which at present uses the title that one should put that connection out of one's head altogether. The business of the day is, happily, not much concerned with fundamentals and it would be a bad day for the country if such things became uppermost. What is alarming is that apparent fading of the central conceptions of Church and Crown. The Crown means the monarch – who, people are always saying, is 'symbolic' or even (and fatally) 'only symbolic', it also means not *the* government but Government. There is plenty of government – some say too much – but the conception of the duty of obedience to it might be thought to have grown a little faint, as if all kinds of subordinate rights or whims or greeds took overwhelming precedence. Of course a civilized government is one which is powerful and stable enough to guarantee just such rights, and a Christian government would be one which accepted the necessity of the Church as well as of the State, and saw these rights in Christian terms. This has never been more than a faint vision, and ages of faith have been as brutal and corrupt, both in church and state, as our own; it is the way of the human race. Those who cry for Disestablishment now are as often as not people who think that governments should jump to do the will of Popes or prelates or Christian consciences in committee, as if their own judgement, knowledge and responsibilities were not what was at stake. The historical record of the rule of Popes and saints is not a good one. Government is difficult enough without their help. If the Church keeps consciences alive then people will act in accordance with their own judgements – foolishly very often, and in accordance with the ordinary canons of human behaviour.

Liturgical revision – to which the Archbishop devotes a chapter – has its political aspects and there can be little doubt that what has happened has made the re-orientation of the Church of England on its historical foundations immensely more difficult. This must mean that any prospect of a renewal of the political doctrine which sees England as turning on the pivots of Crown and Church – faint enough already – has become dim indeed. The Archbishop is conscious of the psychological impediments, in the world as it is, in the way of persuading people to think seriously about questions of unity and authority, and of course there is a lot of common sense in the suspicions that are entertained about these conceptions. The questions however remain and will remain, however awkward they become.

The Church of England used to be 'unquestionably loyal' – in Ken's words. It no longer is so. The cleric who says 'I was not ordained to decorate civic occasions' – a phrase the Archbishop invents for one who is uneasy about these matters – of course has a point but he has lost his grip on other points. The commonwealth does matter; it matters almost supremely, and it matters what sort of commonwealth it is seen to be. It matters even that there should still be men who are prepared to lay down their lives for their friends and who is to say that such things are not more important than the merely ecclesiastical considerations which prevailed at St Paul's in connection with the Falklands service? The people who make up Church and State are the same, or at any rate those who are members of the Church are also members of the State, but one of the many false and destructive tendencies of the Alternative Service Book is the suggestion that the People of God can put their loyalties where they please. 'Supporters of the Prayer Book', the Archbishop says, 'constantly assert that they are not wishing to abolish the ASB, despite many contemptuous things said about it.' For my part, I should be delighted if it could be abolished and the politics as well as the language of the Prayer Book made the basis of any future revision: and this for the sake not of the past but of the future.

The Devil's Hoof-marks

Ecclesiastics who engage in politics usually consider themselves to be above politics. We are usually given to understand that they are speaking for the Church, and they proceed to their pronouncements without asking us to reflect a little on that confusing expression.

The Church of England has a book – now often treated with scant respect by those pledged to maintain its teaching – in which the perspectives of Church and State are clearly set out. Odd that it should be so rarely mentioned by our principal shepherds in their more resounding messages.

Whatever the Church of England may be, in terms of the book of Common Prayer, it is not a body of people who express 'Christian opinions' on unemployment, inner cities, nuclear weapons, or indeed on any other subject, sacred or profane.

A company of faithful people is one whose members have to do their duty in that station of life to which they are called: this would not include, for most of us, settling questions of strategic importance in the economy or in war or, for any of us, pretending to an expertise we do not possess. It would certainly include carrying out our duties to God and to our neighbour.

What arrogance and, indeed, what silliness to suppose that only a self-appointed 'Christian' can see that war, greed, oppression and famine are not quite the thing.

If the denunciation of such commonplaces is a prophetic function, then the world is full of prophets, most of them more moved by the interest of a political group, or by the hope of publicity, than by the Christian faith. And moral disapproval, such as ordinary sensible people may find themselves expressing, turns out on analysis to be a suspect mixture of self-interests of which, on the evidence, we can hardly suppose ecclesiastics to be free.

The Prayer Book, designed for a world in which all members of the commonwealth were supposed to be Christians, was in no danger of speaking as if clergy and congregations were likely to have special insights into affairs of state. Some might and most wouldn't: these are the ordinary facts of life.

Godly, righteous and sober all should be, most were not and are not. The chances of their knowing what is best for themselves, let alone for the world at large, must be rather small. Meanwhile, it was soberly recognized that the peace and prosperity of the commonwealth had to be maintained as best it might be, and the governors obeyed. One could not claim to be rendering to God the things that are God's without rendering to Caesar the things that are his, and so it is lawful for a Christian man to bear arms at the command of the magistrate, but not otherwise.

Of course such assertions must appear to some a blasphemy against personal opinion, which is now so much more sacred, for most people including many who profess and call themselves Christians, than the Creed. Others may be able to explain that, but I cannot. To me it appears that, amidst all the troubles of the sixteenth century, the Prayer Book managed to define with incomparable tact and good sense a context in which a communion of Christians could live at peace in spite of the unworthiness of its ministers and members.

All particular churches have erred, not least that which produced the Alternative Service Book. One of the many Devil's hoof-marks in that book is that in it the bishops have promoted themselves above the Crown.

Why? Perhaps out of jealousy of Rome which, as the heir of the Roman Empire, has often confused spiritual and political power. Certainly out of feelings of superiority towards the ordinary world of day-to-day affairs – hardly a proof of Christian humility. It is this vanity which makes so many congregations now little enclaves of allegedly 'converted Christians' instead of gatherings of wheat and chaff like the rest of us.

It may be that the reform most needed in the Church of England is to re-instate in their former prominence the prayers for the Queen, which are prayers for the well-being of the whole kingdom.

Disestablishment

There is always enlightenment to be had by looking in Tony Benn's direction, and today he comes at us waving the English Church Bill, which proposes: 'an Act to terminate the Establishment of the Church of England'. It can hardly be said that the idea is a novel one, but for all that it *may* be timely.

There can be no doubt that the Church of England is drifting towards disestablishment. Does it matter? The last lot of changes in the legal relationships between Church and state gave the Church a bigger hand in the appointment of bishops and a free hand in devising new forms of service. Opinions differ as to how well the Church has acquitted itself.

Much remains to be done if we are to have disestablishment. We must sack the bishops from the House of Lords. We must abolish the residual power of the state in Church appointments. There are some delicate questions about what is usually thought of as Church property, and raising them may not have exactly the consequences which the disestablishmentarians have in mind. It will be necessary to depose the Queen as Governor of the Church; the bishops have already given themselves precedence over her, in a little paper fantasy in the Alternative Service Book. Future monarchs would have to be so liberated as to be able to make a multi-cultural choice of religions, or officially to have none, like any decent godless citizen. The Coronation service would have to be abolished, or turned into a prayer meeting of whatever sect or religion the monarch happened to favour.

Changes in all these matters would, like the modest moves towards liberation already achieved, excite mixed reactions, the pain and pleasure being perhaps rather differently disposed. The prevailing interests in the Church would no doubt welcome the liberties on offer, such as they are. They would be less enthusiastic about the losses, including the threats to property or supposed property.

All these matters would be for Parliament to decide; it would not be open to the Church to pick and choose. The question of disestablishment is for all of us, the democratic opinions of individual churchmen counting with the rest.

There is much to be said for the view that the interventions of the Church, in matters of public policy, should be for individual churchmen rather than for the Church as a body. In fact 'the Church', as a whole, rarely – one might say never – does intervene in such matters. What we have instead is the odd bishop, or a committee acting more or less under an ecclesiastical aegis, offering what they claim is a 'Christian' opinion. There is in fact no such thing; opinions are either true or false and it matters not who pronounces them, except for the purposes of the ordinary gang warfare of politics. That is why there is reason to think it would be better if the Church kept to the business of teaching the Christian religion – a subject on which some even of its eminent figures seem to be more than a little shaky – and left it to the laity they have instructed to make what use they can in the professional or other affairs in which they are severally skilled, of the knowledge thus acquired. Public questions need all the talent that can be addressed to them, and the widest possible knowledge from whatever source. There is no point in queering the pitch by giving a special prestige to the views of a bishop or a Church committee.

There is a good deal of confusion about these matters. Church spokesmen are apt to see themselves as the forces of light, grandly pitted against the state as representing the forces of darkness. It is a misconception. The Church, in the proper theological sense of the term, is truly set against the world. The world, however, is not the state. It is the ordinary folly and wickedness of fallen mankind, present in ecclesiastical institutions as elsewhere. Vanity, humbug, love of power, a pretension to knowledge one does not possess, may be found even in bishops. The state may not be exactly a candle burning in a naughty world but it is a necessity for all of us. Parliament stands there as the historic guarantee of the discussability of all our common interests, and the Crown in Parliament as the focus of all our loyalties.

Much is talked about the seedier elements of the Reformation settlement, as if the whole history of all particular churches, and not least the Roman, were not full of seedy episodes. Some even imagine that no prince ever meddled in Church affairs before the Reformation, or in Catholic monarchies after that date. However all that may be, the survival of the British monarchy as a Christian institution does look slightly odd in the late twentieth century. It is not on that account necessarily a bad thing. It is not a disgrace to have maintained continuities which have disappeared elsewhere. Rather, it is a sign of the ability of the people of Britain to stay together somehow, in spite of well-fought-out differences.

It can be argued that democratic government involves the equalisation of all opinions. In a sense this is so, but the matter is not as simple as that. We all feel free to make judgements of value which conflict with any such interpretation of our situation.

Even those who choose not to think of the present age as *post*-Christian would have to admit that in 2,000 years the Christian faith has carried forward in its institutions much of the ancient world, and something even of other cultures with which it has been in contact, and that there is little in our common values of which traces are not to be found in those sources. The 'individual conscience' of which so much is heard can be only a tiny variant of the collective European conscience. It may be offensive to the scrupulous to call Britain a Christian country but of course, as compared with India or China, for example, that is what it is.

It is hard to see why the Christian elements in the constitution should be thought to do any harm to the Church, or to any of us. The case has not yet been argued, so far as I know, but it will have to be, if we are to have disestablishment. One consequence of the formal de-Christianisation of the state in European countries which are neither more nor less Christian than our own has been the development of political parties with a more or less overt connection with the Church in its local, usually Roman, form. This is something we could do without. If one party claims to be explicitly Christian, another will surely become explicitly non-Christian. That would clarify nobody's conscience, and would be profoundly disturbing, one would have thought, to individual Christians in all parties.

It would be something if Mr Benn's Bill provoked some serious thought among churchmen.

The Truth Shall Make You Free

The Lambeth Conference may not interest everyone, but anyone who has even a glimmering of the way in which the Church of England is caught in the wider troubles of our time will find in it a matter for reflection. The Anglican Communion, in its present form, was left in the wake of the retreating British power overseas as the Roman Church was, over so much of Europe, when the legions were recalled to defend the Capitol. There is no need to insist on the differences. The Church of England was left with responsibilities and without authority. The Churches scattered over four continents, in widely varying circumstances, adapted themselves to the independence of their territories, but remained bound in communion with the English Church and with one another. Hence the Lambeth Conference, which includes a significant minority of churches in lands which were never in political obedience to the British Crown.

Anglicans now often speak of themselves as a 'denomination', but the Church of England has always claimed to be something different – the only true successors, in England, of a line stretching back unbroken to the Apostles and to Christ himself, that 'visible Church' which Article XIX asserts is 'a congregation of faithful men, in which the pure Word of God is preached, and the Sacraments be duly ministered according to Christ's ordinance in all those things that of necessity are requisite to the same'. This is hardly the place to air that contrast with the Invisible Church which played so large a part in Reformation theology. It is the visible Church – always less impressive because flesh and blood like the rest of us – which was represented at Lambeth. A President should be eirenic and the Archbishop of Canterbury was, preferring the New Jerusalem of Revelation to the actual world in which the Conference was transacting its business, and into which Christ tells us he came 'not to send peace, but the sword' (Matt. 10:34), not peace 'but rather division' (Luke 12:51). It is not that the tiresomeness of the ordinary world forgotten, in the Opening Address; indeed a careless reader might suppose that the speaker's eye was as much on the fashionable as on the eternal. 'How can we see the heavenly vision and at the same time tolerate women and men, God's masterpieces, belittled by reason of their colour, sex, or social class?', he asks, even adding – with, surely, an excess of that benignity for which he is noted: 'It has been one of the great strengths of the World Council of Churches... that it has always seen the search for Christian unity in this *wider* [my italics] context.'[1] Yet, read as a whole, the Address bears evidence of profound and proper uneasiness, a sense of 'the need to recognize the persistence of conflict in Christian history', and of the impossibility of satisfactory solutions to the Church's problems, though it is far from clear that the Archbishop does not expect non-ecclesiastical institutions, and governments in particular, to do better with the problems he puts to them.

It is difficult to reconcile the actual confusions in the visible and actual Church with what the Report on Christianity and the Social Order – one of the four reports contained in this volume – calls 'the role of the Church, locally, regionally, and internationally... to speak prophetically to the world... to oppose all misuse of power whether by individuals, the tribe, the party, the majority or the minority'. By what authority can such an ecclesiastical body – or rather its representatives – speak? An individual Christian, clerical or lay, may so speak, but to transfer this judgement of what are in effect political problems of a highly complex nature to an organization assumes that the organization has a knowledge of the truth in these multifarious affairs which cannot in the nature of things belong to it. The Chairman of the committee which prepared this report was the Archbishop of York – hardly the most reassuring of names, for many churchmen. We all live on a diet of inaccurate news, supplemented by odds and ends from our own sources. To jump from that to an assumption of authority to judge the actions of countries of which we know even less than we do of our own must be a gross presumption. And in our own country, our role is limited to a very little rational action, and almost unlimited expression of ill-informed opinion. For my part, I should be more reassured by a Church which directed our attention to our neighbours, to the daily life we actually lead.

---

1 The Lambeth Conference 1988: The Reports, Resolutions and Pastoral Letters from the Bishops.

The good Samaritan, after all, was attending to a man awkwardly placed before his own eyes, so he knew what he had to do.

Should not the Church treat with reserve the media world, a picture created for us by predominantly commercial motives, to entertain and scandalize rather than to enable anyone to do anything sensible? We all have to live with it, but we should not mistake it for reality. One learns with apprehension that there was 'an unprecedented interest of the media in the personalities and work of the Conference' and that there were 220 'accredited media representatives' served by what are oddly described as 'a team of 46 professional church communicators'. Those who live by the media will perish by the media; a Church which needs advertising men and press men to communicate will present the phoney face of politicians and commercial establishments. To a depressing extent it already does so. How does one person speak to another? The disastrous course of the Church of England, over the last ten years or so, has been dominated by the notion that there is a mode of management of speech which facilitates its intelligibility. Not the truth of what is said, as it seems to the speaker, but its acceptability to the largest possible audience, has been the concern of many of those most prominent in the Church. Their concern has not been to teach the faith of their fathers but to modify it in way which will ensure that it does not seem strange to a population largely distracted by the superficialities of what is merely topical. There used to be eternal truth; now, in the mouths of these mis-leaders, there is only the contemporary. But, amidst the din of the modern world, it is more than ever necessary *reculer pour mieux sauter.* A Church which tries to keep pace with the world, rather than to be set against it, is no longer the Church.

It is of course the claim of the apostles of contemporaneity that those who do not run with them are living in a past which is no longer 'relevant' to spiritual concerns. It is an odd view, from an institution whose authority threads its way through two thousand years of history. This is the continuity which has to be established and maintained by the Anglican Communion, if it is to be recognized for what it says it is. The task is increasingly hard, in a world in which instruction is unpopular and learning an élitist pretension. All these difficulties exist at home; they are multiplied in a Communion which spreads its bounds wider and wider among people with wide cultural differences. The language of Christianity is, inevitably, Judaeo-Graeco-Latin, and this starting-point cannot be changed retrospectively. When the Conference wrestled with cultural problems it could be suspected of being more concerned to avoid offending susceptibilities than with the transmission of the historic faith. It is not only the cultural differences between the English centre of Anglicanism and its geographical peripheries which are in question. The problem is defined as the general one of 'finding an authentically local Christian identity'. This process is said to happen 'within Churches in what has been thought to be a single culture, when disadvantaged or powerless people in England or North America – working-class people, Black people, women – begin to discover how to be Christians in their own style'. This last rather flighty expression avoids the problem of transmission. And of course a working man in the North of England depends upon the same sources as the rest of us. We know what use has been made of this sort of talk to suggest that the historic books of the English Church should be scrapped. Resolution 22 puts the matter grandly: 'Urges the Church everywhere to work at expressing the unchanging Gospel of Christ in words, actions, names, customs, liturgies, which communicate relevantly in each contemporary society'.

This evades the whole question. The 'unchanging Gospel' is certainly not to be transmitted without the help of words: the Bible itself is a stumbling-block. Its words cannot 'communicate relevantly' to people intent only on being 'Christian in their own style' and not on learning from the past. No educated person supposes that he is going to begin to grasp the orientations of Buddhism, Islam, or Hinduism without prolonged study. Anything which invites people to think that the absorption of a glimmer of Christianity into a heathen culture is something entirely different, should think again. The risk in a world of instant communications, is that this historic faith is not so much transmitted as thrown into a melting-pot. What must emerge is one more ingredient for a world-wide ideology whose communion is in the media, not in the Church.

The Archbishop no doubt sees the danger of such unity, and can only express the hope, as his role demands, that 'the search for Communion among Christians gives us a pattern for the wider communion of all humanity'. There are signs that things may work the other way round. Whoever sits in the middle of the Anglican Communion is going to be busy. Like an official of UNO or of NATO, he has to think of adjustments, reconciliations, compromises. There are all the usual organizational hazards. Such an official is not 'a man speaking to men', like a poet or a priest, but a practical man who has to get by as best he can. The vices of authority are well known, but where there is no authority there must be cajolery and flattery. The language of the Conference is not free of this. The world has become too wide for plain speaking, perhaps for speaking at all of anything more than superficialities. It is as if the Church had goods to sell, rather than a truth to be proclaimed whether people liked it or not. Whether or not it was necessary for the bishops to come to Lambeth, it was necessary for them to go home. And not least, the English bishops, not – one may faintly hope – to be 'Christians in their own style' but in the style of the English Church, which a number of them have so long treated with contempt.

Resolution 22 'recognizes that culture is the context in which people find their identity'. I am not sure that I understand this, but when the English bishops got back to their dioceses they could have done worse than reflect on where they are caught in the network of space and time. The resolution 'affirms that God's love extends to the people of every culture' – a proposition hardly in doubt – and that 'the Gospel judges every culture according to the Gospel's own criteria of truth'. There is good and bad in all of them, I expect that means. But what is really at issue is how far a man in one culture can speak to a man of another. The limitations of understanding are strictest precisely in those fields with which religious discourse is concerned. The possibilities of misunderstanding are great. A profound knowledge of culture B is required before the man from culture A can know how to address the man from culture B on these subjects, and the man in culture B has, in fact, to assimilate profound elements of culture A before he can begin to adapt the message to his surroundings. The sleight-of-hand at Lambeth seems to have been to pretend that these difficulties hardly exist, even though it is admitted that 'there is no form of Christian life and language which is quite free from the influence of the culture in which it exists'. The understatement conceals the differences between a culture with an age-long Christian inheritance and one whose language and background is a world of quite different meanings.

Though the thought must be unfashionable, there is certainly a need, in every culture, for a learned class who can appreciate the problems of the transmission of meanings, and make themselves familiar with significant parts of the literature of the Christian past. This may seem a tall order, at a time when, even in the Church of England, such people are becoming scarce. The fashion has been rather for clerics who would teach before they have learned, and who excuse themselves by pretending that they need no more than the media-soaked language of their more ignorant parishioners.

We have lived under a regime which has not only been careless about the transmission of traditional meanings but wilful in the promulgation of texts, both of Bible and Prayer Book, where these meanings are thrown to the winds in the lying name of universal intelligibility. Reading the resolutions passed by the Conference, and no doubt no more binding on us than on anyone else who chooses to ignore them, one cannot but deplore the tricks which put 'human rights' in place of divine law, and political programmes before obedience to the Gospel, the imagined well-being of societies before concern for the journey of life which it has been the proclaimed function of the Church to guide. 'To calculate the events of each particular action is impossible', as one of the wisest of the bishops of the English Church remarked, yet the Conference has found the itch to meddle in political matters, in which there can be no certainty, irresistible. 'It is very possible' – to quote my bishop again – 'that a man, in obeying the commands of his lawful governors, might transgress some law of God contrary to them; which is not possible for him to do, by a patient suffering and non-resistance for conscience sake.' Perhaps also, the Lambeth bishops should have taken more notice of a further warning from the same source: 'Tenderness and benevolence are often motives to the best and greatest actions; but we must not make them the sole rule of our actions; they are passions rooted in our nature, and, like other passions, must be restrained and kept under, otherwise they may possibly betray us into as great enormities as any other unbridled lust.'

THE NINETIES

C.S. Lewis

Lewis was born in 1898, the son of a Belfast solicitor. He was educated first at home, then in England at a preparatory school, at Malvern (for one term only), and by a private tutor. So to Oxford. It was 1917. Lewis had volunteered, and he was in effect an officer cadet, soon in 'barracks' at Keble. He returned to Oxford after a brief spell on the Western front, where he was wounded, and at Oxford he stayed until 1954 when he was appointed to a chair in Cambridge. He seems hardly to have set foot on the European mainland, after his wartime excursion, and indeed to have seen remarkably little of England. He died in 1963.

The story A.N. Wilson has to tell in *C.S. Lewis: a biography* is more complicated than that. Empson thought Lewis 'the best read man of his generation, one who had read everything and remembered everything he read'. He was indeed a man of words, reading, writing and arguing incessantly, when circumstances permitted. His pre-university tutor thought he should consider the Bar as a career: 'He has every gift, a goodly presence, a clear resonant voice, an unfailing resource of clear and adequate expression.' Lewis, on the other hand, saw himself, then and for some years afterwards, as 'a poet, first and foremost, and this view was confirmed by no less a person than William Heinemann himself, who assured him, as he took the MS of *Spirits in Bondage: A Cycle of Lyrics* (1919): 'Of course, Mr Lewis, we never accept poetry unless it is good.' Lewis had the delicacy to publish the poems under a pseudonym. Before he returned to Oxford after the war, he had already decided on an academic career. He took a first in Mods, a first in Greats, and the Chancellor's English Essay Prize. He was now to be a philosopher, but stayed for an extra year and took a first in English Literature. His first job was as a temporary lecturer in philosophy in his old college, Univ.; then, in 1925, he was elected to a fellowship in English at Magdalen. He was still 'preparing for Lewis the great Romantic poet to burst upon the world', but discreetly did not want his gifts in that direction to be known in Magdalen and published his second volume of verse, in 1926, under the same pseudonym as the first.

The way he found to greatness turned out to be something quite different, where the fluency which might have served him as a barrister had more success. He was to be 'a phenomenon who had a life of his own in the minds of the reading public': 'C.S. Lewis the popular Christian apologist, who was reaching so many readers in Europe and the United States'. Best-sellers prove more about the state of their vast readerships than about themselves. 'There has been a great deal of soft soap about God for the last hundred years,' says Wilson. But has not the soap grown softer still has time has gone on, and have not Lewis's writings, by their very fluency, had a part in the deteriorations of the last half-century? 'To those closest to him Lewis did not seem ever to have been a very convincing apologist,' Wilson writes; his 'American admirers' – his 'mail-bag' was 'huge' – thought otherwise. Claims that X or Y are Christian writers are always more or less absurd. Hopkins said, 'Christ is your only literary critic,' and it may be added that He does not run a book club. But Lewis certainly achieved the distinction of being represented, on an upper floor of Wheaton College, Illinois – Billy Graham's old college – in the collection of memorabilia of such Christian writers as George MacDonald, T.S. Eliot, Charles Williams and Tolkien. It is evidence of some sort of fame. A.N. Wilson sees 'unmistakable and remarkable evidence of something like sanctification which occurred in him towards the end of his days', but that I do not pretend to be able to judge.

Wilson himself is anxious that we should not 'canonise' Lewis 'as a plaster saint', and this biography should certainly reduce that risk, for any reader who might be subject to it. On the other hand, I find baffling the biographer's insistence that Lewis was 'a Romantic egoist in the tradition of Wordsworth and Yeats'. I did not know that there was such a tradition, though I daresay it exists in some critical school somewhere; and I find it difficult to grasp what the three writers are supposed to have in common. Egoism they certainly all had – as we all have in greater or less degree – and Yeats and Lewis might both be said to be hoaxers, in different styles, but that is hardly an accurate classification for Wordsworth, much the most serious character of the three as well as incomparably the most important writer. Lewis is surely rather to be seen as belonging with Dorothy Sayers, or at best with Charles Williams and Tolkien, all of whom figure in this book. A biography such as this, however, is not really an occasion for conclusive judgements about the author's literary status, but for exploring how a very odd – and able – Ulsterman fared in Oxford, a place not without its own oddities.

Wilson is determined that this shall be no mere tale of outward dealings. From the first page of the Preface we take one of those plunges into childhood which have been *de rigueur* with biographers since Freud, no doubt because, however shaky the scientific basis of that guru's pronouncements may be, they promise excitements which have a wide appeal, sometimes to the exclusion of more objective realities. Wilson can hardly be faulted on that account, for we are not spared information about Oxford customs and wrangles, and the subject of his biography is shown to be one who somehow failed to make many of the adjustments which are the ordinary concomitants of growing up. Apart from the implications of Lewis having discovered Narnia in a wardrobe where he played with his brother at home in Belfast, it is difficult not to make much, as Wilson does, of the connection between the course of Lewis's life and the plain fact of the death of his mother when he was nine years old. Naturally the happiness he enjoyed, with his mother, in those early years, takes us into an obscure and rather vague territory, but it seems to have been real enough, while the evidence of his long-continued hatred of his father is indubitably historical and abundant. It remains astonishing that, at the age of twenty, when he returned to Oxford after the war, as an undergraduate, he was accompanied by a lady of forty-five from whom he was not to be parted until her death more than thirty years later.

This liaison has been variously interpreted, but there is no doubt – and Wilson has none – that what began as the finding of a substitute mother was soon complicated by what is normally quite a different relationship, and that this large ex-combatant did not feel the need for any of the developments which ordinarily turn an adolescent's attention towards his contemporaries of the opposite sex. Mrs Moore was the mother of a fellow cadet, and the two boys, before going to France, agreed that Clive – who never used his own Christian name but was known as 'Jack' – would 'look after' her should her son be killed. Her son was killed, and it is possible, even likely, that Jack's relationship with her would have developed differently had he lived, though the emotional aberration – if it is allowed to call it that – seems already to have been established, in its main lines, before the news of Paddy Moore's death came through. Before Jack had undergone – in Oxford – 'his only piece of practical training for trench warfare', 'he had reached the point where he could not bear to see his father *à deux*,' and Mrs Moore, who was separated from her husband, thought then to be 'somewhere in Ireland', was letting it be known that the man was a monster: she referred to him as 'The Beast'. 'Jack was given to understand that he had treated her badly and failed to give her enough money. The Lewis family knew nothing of this and assumed that Mrs Moore was a widow.' Jack of course knew about 'beasts', for his own respectable father was one, according to him, though it must have been of a different kind.

Wilson gives all the details of Janie Moore's domestic arrangements in Oxford, from Jack's first undergraduate days when she was in lodgings, already partly dependent on him, to the various states of joint domesticity during the years when the two lived together at the Kilns. The common feature, so far as Jack was concerned, was that he attended to Janie's wants and needs daily, and satisfied his own more obscure needs, whether as undergraduate or don, in a state of semi-detachment from college and university. There he blustered and talked big; in his own retreat, with his mother-and-mistress-in-one, with whom his relationship was for some years embarrassed by the presence of Mrs Moore's daughter, who had sometimes to be sent out so that they could be on their own. In his domestic role he was submissive beyond the wont of husbands, and never failed to respond to the frequent and peremptory calls from the kitchen, whatever academic or other work he may have had in hand.

This might have been a preparation for saintliness, but he was not there till long afterwards – not, indeed, until after the death of Janie, and indeed after the death of his second *de facto*, and first legal, wife. The latter was an American, with whom he had been in transatlantic correspondence – he in the role of the famous Christian apologist – for some years. Mrs Gresham, herself a poet, was, like Janie, rescued from an unsatisfactory husband. He was fifty-four, and she thirty-seven, when they met, and with her, too, he lived till she died, which was in 1960. Lewis approached Christianity in stages. When he was confirmed, as a boy, he was – perhaps not surprisingly in one naturally argumentative – an atheist. His first conversion, in 1929, 'as befitted a man who had sung the pleasures of the ordinary . . . occurred on a bus going up Headington Hill, on his way back to Mrs Moore's house'. It was, Wilson says, not a conversion to Christianity, but 'a recognition that God was God.' It was in the early 1930s that he 'came to an acceptance' of '"mere Christianity"'. The story of this phase seems not to have been frankly told in *Surprised by Joy*, in which he elected to 'draw a veil over the two greatest facts in his emotional history: his relationships with his father and Mrs Moore'. 'Probably,' Wilson speculates, 'his way of looking at himself had become so idiosyncratic that he was not *able* to see the significance of these two relationships in his religious, as well as his whole emotional, development.' The third stage – 'the second, or more radical phase of conversion, twenty or more years after the first' – appears to have been in some sense deeper. 'His intimates,' Wilson tells us, 'were the last people to know what was going on *inside* Lewis... It was this inability to be personal – to be, in one sense, natural – which led so many of Lewis's friends to be surprised by sides of Lewis which emerged in his work.' The outward events of his life, after this third stage, seem to bear out Wilson's judgement that he was 'in a tremendous muddle'.

Lewis was unpopular 'in the English Faculty in Oxford, and indeed in the University at large'. 'He disliked his colleagues at Magdalen.' 'Even colleagues who were Christians... noticed that his variety of Christianity did not extend to meekness, or even necessarily to politeness.' A notable debate took place in 1948 in the Socratic Club, when Elizabeth Anscombe – represented by Wilson as being as tough and unscrupulous in argument as Lewis himself – 'thoroughly trounced' him in argument, and showed up his inadequacy as a philosopher. This occasion seems to have had an extravagant effect on Lewis, arousing 'not least', according to Wilson, 'his fear of women'. 'Once the bullying hero of the hour had been cut down to size, he became a child, a little boy who was being degraded and shaken by a figure who, in his imagination, took on witch-like dimensions.' Lewis, who is said to have preferred boys' books in the second half of his life, became a real – if perhaps somewhat unwholesome – success as a children's writer with *The Lion, the Witch and the Wardrobe*, 'being stung back into childhood', Wilson plausibly informs us, by his defeat at the Socratic Club.

It is difficult to know what to make of Lewis, whom Lord David Cecil declared to be 'a great man', yet who seems to have had only a minimal self-knowledge and who had a capacity for getting things 'plumb wrong' in human relationships. It was certainly a man of unusual talent who produced some sixty books, including *English Literature in the 16th Century, excluding Drama*, the famous books of theologically-uninformed apologetics, and a series of best-selling children's books. Yet the impression one gets, from this biography, is that the man was a shambles. Wilson asserts that there was nothing '"donnish" about Lewis's intelligence. In all his talk, and in his writings, he addressed the sympathetic, lively-minded "general reader" or "average man".' There is something in this, but it is impossible to resist the conclusion that his success did not come from any gift for rapport with ordinary people, or from any unusual penetration of mind or ability to simplify complicated matters, but rather from a superficiality with which his readers felt quickly at home.

Michael Ramsey

It cannot be easy to be Archbishop of Canterbury. The holder is open to all the confusions of public life, yet has to follow threads which are invisible to many of those who do business with him or question him as to the meaning of his pronouncements. As the successor of St Augustine, he has to look back on two thousand years and more of history; as the butt of politicians and journalists, he has to justify himself to a world in which the language of Christianity has become merely vestigial. The complexities of the situation are endless.

Michael Ramsey set out on his journey to this perilous office in 1904, as the son of a Cambridge mathematics don. His mother had been educated at Oxford – early days for such a distinction though those were, for a woman – and was a suffragette and a socialist. There were four children – an elder brother and two younger sisters. The elder brother, Frank, was early and universally regarded as brilliant; he was a mathematician and everything that the son of a mathematics don should be. The two sisters seem not to have mattered so much to him, and they found him odd. 'His younger sister remembered,' Owen Chadwick tells us in *Michael Ramsey: A Life*, 'that suddenly he might leave the table with a wild mad look, and rush into the garden. In the night he might be heard running up and down his attic bedroom banging the wall at each end, and keeping other people awake.' The younger sister was right – he *was* a bit odd. 'He had a physical clumsiness in the management of his hands. He learnt to eat tidily later than most children.' Much later, when he was a professor at Durham, he was seen – as observers thought – learning to ride a bicycle: 'but the truth was that whenever he rode a bicycle he looked as though he was learning to ride.'

The religious orientation of the Ramsey family is significant. There were prayers every day after breakfast. Father, who of course presided, was a Congregationalist, and it was to a Congregational church that father, mother and children went each

Sunday. Mother was the eighth of nine children of a vicar, and with her Michael became acquainted with her preferred form of Anglo-Catholic worship. He learned little at the dames' schools to which he was sent, and for a year was taught at home by his mother, but that 'made him squirm' and he pulled horrible nervous faces. So he was sent to King's College Choir School as a 'mouldy day-bug', and here the chaplain, Eric Milner-White, is said to have interested him in religion. Michael certainly took to Milner-White – the inventor of the service of carols and nine lessons – whose photograph was on his wall when he died. There was, at the Choir School, still no sign of an academic progress which even began to match up to Frank's, and there followed an unhappy time at a boarding-school where one of his mother's brothers was headmaster. Michael cannot have been doing so badly all this while for in 1918 he only just missed a scholarship to Winchester, and won one to Repton, where on the cricket field as perhaps elsewhere he had, on his own confession, 'a curious strain of not attending to things which failed to grip my interest'. There the headmaster was none other than the man who was to become his immediate predecessor as Archbishop of Canterbury, Geoffrey Fisher. Fisher presumably *could* take an interest in indifferent matters, for he was an administrator-archbishop as against Ramsey's 'Man of God'. Both, presumably, were also men of themselves, Fisher as slightly fussy and self-important, Ramsey in the more engaging way of following his own devices, appearing unconcerned about his many oddities and, to an extent unusual in high office, keeping silent when he felt like it.

After Repton Ramsey went to Magdalene College, Cambridge – his father's college. There he took a second in Classics and a first in Theology, and became President of the Cambridge Union, which does not suggest that he suffered from any morbid tendency to silence when he had an audience to listen to him, and it is said that, had he not become a priest, he would have been a lawyer. There can be no doubt of the genuineness of his vocation, but his temperament inclined him to academic rather than parochial work. Not only was he uninterested in the minutiae of existence but, as reported by Michael De-la-Noy in *Michael Ramsey: A Portrait*, 'was not very approachable, not in the way a normal parish priest would be'. He was ordained deacon at the age of twenty-three and for two years served as an assistant curate in Liverpool. As soon as he was priested, at the age of twenty-five, he became a sub-warden of Lincoln Theological College, and he remained there for six years. There followed two years in charge of a church in Boston, Lincolnshire, and he then became vicar of the small, untypical parish of St Benedict's, Cambridge, where he could be seen charging through the streets with his underpants showing through his trousers. He had already written a distinguished book, *The Gospel and the Catholic Church* (1936), while he was still at Lincoln, and after two years at St Benedict's he became, at the age of thirty-five, Van Mildert Professor of Divinity in the University of Durham, and a canon residentiary of the Cathedral. Two years later he married Joan Hamilton, though not before he had consulted his sister Bridget, happily 'a doctor working in that sort of area', about 'the facts of life': he was 'very ignorant', his sister reported. It is perhaps a donnish trait to consult an expert on any subject, though few, one imagines, need to carry the process so far. Joan seems to have been, through all the changes of Ramsey's life, the perfect wife for this unusual character – intelligent, capable and sympathetic with all she met. Ramsey stayed in Durham for ten years, as a professor, and then, notorious Anglo-Catholic though he was, he was elected Regius Professor of Divinity at Cambridge on the proposal of two Nonconformists. This might well have provided eminently suitable occupation for the rest of his working life, but after two years, at the age of forty-seven, he became Bishop of Durham and took his seat in the House of Lords. 'They've made me Bishop of Durham,' he is reported to have said to several people in the streets of Cambridge: 'Oh, hell!'

The Ramseys loved Durham and Michael's years there were a success, and not only with churchmen and academics. He would chat up the people at a parish bunfight 'with a mixture of silence and belly-thumping laughter and beams all round and leg-pulling but with care and affection,' Chadwick says:

> but mostly he did not need to talk... people came up and talked to him, and he would nod and smile benevolently and say happily, Yes, Yes, Yes... He became a friend of Jack Lawson (Lord Lawson) who was a faithful Methodist, and of Sam Watson the Durham miners' leader, whom he came to know intimately. He always attended the Durham miners' gala.

After four years he was appointed, at the age of fifty-one, Archbishop of York, where he stayed for five years until he became, in 1961, Archbishop of Canterbury.

While De-la-Noy gives an excellent account of Ramsey's career and finds room for many enlivening details, Chadwick's larger and much more scholarly book gives, at every stage, admirably lucid analyses of the issues he faced, his attitudes to them, and of the attitudes of the churchmen, academics and political personages who were involved in them. This is a work which students of the history of the English Church will long find indispensable. After an opening hundred pages on 'The Making of a Christian Leader', which takes the story up to Ramsey's election to Canterbury, Chadwick packs into three parts, the arrangement of which could not be bettered, an immense amount of information about the great variety of matters with which the Archbishop had to deal, at home, in 'The Worldwide Community' and in his relations with the Orthodox, Roman and other Protestant Churches. He concludes with a fifth part on 'The Man of God' and this includes an account of Ramsey's years in retirement, in turn at Cuddesdon, Durham, York and, finally, in Oxford, where, still accompanied by Joan, he was in St John's Home, run by the All Saints Sisters in Cowley. Both he and his wife were by then in need of help, and it is evidence of his residual liveliness that, while they were still waiting for a vacancy in the Home, he wrote: 'Two people who were expected to die have not succeeded in doing so but the Mother goes on using optimistic language.'

It would be frivolous, in the face of Chadwick's magisterial summaries, to attempt to separate the many strands of Ramsey's activity at Lambeth. Each of them carries a long tail of history and theology. The impression left by both books is of a man who did not change the course of history but played his part in it with outstanding integrity. Ramsey had no exceptional foresight, and more than once something which started from his liberalism and charity ended, either in his day or soon after, by going too far for orthodoxy. He approved of the recommendations of the Church's report on divorce, 'Putting asunder', but found that it led to the Divorce Reform Bill of 1968-69, for which he refused to vote on the Second Reading. When the General Synod came into existence, in 1970, Ramsey commended the new institution: yet, though he did not go back on this, he came to have a lively appreciation of the drawbacks, certainly not less now than they were in his day. He was not administrator enough, nor indeed statesman enough, to see what would happen. He was suspicious of the Prime Minister's and the Crown's role in the appointment of bishops, though he managed well enough in those quarters, but no one could say that the advances which have since been made towards a more ecclesiastically-managed system have resulted in an improvement of the quality of the bench. There are other subjects of which the subsequent history might make some question Ramsey's wisdom in some particulars, but his attitudes were those of a man set against rigidity and illiberality. Chadwick, who describes the attempt to unite with the Methodists as 'the big failure of Ramsey's life', none the less adds that 'the historian of these events finds it hard to see how Ramsey could have acted other than he did.'

Most of all to be regretted was Ramsey's failure to see the dangers of the movement which has resulted in the virtual relegation of the Book of Common Prayer. Ramsey had been profoundly and adversely impressed by Parliament's refusal to approve the revised Prayer Book presented in 1928. He came to think that the state should give the Church freedom in doctrine and worship, and this freedom was given only 'during and after his last moments as Archbishop'. The results, with the adoption of the Alternative Service Book in 1980, have been disastrous, although our historian seems not to share this view and Ramsey himself was happy to use the new book at the end of his life. 'He did not,' as Chadwick says, in another context, 'regard words as an essential means of communicating between human beings.' This perception is at once profound and incomplete, and the incompleteness is perhaps to be explained by some deficiencies in his make-up. His lifelong reading habits do not suggest much awareness of those spaces between the ultimate silence and exposition, which are filled only by great literature, and by poetry in particular. Cranmer, admittedly in a different phase of the language, lived in all three areas, which for him were not separated. No one who has any inkling of these matters could suppose that liturgies which have grown historically out of profound necessities can be replaced at will with either malice or good will aforethought.

The account Chadwick gives of Ramsey's travels as archbishop, and of his activities in Africa and at the Lambeth Conference, shows how far the duties and opportunities of his office had carried him from the days of the World Council of Churches at Evanston (1954), with its 'insincerity of pretending that platitudes were pronouncements of world-shaking import.' Ramsey 'hated what he saw at Evanston'. He avoided insincerity, we may be sure, in his personal contacts on his many journeys, but he may have tolerated, or perhaps even not recognized, many of the misunderstandings and failures of communication which are inescapable in the conferences of people of widely different backgrounds attempting to discuss matters which go to the root of traditions, to the root of minds and beyond. The effects of the twentieth-century facility of movement and speech between continents have to be reckoned with, and they include both a vast but still incomplete and largely indigestible supply of information and a thinning of meanings the transmission of which requires a certain likeness of minds. Ramsey was a man deeply rooted in English ways and – apart from his administrative weaknesses, which cannot be overlooked in an office which requires much ability of that kind – was extremely well qualified to lead the Church of England of his day. But one is left wondering whether, with his deep sense of the local and the historical, he would not have done it better had he not been distracted by the affairs of a worldwide communion billowing to and fro under the force of a diversity of cultural movements. The Church of England needed – now needs still more – someone who is allowed to keep his mind on the historic functions of the Archbishop of Canterbury. It is enough for one man – even the most gifted – and the presidence of the Anglican Communion should be a function for someone else.

Change and Decay

'A good sermon morning and evening, and no bloody nonsense about Holy Communion': that was the prescription of a Wiltshire farmer I knew. It did not occur to him, a generation ago, that the form of service could be other than the one he had been familiar with since childhood. Meanwhile, in other places, all kinds of funny things had long been going in. The clergy of the Church of England, like its laity, has never been famous for discipline. And if since 1980 there has been a pressure to conform which had almost disappeared from the Church, it has been a pressure to conform to *alternatives*, which has a pleasing smack of dissidence about it.

The disarray of the last ten years is variously judged, and however pleasing it has been to some it has not stopped the decline of Church membership. With the prospect of a new mind in Canterbury, it is a good time to review what has been happening, and nothing could be more timely than this short history of *The Development of the Anglican Liturgy, 1662-1980* by R.C.D. Jasper, who was a member of the Liturgical Commission from its appointment in 1955, and its chairman for the fifteen years which ended with the production of the Alternative Service Book.

Dr Jasper's history is divided into two parts: the first a summary history of the years to 1955, the second an account, at once fuller and, understandably, more personal, of later considerations. Both parts are, it goes without saying, backed by Dr Jasper's exemplary learning, and they are written with a lucidity which makes them readily accessible to laymen. The first part starts with the events of the Restoration, when the mood was for the recovery of unity, ecclesiastical as well as political, after the divisions of the Civil War. Presbyterians and Laudians tried to reach an accommodation, and there was agreement on minimal alterations of the Prayer Book, which had been banned under the Commonwealth and received with satisfaction on its reappearance. The eighteenth century produced an undergrowth of liturgical ingenuities from the Non-jurors with their Usages to Whiston who, though a scholar rummaging in the past was, as an Arian, significantly in sympathy with the Deism which was the fashionable aberration of the century. The innovator who was at once theologically orthodox and profoundly concerned about pastoral matters was Charles Wesley, who did his best to keep his followers close to the Prayer Book.

The forms of ecclesiastical restlessness which took place in the nineteenth century did not seriously threaten the use of the Prayer Book in the Church of England, and *The Book as Proposed in 1928* was an attempt to confine revision to what some held to be essential. The history of the Liturgical Commission from 1955 is different. An initial conservatism gave way to an academic radicalism of which Dr Jasper was one of the chief as well as one of the most persistent exponents. Every argument was used to justify change and one might say that 'the point that there could be no spiritual benefit in repeating archaic words and phrases' was taken as suggesting that there might be great benefit in repeating modern ones instead. The credulous 'with-it-ness' of the 1960s gave this a fashionable look. Another major influence was the revision of the Anglican liturgy to suit the tastes of former imperial countries and of the small group of English scholars who advised them. Alterations made in the light of the line of scholarship to which Gregory Dix had given currency were seized on to make the point that the BCP was no longer an adequate symbol of Anglican unity. Nobody seems to have asked whether it might not, with minimal alterations only, be the best hope for the unity of the Church of England.

Modern scholarship has indeed made some reconciliation possible between what were once mutually hostile doctrines of the Eucharist, but since the BCP has long been recognized as holding these different views in suspense, that does not in itself provide a sufficient argument for a new form of service to serve as a statement of doctrine. There is, anyhow, little to be said for changing the liturgy to keep up with the changing fortunes of scholarly brawls, at the expense of pastoral arguments, which must give great weight to the benefits of continuity. It took the Liturgical Commission twenty-five years to undermine the BCP. A similar amount of effort, applied to pastoral matters, would probably have suggested building on the familiar book, with little more than the simplifications which would have brought it nearer to the way it was actually used, and made it easier for beginners to handle – easier, too, than the current volume of many alternatives.

In the final paragraph of Dr Jasper's book it is suggested that the 'low-keyed' language of the ASB is fine if 'the clergy work imaginatively with it... *we have to create* from ASB... what we have been accustomed to feel in our early literature.' This surely certifies the inadequacy and artificiality of the 1980 book.

The writer and the Word

At the beginning of this book, *Incarnation: Contemporary Writers on the New Testament*, is a page blank but for four names: Simone Weil, W.H. Auden, Flannery O'Connor, and Robert Fitzgerald. Not a dedication but a reminder: perhaps these are people the editor, Alfred Corn, would have liked to ask to contribute to his collection. The actual contributors – twenty-three including the editor himself – are either novelists, or poets, or both, and a number of them are – for whatever that may signify in terms of currency – winners of literary prizes or contributors to *The New Yorker*. Several of them are, or have been, teachers of creative writing. In general, they may be said to represent no fugitive or cloistered virtue but rather literary practices more or less tolerated in our age.

There must be readers who will think this is an odd quarter to go for illumination on the subject of *Incarnation*. The authors in question have in common, however, a peculiarity by no means taken for granted in the literary world in the second half of the twentieth century: all of them have been willing to make public his or her reflections on one or other book of the New Testament, in furtherance of providing an answer to the editor's question: 'Just what is the importance of these ancient scriptures to contemporary imaginary writing?' It might be thought that there is a certain condescension in this question, which suggests that the reader may be expected to trust the discoveries of the contemporary literary imagination more than the original texts. Such readers are perhaps not uncommon, but one does not have to be a fundamentalist to think such a view fallacious, if only because texts which have lodged for nearly two millennia somewhere near the centre of the Western mind are *ipso facto* more important than the best of our current productions. What emerges is twenty-three bits of impressionistic criticism – not itself an enduring form of literature – which must throw some light on the current confusions, or add to them.

Alfred Corn's introduction starts with some impeccable reasons for distrusting fundamentalists. 'One of the disturbing things,' he says, '...is that they seem not to read the Bible enough, or not comprehensively. Seizing on one verse or chapter and letting everything follow from that suggests a lack of perspective. It ignores the careful balance established among a series of books composed by different hands over roughly a forty-year period in the second half of the first century.' Quite so. But this insistence on context tells against the editor's own device of seeking the reaction of individual writers to isolated books. Some sense of a wider context is implicit in all criticism, but the books of the Bible are inescapably a special case. It is impossible to read them without rousing memories not only of other texts but of the ways they have been read for so long, and this goes for the most un-churched as for the Pope of Rome. Their history is part of their meaning. Indeed, all our history is part of their meaning, and beside this unknowable bulk any individual reaction is of almost infinitesimally small importance.

It must be said that this difficulty is seen with more or less clarity by all the contributors to this volume, not least, of course, the editor himself. The bits of autobiography which many of them let slip are illuminating. Corn describes a vision he had some eight years ago when, as a 'self-described atheist', he 'was taking a walk in the Grove Street cemetery in New Haven... out enjoying the pink-and-white blossoms on the cherry trees.' Armed in the best late-twentieth-century manner with a portable player, he sat down on one of the flat tombstones and put on 'a tape cassette of Bach keyboard music'.

> And suddenly I knew with complete certainty that the world and everything in it was a Creation, so complex as by contrast to simplify the Bach fugue into a child's bare, unaccompanied nursery song.

Corn's account of this occasion disposes any suspicion his introduction may have given rise to that he entered upon the compilation of the volume with no more reflection than is required to set on foot a slightly trendy literary exercise. His reference to himself at the time as a 'self-described atheist' might be intended to suggest that our descriptions of ourselves are not to be relied upon, but does not that in turn cast a doubt on the validity of the subjective method on which the book is constructed?

Corn has found a home in the American Episcopal Church

'where the inherited strands of Catholicism and Protestantism both are active and in fruitful dialogue.' Whatever point of belief or incredulity other contributors may find themselves in at the time of writing their pieces, there can be no doubt about the part their respective upbringings have had in forming their orientations. It is not the nature of the homework the editor set them to give us much in the way of information about the diverse journeys which are hinted at, and it is no doubt as well that invitations to so many novelists and poets did not offer them the temptation of competing with St Augustine. 'Not all of the contributors are practicing Christians, or even Theists', the introduction tells us. 'Two of them are Jews who had important comment to offer on these texts or on Christianity at large.' The diversity of starting point has more significance here, not surprisingly, than the diversity of the writers as *writers*. Robert Hass has 'shed his Catholicism', but it remains abundantly clear that it is Catholicism that he has shed. Rita Dove starts from an African Methodist Episcopal establishment, and ends with an insistence that 'anyone who feels the need to connect the outside world with an interior presence must *absorb* the mysterious into the tangle of contradictions and longings that form each one of us.' Amy Clampitt tells us of her beginnings in 'a little country church' of a community which had been settled by 'members of the Society of Friends or Quakers... who in a welter of late-nineteenth-century evangelism had lost track of precisely who they were.' John Hersey still finds that what 'would not do for [his] Social Gospel parents... won't do for their agnostic son.'

It seems to me that the interest of this volume lies rather in the impressions it contains of the impact of Christianity at large than in any comments on particular books of the New Testament, worthy of attention as some of those comments certainly are. Perhaps that is not quite the way to put the matter. Christianity is hardly at large: the light it gives may rather be said to glimmer or blaze within whomever it does glimmer or blaze for a longer or shorter time. Yet there is a sense in which our limited shreds of perception of this mystery – for it is surely a mystery or nothing – walk up and down the world seeking whom they may devour, or whom they may bite to open a crack through which light can flow. It would be wrong to expect more from even the most hopeful contributors; I find myself unable to judge whether we should expect as much.

The question remains, whether there can be any special function for novelists and poets, as a class, in this uncertain process. One can speculate on the literary consequences of such an attempt as is here made to define such a function. There is a presumption which is not altogether reassuring in Larry Woiwode's suggestion that there is, in Acts, 'a packed compression' which 'is a forerunner of writing of the kind we won't witness in its full-blown application until our own stark, purged fiction of the twentieth century.' Dana Gioia, for all the creditable caution of his approach to Philippians, is surely on the way to imperilling his literary integrity when he talks as 'a poet writing about the New Testament' and yet worries about the reader's 'life-time of preconceptions' and in a particular sense those of his audience, 'including most American intellectuals', for whom the New Testament 'is a great moral document in which great truths are unfortunately tangled up with discredited supernatural legend.' And he is surely making a display of literary airs in suggesting that 'imaginative writers' like himself are able to bring an unusual 'innocence and humanity' to the understanding of Paul, and in attributing to the writer's imagination 'its higher sense of the intuitive discovery of reality'.

Yet this last portentous phrase of Gioia's goes to the root of the problem with which this volume confronts us. In our day 'writer', whether imaginative or not, is primarily a trade category, and 'writing' flourishes, as a trade, as never before in recorded history. Where is one to draw the boundaries of 'imaginative writing'? Does it include advertising copy? Some advertising copy writers are as imaginative as some novelists. Does it include the endless rubbish put out night and day under the title of plays, reminiscences of alleged 'experiences', songs, and, not infrequently, of 'news'? If 'imagination' has a 'sense of the intuitive discovery or reality', where does lying begin? Is the vast trade world of 'poetry' itself free of it? Is the business of teaching 'creative writing'? Is 'literary criticism' untainted? If imagination opens the mind to reality what becomes of our criteria of truth? And what are those criteria? The question is as old as human debate, and will be asked as long as the world lasts.

It is the recognition of this dilemma which is at the bottom of all religion, and the exponents of religions are no more free than the rest of mankind from the temptations of mere plausibility. The New Testament – or more properly the whole of history which begins with the first chapter of Genesis – stands at the centre of the most persistent attempt made, in the Western world, to account for the human condition. The 'personal responses' in which the editor is primarily interested certainly illustrate that condition. Can they do more? He asserts, with impeccable orthodoxy, 'that the practice of sacrifice, at the small scale and the large, is central to any valid "imitation of Christ".' The volume as a whole suggests that an appropriate sacrifice, 'at a small scale', would be the vanity of authors – and not only those represented in this book.

AN APPENDIX OF POEMS

In Honour of J.H. Fabre

My first trick was to clutch
At my mother and suck
Soon there was nothing to catch
But darkness and a lack.

My next trick was to know
Dividing the visible
Into shapes which now
Are no longer definable.

My third trick was to love
With the pretence of identity
Accepting without proof
The objects 'her' and 'me'.

My last trick was to believe
When I have the air
Of praying I at least
Join the mantis its prayers.

A Letter to John Donne

On 27 July 1617, Donne preached at the parish church at Sevenoaks, of which he was rector, and was entertained at Knole, then the country residence of Richard Sackville, third Earl of Dorset.

I understand you well enough, John Donne
First, that you were a man of ability
Eaten by lust and by the love of God
Then, that you crossed the Sevenoaks High Street
As rector of Saint Nicholas:
I am of that parish.

To be a man of ability is not much
You may see them on the Sevenoaks platform any day
Eager men with despatch cases

Whom ambition drives as they drive the machine
Whom the certainty of meticulous operation
Pleasures as a morbid sex a heart of stone.

That you should have spent your time in the corruption of courts
As these in that of cities, gives you no place among us:
Ability is not even the game of a fool
But the click of a computer operating in a waste
Your cleverness is dismissed from the suit
Bring out your genitals and your theology.

What makes you familiar is this dual obsession;
Lust is not what the rutting stage knows
It is to take Eve's apple and to lose
The stag's paradisal look:
The love of God comes readily
To those who have most need.

You brought body and soul to this church
Walking there through the park alive with deer
But now what animal has climbed into your pulpit?
One whose pretension is that the fear
Of God has heated him into a spirit
An evaporated man no physical ill can hurt.

Well might you hesitate at the Latin gate
Seeing such apes denying the church of God:
I am grateful particularly that you were not a saint
But extravagant whether in bed or in your shroud.
You would understand that in the presence of folly
I am not sanctified but angry.

Come down and speak to the men of ability
On the Sevenoaks platform and tell them
That at your Saint Nicholas the faith
Is not exclusive in the fools it chooses
That the vain, the ambitious and the highly sexed
Are the natural prey of the incarnate Christ.

Easter

One good crucifixion and he rose from the dead
He knew better than to wait for age
To nibble his intellect
And depress his love.

Out in the desert the sun beats and the cactus
Prickles more fiercely than any in his wilderness
And his forty days
Were merely monastic.

What he did on the cross was no more
Than others have done for less reason
And the resurrection you could take for granted.

What is astonishing is that he came here at all
Where no-one ever came voluntarily before.

The Temple

Who are they talking to in the big temple?
If there were a reply it would be a conversation:
It is because there is none that they are fascinated.
What does not reply is the answer to prayer.

In Memoriam Cecil De Vall

late garrison chaplain, Barrackpore

You can count me as one who has hated
Out of spoiled love rather than malice.
Let me lie now between tufts of heather,
My head in the grass.

The sky is too high, I prefer to be far under it
The road is happily distant.
No angel shall catch me here, nor tourist
Abase me with his talk.

Out from this patch of dust the flat plain
Extends like Asia under a blue sky.
It is no misanthropy that binds me here
But recognition of my own failure.

I ask no better than that
The long convolvulus shall grow over me
And prickling gorse
Keep the children away.

Soon the fallen flesh will begin to crawl
Making off in the worm's belly
Into the undergrowth, and the polished flies
Will riddle me like hat-pins.

I bid their rising lives welcome because
It is better to be many than one;
The mirrors of blue-bottle and worm
May reflect to more purpose than I.

Curl my fin where the shark
Lurches in the blue Mediterranean;
Open my wizened eye
Like a lizard under a tropical leaf.

As I bite the dust of this flat land
For the last time, with dissolving chaps,
Keep me free from all such reflection
Lest the mind dazzle as it goes out.

I do not wish to recognise Christ
As I enter the shades.
What other company could I have
In darkness of my own choosing?

Perhaps it is no more than a recollection
– The banks of a river,

The heavy vegetation wet with the monsoon,
My friend on the verandah?

He brought out the long whiskies and proved
That God hated nothing that He had made:
At no time did I take at his hands
Any but his own hospitality.

Fill my mouth with sand, let the passer's boot
Unwittingly fold my skull.
I have resigned the pretensions
Of the individual will.

From the darkened shores of the river
The dogs howled;
I was alone with the famished and the dead.
Whatever stirred in those shadows was not God.

The Person

What is the person? Is it hope?
If so, there is no I in me.
    Is it a trope
Or paraphrase of deity?
    If so,
I may be what I do not know.

Do not be proud of consciousness
For happiness is in the skin.
    What you possess
Is what another travels in.
    Your light
Is phosphorus in another's night.

It does not matter what you say
For any what or who you are
    Is of a day
Which quite extinguishes your star –
    Not speech
But what your feelers cannot reach.

There is one God we do not know
Stretched on Orion for a cross
    And we below
In several sorts of lesser loss
    Are we
In number not identity.

Homo Sapiens is of No Importance

And it may be that we have no nature
That he could have taken upon him.
Plato of course discussed it.
Deborah sitting under a tree
In a time of matriarchy:
Blessed be thou among women,
Blessed be the hand, the hammer,
Blessed the tent-peg as it drove through Sisera,
Blessed the connection between two interiors,
Blessed the wire between the switch and the bulb.
Not for the mind of Jael but for her hand
Not for the hand but for the hammer
Not for the hammer but for the tent-peg
Not for the peg but for Sisera dead
Not for Sisera dead but for his army routed
Not for that but for the momentary ease under a tree
Not for that but for the tree itself
Not for the tree but for the sand blowing by it
If there was any nature it was in that.

The Usk

Christ is the language which we speak to God
And also God, so that we speak in truth;
He in us, we in him, speaking
To one another, to him, the City of God.

I

Such a fool as I am you had better ignore
Tongue twist, malevolent, fat mouthed
I have no language but that other one
His the Devil's, no mouse I, creeping out of the cheese
With a peaked cap scanning the distance
Looking for truth.
Words when I have them, come out, the Devil
Encouraging, grinning from the other side of the street
And my tears
Streaming, a blubbered face, when I am not laughing
Where in all this
Is calm, measure,
Exactness
The Lord's Peace?

II

Nothing is in my own voice because I have not
Any. Nothing in my own name
Here inscribed on water, nothing but flow
A ripple, outwards. Standing beside the Usk
You flow like truth, river, I will get in
Over me, through me perhaps, river let me be crystalline
As I shall not be, shivering upon the bank.
A swan passed. So is it, the surface, sometimes
Benign like a mirror, but not I passing, the bird.

III

Under the bridge, meet reward, the water
Falling in cascades or worse, you devil, for truthfulness
Is no part of the illusion, the clear sky
Is not yours, the water

Falling not yours
Only the sheep
Munching at the river brim
Perhaps

IV

What I had hoped for, the clear line
Tremulous like water but
Clear also to the stones underneath
Has not come that way, for my truth
Was not public enough, nor perhaps true.
Holy Father, Almighty God
Stop me before I speak

– *per Christum.*

V

Lies on my tongue. Get up and bolt the door
For I am coming not to be believed
The messenger of anything I say.
So I am come, stand in the cold tonight
The servant of the grain upon my tongue,
Beware, I am the man, and let me in.

VI

So speech is treasured, for the things it gives
Which I can not have, for I speak too plain
Yet not so plain as to be understood
It is confusion and a madman's tongue.
Where drops the reason, there is no one by.
Torture my mind: and so swim through the night
As envy cannot touch you, or myself
Sleep comes, and let her, warm at my side, like death.
The Holy Spirit and the Holy One
Of Israel be my guide. So among tombs
Truth may be sought, and found, if we rejoice
With Ham and Shem and Japhet in the dark
The ark rolls onward over a wide sea.
Come sleep, come lightning, comes the dove at last.

The Test

There is no body but the body of
The person who is offered up to love:
Rare body and rare person, for without
Extreme love every person is in doubt.
Where there is none, the scavenger desire
Will still find the material for his fire:
He lacks only the metaphysic twists,
For who can be, if no-one else exists?

A Renaissance

Now that the theories of Freud
Are recognised as null and void,
The dialectic of Karl Marx
No longer gives out any sparks,
Time to return to simple fact
Which has all theorising whacked.
The human race is always wrong:
The evidence for that is strong,
And has been, ever since the day
When Adam first had his own way,
Which was, however, not his own.
The Tree of Knowledge was full-grown
When he began his foolish quest
For what he thought would suit him best.
The best was there already, he
Had need only of eyes to see.
Few are content with that, preferring
Ideas to set the head-piece whirring.
And then the mouth: how nice to hear
One's own inventions made so clear.
His first idea was smart: he told
His Maker he was not so bold
As to be naked in His sight:
Surely God would think that was right?
But God knew everything, which makes
It difficult to pass off fakes.
This trouble has persisted since

That day, and still it makes one wince
To think that nothing can be thought
Which will add up to more than nought.
Instead of thinking Adam found
He had to dig the stubborn ground,
While Eve had babies in a row
And sorrow too, they hurt her so,
And both were peeved to find that pleasure
Extinguished their accustomed leisure.
Too bad that disobedience
Should count against people of sense!
They thought, and soon their vanity
Infected the whole family,
Till Cain killed Abel and so ended
The notion man could be befriended
By other creatures of his kind
– Or should have done, but that the mind,
They proudly thought, could put that right.
Philosophers sat up all night
For generations after that
To prove that the round world was flat,
That people were born free and could
Find their own way out of the wood.
God had foreseen that too, foreknew
The silly things that they would do,
And, as intended, sent his Son
To throw new light on everyone.
Some such solution was expected
But vaguely, and what God projected
Was not a human thought at all.
Men thought God's story rather tall:
Conception without human help
Which yet produced a human whelp.
Absurd! God did it to reprove
A misconception about love
Which was endemic from the first.
So bang! Another bubble burst.
Christ walked in all humility
Upon the earth, and man was free,
Or could be, if he did not find
The reason in his own poor mind.
God! What a God! So great and small

Must bow before Him after all!
A likely story! All the grand
People refused to understand,
As well they might. It was not funny
To be assured that power and money
Counted for nothing. But the Son
Went on His way, God's will was done.
He put himself upon a cross
To prove that gain was only loss,
And afterwards everyone said
He could not come back from the dead.
But that is what He did, and few
Believed the story could be true,
And yet it was: the Resurrection
Was not a human insurrection
(They always fail), but He who rose
Went to His Father as He chose.
The Devil sneaked around and said,
As is his custom, God was dead,
Or up to tricks which he, the Devil,
Thought not entirely on the level,
He took the side of humankind:
The human will, the human mind,
Slightly adjusted, could devise
Reasons for everything, first prize
For everybody, and a place
Far better for the human race
Than that old garden where all knowledge
Grew on a tree, not in a college.
So man grew wiser, theory
Replaced the things we touch and see,
And language in the end referred
To everything without a Word;
Number came in and counted all
Hitherto thought innumerable.
The world became a counting-house.
God saw it all, and then a mouse
Squeaked, a cock crowed and so a man
Remembered how it all began.
Back to square one. A human heart
Popped up and made its owner start.
Worse still, the world again had Art.

For Thomas à Kempis

ne amore visibilium traherentur
ad infima

Old monk, I cannot drain the world of sense,
Nor despise beauty, which says everything,
For use says nothing, and there must be praise
For all created things, and recompense,
Surely, in all that world which, vanishing,
Leaves marks upon the squalor of our days?

Even the human body, not immune
From beauty or from kindness, touches us
With splendour which was found in Paradise
Eastward of Eden, and may still attune
Our instant eyes to catch the marvellous
Which is not anybody's greedy prize.

The fine proportion which is in the deer,
And everything that man has never made,
Corrects the mind which watches silently.
Contemplatives? They are found even here,
Where the mind registers the light and shade
And even flesh may teach humility.

So, Thomas Hemerken, you should complete
Your praise of nothingness with praise of all.
The girl dressed only in her falling grace,
From perfect shoulders to as perfect feet,
Lacks nothing, and her beauty seems to call
With one design in every track and trace.

Image of God, for so she is! He chose
So to portray desire of union
With the invisible, to which all tends.
The spirit clothed in flesh cannot disclose
Itself, whatever other will is done,
Except in what it wears for human ends.

All is concealed, indeed, unless it speaks
The language of the flesh and speaks in love,
Counting itself as nothing lost in all.
And so, through ordinary days and weeks,
We may see everything, around, above,
The oak-tree's rising and the acorn's fall.

And yet the whole green world cannot prevail
Upon the mind love has discomfited,
For speaking there must be, another voice.
Who hears? Who speaks? If, indeed, meaning fail,
The spirit is unreading and unread,
Cannot despair and can still less rejoice.

Flesh understands, or spirit cannot teach:
The Devil has no way but emptiness.
Beware, Thomas à Kempis, Hemerken
Can know no more than human sense can reach.
All is in balance, neither more nor less,
So just, in Love, but singular in men.

Sources

THE FIFTIES

Published in *Theology*: 'A Political Note', March 1951; 'A Literary Note', August 1956.

Published in *Frontier*: 'Responsible Positions', April 1958; 'Newman's Politics', July 1958.

'Church and State', *The Church Quarterly Review*, January-March 1957.

THE SIXTIES

'Church and Town', privately printed, ?1964.

'What Kind of English?', *Church Times*, 4 February 1966.

'Native Ruminations', essays privately printed (Knole Park Press, Sevenoaks), 1967.

'Is there a Church of England?', *Frontier*, August 1969.

THE SEVENTIES

'The Schism between Church and State', *Scotsman*, 25 November 1972.

'Politics and the Pulpit', *TLS*, 23 April 1976.

'Some English Divines': the General Preface to *The English Sermon*, 3 vols, Carcanet Press, 1976; Introduction and prefaces to Vol. II.

Published in *PN Review*: 'A Four-Letter Word', vol. IV, no.1, 1976; 'Intimations of the Eternal', vol. IV, no.2; 'Coleridge Revisited', vol. V, no.1, 1977.

'A Viewpoint on the Book of Common Prayer', *TLS*, 7 December 1979.

THE EIGHTIES

Published in the *Spectator*: 'Tinkling Symbols', 5 December 1981; 'A Gentle Warning', 2 May 1981; 'An Abdication by the Church', 7 March 1981; 'The Reverend Member?', 13 February 1982; 'Notes on Church and State', 1 August – 5 September 1981; 'The Archbishop's Travels', 10 April 1982.

Published in the *TLS*: 'The Alternative Service Book', 14 November 1980; 'Overheard by God', 24 April 1981; 'Martin Browne and Religious Drama', 22 May 1981; 'Religion and Public Doctrine', 6 February 1981; 'Richard Baxter', 6 August 1982; 'George Herbert', 8 April 1983.
Published in *The Salisbury Review*: 'Richard Hooker', Winter 1983; 'The Church as Sect', January 1985.
Published in *The London Review of Books*: 'Harry Williams', 2-29 December 1982; 'Hensley Henson', 1-14 September 1983.
Published in the *Independent*: 'The Devil's Hoof-marks', 11 July 1987; 'Disestablishment', 18 May 1988.
Published in *PN Review*: 'Christian Sobriety', vol. 9, No.4, 1982; 'The Truth Shall Make You Free', vol. 16, no.1, 1989.
'The Prayer Book Controversy', *Michigan Quarterly Review*, Summer 1983.

THE NINETIES

Published in *The London Review of Books*: 'C.S. Lewis', 22 February 1990; 'Michael Ramsey', 22 March 1990.
'Change and Decay', *Spectator*, 19 May 1990.
'The writer and the Word', *The New Criterion*, August 1990.

Index of Names